BOUTIQUE ATTIRE

THE ART OF SEWING

BOUTIQUE ATTIRE

BY THE EDITORS OF TIME-LIFE BOOKS

TIME-LIFE BOOKS, NEW YORK

TIME-LIFE BOOKS

FOUNDER: Henry R. Luce 1898-1967

Editor-in-Chief: Hedley Donovan
Chairman of the Board: Andrew Heiskell
President: James R. Shepley

Vice Chairman: Roy E. Larsen

MANAGING EDITOR: Jerry Korn
Assistant Managing Editors: Ezra Bowen,
David Maness, Martin Mann, A. B. C. Whipple
Planning Director: Oliver E. Allen
Art Director: Sheldon Cotler
Chief of Research: Beatrice T. Dobie
Director of Photography: Melvin L. Scott
Senior Text Editors: Diana Hirsh, William Frankel
Assistant Planning Director: Carlotta Kerwin
Assistant Art Director: Arnold C. Holeywell
Assistant Chief of Research: Myra Mangan

PUBLISHER: Joan D. Manley
General Manager: John D. McSweeney
Business Manager: Nicholas J. C. Ingleton
Sales Director: Carl G. Jaeger
Promotion Director: Paul R. Stewart
Public Relations Director: Nicholas Benton

THE ART OF SEWING
EDITORIAL STAFF FOR
BOUTIQUE ATTIRE:
Editor: Fred R. Smith
Assistant Editor: David L. Harrison
Designer: Virginia Gianakos
Text Editors: Betsy Frankel, Gerry Schremp
Picture Editor: Kaye Neil
Chief Researchers: Wendy A. Rieder,
Gabrielle Smith (planning)
Staff Writers: Sondra R. Albert,
Marian Gordon Goldman, Angela D. Goodman,
Susan Hillaby, David Johnson, Marilyn Kendig,
James Randall, Sandra Streepey,
Reiko Uyeshima, Timberlake Wertenbaker
Research Staff: Karen Bates, Sally French,
Laura James, Ginger Seippel, Cinda Siler
Art Staff: Anne B. Landry (art manager),
Angela Alleyne, Penny Burnham, Patricia Byrne,
Catherine Caufield, Jean Held, Jill Losson
Editorial Assistant: Anne Gordon

EDITORIAL PRODUCTION
Production Editor: Douglas B. Graham
Assistant Production Editors:
Gennaro C. Esposito, Feliciano Madrid
Quality Director: Robert L. Young
Assistant Quality Director: James J. Cox
Associate: Serafino J. Cambareri
Copy Staff: Eleanore W. Karsten (chief),
Kathleen Beakley, Ricki Tarlow,
Florence Keith, Pearl Sverdlin
Picture Department: Dolores A. Littles,
Susan Hearn
Traffic: Carmen McLellan

THE CONSULTANTS:
Gretel Courtney taught for several years at the
French Fashion Academy in New York City. She
has studied patternmaking and design at the
Fashion Institute of Technology in New York and
haute couture at the French Fashion Academy.

Annette Feldman is a knitting and crocheting designer, both for clothing and interior decoration.
She is the author of several books, including *Knit,
Purl and Design; Crochet and Creative Design;*
and *Beginner's Needlecraft.*

Tracy Kendall has for many years designed sets
and costumes for commercial films and advertis-
ing. She is currently a fashion stylist.

Julian Tomchin is a textile designer who has re-
ceived the Vogue Fabric Award and a Coty
Award of the American Fashion Critics. A grad-
uate of Syracuse University's Fine Arts College,
he has been chairman of the Textile Design Department at the Shenkar College of Fashion and
Textile Technology in Tel Aviv and now teaches
at the Parsons School of Design in New York.

Valuable assistance was provided by these
departments and individuals of Time Inc.:
Editorial Production, Norman Airey; Library,
Benjamin Lightman; Picture Collection, Doris
O'Neil; Photographic Laboratory, George Karas;
TIME-LIFE News Service, Murray J. Gart;
Correspondents Margot Hapgood and
Dorothy Bacon (London), Ann Natanson
(Rome), S. J. Diamond (Los Angeles), Roy
Rutter (Madrid), Martha Green (San Francisco).

CONTENTS

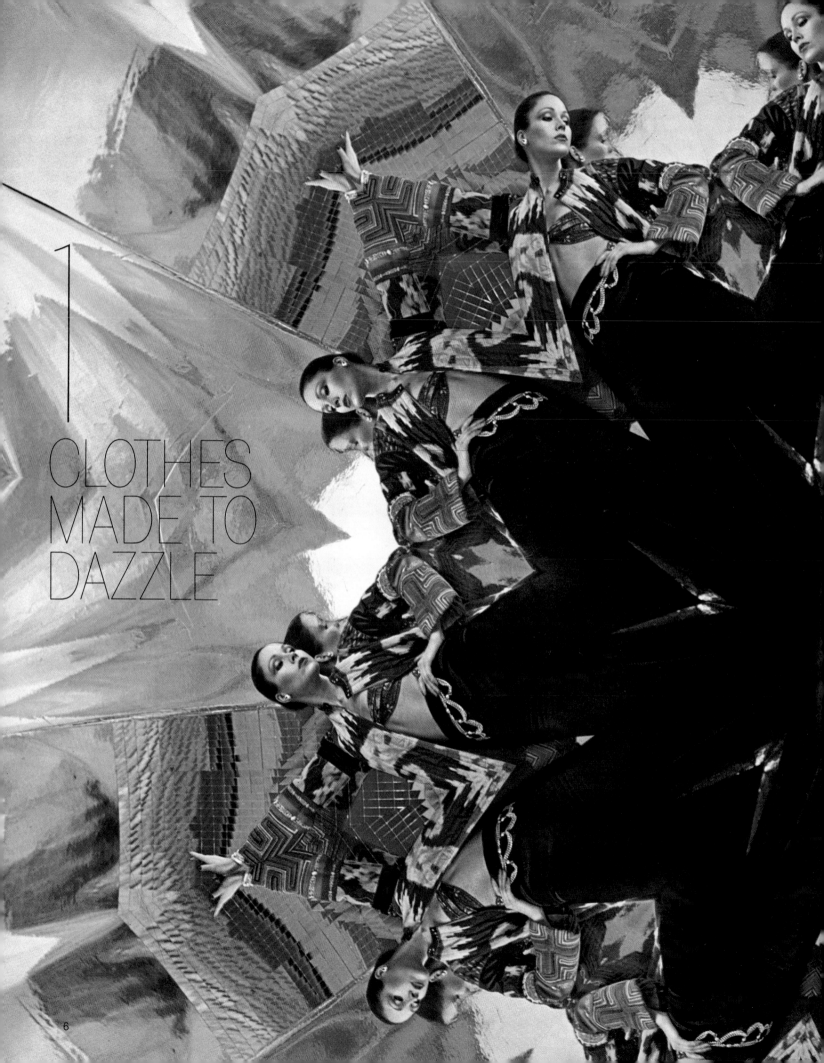

1

CLOTHES
MADE TO
DAZZLE

When Mary Quant opened a small shop in 1955 in London's bohemian Chelsea section, announcing she would sell "a bouillabaisse of clothes and accessories and peculiar odds and ends," she not only launched a new fashion concept, but also gave the word boutique new meaning. Until then a boutique had always been a small, elegant Parisian shop that sold expensive clothes made by the fa-

FASHION EMBELLISHED WITH FUN

mous couturiers. Quant's Bazaar boutique, even though just as small, was different in every other regard.

Bazaar clothes were original, often one-of-a-kind garments, startlingly cut from inexpensive fabrics. They were brightly ornamented with braid, appliqué, lace and various other touches of hand craftwork; and they were dyed in striking colors that were not only bright but frequently clashing. Most of all, the new trappings were both fun to wear and sold at a modest price even working girls could afford.

Boutique still means fun. The idea developed by Quant has now grown up and left its Chelsea home, spreading not only across England, but to France and the rest of the continent, to America, Australia and Japan. The innovative force that energized the original concept continues strong, but time has made it more eclectic. Today, boutique fashion takes in Western-style jeans and nostalgic '40s-style blouses with wide, padded shoulders, as well as Third World garb like West African dashikis, North African caftans and Mao jackets.

Fortunately for the home seamstress, much boutique wear is built around basically plain fabrics and simple-to-sew styles that are made striking and imaginative by colors from tie dyeing, batiking or painting and embellishments such as embroidering or quilting. Using these and other crafts, even a beginner can produce unique clothes with the special boutique look that sets styles all over the world.

Mary Quant and her friends did not dream when they opened their innovative shops that boutique wear might someday go global. At the time, all they wanted to do was design "now clothes" for "now people," most of whom seemed to them to live in and around Chelsea.

Even tackling one London neighborhood took courage, for English girls had traditionally been imprisoned in dowdy gray school uniforms—until they reached the age when they were allowed to wear their mothers' equally drab woolen suits and pale chiffon or brocade evening dresses. But change was in the air. The bombs that rained down on London during World War II had forced Englishmen of different social and economic levels to seek shelter in the same air-raid shelters, and this intermingling helped to lower old class barriers. By the mid-1950s the iconoclastic generation characterized by Britain's "angry young men" was openly attacking the class system, in literature and art and in films that glorified the underside of English life. Newfangled rock 'n' roll stormed into London with English imitations of American rock singer Elvis Presley. Everything, in fact, seemed new—except clothes, which were as drab as ever.

But the revolution in fashion was already afoot in swinging London, and Mary Quant led the shock troops. Long before the boutique era began she had started rebelling against Establishment styles. At age six she cut a bedspread into a dress with nail scissors, and later she polished her talents at art school. After a stint as a milliner's assistant, she teamed up with her future husband, Alexander Plunket Greene, to buy a little attached house in Chelsea. The basement became Alexander's campy restaurant club, the ground floor Quant's Bazaar boutique. Both were an overnight smash. People sometimes stood six deep outside the Bazaar, and Quant struggled to find the kinds of jolly merchandise she wanted for it. Her solution was to put a sewing machine into her bed-sitting-room and run up her own designs out of fabrics she bought retail. Describing those hectic days and nights, she later remembered: "I had to sell one day's output before I had the money to go out and buy more material." Luckily, each day's output seemed to sell better than the last. She hired a dressmaker to work with her, and then another and another, until her room was so full of sewing machines she could hardly find her bed at night.

What made Quant's fashions—and those of the other young English designers who quickly set up boutiques of their own—such a hit was that they were not only fresh but often outlandishly sassy. Anything that established fashion decreed, the boutiques rebelled against—with verve. Hems that revealed the knee were considered scandalously avant-garde, but Quant and her friends cut their skirts shorter yet—and started the ascent of the mini.

Fabrics like wool and linen were the convention, so the rebels used unexpected —and amusing—materials like oilcloth tablecloths for raincoats, cotton bed sheets for dresses and baize meant to cover billiard tables for jackets and coats. To dress up these materials, the designers appliquéd them with Op art designs in contrasting colors and even cut holes in garments, giving them the look of Swiss cheese. By the early 1960s, the audacious Chelsea look had conquered England. Boutiques sprang up all over the country and were frequented both by the young and by the not-so-young who wanted a trendy new look.

While the women shopped in Chelsea, the men traveled east to London's Carnaby Street, which had become a mecca for Mod attire. There they decked themselves out in shirts with loud polka dots, shiny leather vests and tight hip-slung trousers. Turn-of-the-century Edwardian clothes—velvet jackets with silk lapels, shirts with lace ruffles and high-heeled patent-leather boots —were popularized by the Beatles, who had capped the music revolution begun by Elvis Presley.

The Beatles, in all their quirky boutique splendor, caused as much of a stir on the continent and in the United States as in England. By the mid-1960s fashion buyers and designers from Rome and Amsterdam, New York and Los Angeles had begun to flock to London to buy the new clothes and adapt the styles to their markets. Even that couture capital of the world, Paris, was not above borrowing ideas from Chelsea.

The Chelsea look needed modifying to reflect the Parisian view of fashion as an art, and new designers like Emmanuelle Khanh and Sonia Rykiel took up the challenge. Their colors and fabrics were as theatrical as Mary Quant's, their hems at least as short. But with a scallop here and an appliqué there they created softer, more feminine and frankly sexier-looking boutique wear. Rykiel turned to knits and gave them hitherto unheard-of dimensions by producing pullover sweaters so skinny they looked as if they had been shrunk, cardigan sweaters so long they served as coats.

Across the Atlantic, the idea of small shops for amusing clothes had begun to catch on even before the term boutique was used for them. As far back as 1959, an adventurous young businesswoman named Geraldine Stutz had replaced stodgy styles with smarter fashion and boutique-like selling areas when she assumed presidency of Henri Bendel, the posh specialty shop in

New York. Soon big department stores as well as small out-of-the-way shops were providing boutiques—and boutique fashions.

Innovative Americans picked up and expanded the ideas of viewing fashion as fun and boutique design as the way to enjoy it. They pressed for radical notions: they upstaged the mini with hems as short as those on skating skirts, then switched to hems that swept the floor. But they also went in the opposite direction, applying boutique crafts and styles to clothes that were not just for flower children. In the years that followed, the elements of boutique fashion set the trends in Paris salons and Kansas country clubs as well as Chelsea discotheques. For boutique still stands for improvisation and the freedom to reinterpret designs and materials in individual ways.

In today's boutique fashions, homespuns mix with velvets and handcrafts blend with machine-made gewgaws. Whatever kind of artisanry a home seamstress enjoys or wishes to experiment with—stenciling or knitting or quilting—can be put to stylish use. And since simplicity of line is the hallmark of boutique wear, the seamstress who sets out to create her own garments can wind up the sewing in short order, and concentrate her talents on improvising wonderful ways to adorn her designs with beads or braids, studs or appliqués.

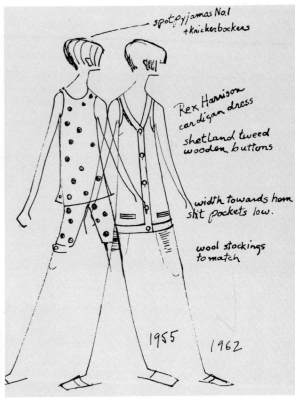

Supergraphics on handbags *(left)*, polka-dotted knickerbockers and sweaters worn as minidresses *(right)* were typical of the sassy designs that made the windows of Mary Quant's boutique, Bazaar, an attraction for Londoners of the 1950s. Such clothes—young, insouciant—had never been seen before, and Quant herself, in her trendy haircut, was the very epitome of the swinging London that introduced the boutique style.

Bright ideas in fancy bred

Boutique designs stretch the imagination. Any period of history, any of the world's bazaars may furnish ideas for styles to be interpreted in ways that suit modern, active life. Handcrafts like studding, appliqué or crochet are put to innovative uses *(left).* Fabrics serve as invitations to patch, trim or dye *(overleaf).*

Whatever the craft, the material or the inspiration, boutique clothes are simple designs transformed by handwork. A home seamstress can turn boutique effects like these into one-of-a-kind fashions and add éclat to a basic wardrobe.

Craftwork creates such novel boutique effects as stud-and-rhinestone decorations on a blue-jean suit, a seascape appliqué on a suede smock and a free-form crochet for a sweater.

Unexpected fabric transformations turn even classic garments into surprising boutique fashions. Parts of an antique quilt, for example, are joined together to produce the handsome Chinese-style jacket at far left. Scraps of a dozen richly patterned materials are pieced to create an elegant collage, then fancifully ornamented with bands of sequins to create front panels for a velveteen jacket. And abstract batik motifs dyed by hand convert an ankle-length T-shirt into a party-going dress.

15

Embellishments applied with a lavish hand provide the dazzle for boutique wear. Masses of shiny metal disks edged with bead ropes glitter on a jersey tunic; macramé fringe flows from a hand-painted silk skirt and shawl, while quilting extravagantly puffs the brocaded metallic fabrics adorning an evening jacket.

2
MAXIMUM STYLE
FOR MINIMAL
SHAPES

Without the facilities and staff of conventional clothing manufacturers, boutique designers have made a virtue of necessity by creating clothes that are simple to cut and simple to assemble. Examined with an analytical eye, a boutique garment is likely to be nothing more than a circle, square or rectangle of cloth, minimally sewn and imaginatively decorated. This idea of elaborating upon the simple design,

CAPITALIZING ON THE LURE OF CAPES

like so much else in the boutique style, is a return to ancient principles. The Mexican poncho, the Arabian burnoose, the Indian sari and Indonesian sarong all belong to this easygoing, unstructured breed of clothing. In fact, echoes of these four garments regularly turn up in boutique collections.

But of all the classic body coverings that have been adopted by boutique designers, probably nothing outclasses the cape, a garment so identified with boutique fashions that it is difficult to think of one without summoning up an image of the other. Why the cape should be so favored is readily apparent: it is the ultimate in uncomplicated garments—it has no sleeves, no waistline, no season or occasion, and it is no trouble to get into. A cape is a circle of cloth, or some part of a circle; it opens in front and is worn tossed over the shoulders as a covering for other clothing.

But there its generic description must stop, for the cape has appeared in an astonishing range of types and has served an equally astonishing array of purposes. It has hidden the bulging profile of pregnant ladies and the daggers of highwaymen. Shepherds have slept under it beside their flocks in the fields, courtiers have worn it to assignations and admirals have wrapped themselves in its wind-cutting folds to direct the course of naval history.

Soldiers in ancient Assyria went into battle in leather capes that were reinforced with metal studs to deflect spears, while in Egypt court ladies often topped their low-cut gowns with gossamer bosom-revealing capelets. Medieval monks wore their capes plain and rough to betoken humility, while kings elaborated them with jewels and fur as badges of their royal office. At her coronation in 1558, Queen Elizabeth of England wore a cape of "clothe of golde, tissued with golde and silver, furred with powdered armyons [flecked ermine]."

The cape continued to be a common article of clothing right up through the 19th Century, especially whenever fashion decreed such cumbersome styles as pan-niered skirts, pumpkin pantaloons and leg-of-mutton sleeves. Then, for a time, it fell from favor—except among those true cape *aficionados,* the Spanish, and except for an occasional eccentric with both the flair and the personal authority to dress as he pleased, like Salvador Dali.

Revivals were attempted now and again. In the 1940s the collections of high-fashion designers Bonnie Cashin and Pauline Trigère began to include the cape—Cashin, because it was the logical concluding element to a particular style of dressing she called "uncut-up coverings"; Trigère, because she loved its facility for hiding anatomical mistakes and at the same time giving the wearer allure. Customers, however, did not rush to buy.

Not until the informal but dashing style of the boutiques took hold did the cape recapture its proper place in the wardrobe. Today it is seen everywhere on women of every age and size and every level of income. A cape will go over anything from slacks to an evening gown; it folds flat for traveling and is as appropriate to stadium seats at a football game as a box at the opera.

Construction of the cape is relatively simple; the only critical point is the shoulder line, which must fit properly for the cape to hang well. There are only the simplest of seams and no darts to be sewed in the yoked cape overleaf—and some of the typical boutique fashions that follow are even simpler. The poncho in fact is probably the most elementary garment invented: it is nothing more than a square of fabric with an opening for the head to slip through.

A cloak for a sweeping flourish

Whether swept about in splendid hauteur or clutched demurely close, a full-length cape makes an eye-turning impression. This one is simply shaped at the shoulders to the wearer's measure and pieced from wedge shapes into a three-quarter circle of dramatic fullness. Ties at the neck serve as both collar and clasp. The only other detail—bands of zigzag topstitching on the ties, yoke, front opening and hem—creates the effect of trapunto quilting on the fluffy mohair fabric.

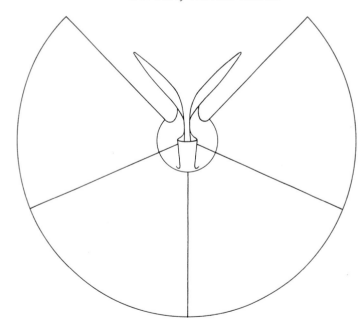

The four wedges that make up the body of the cape encircle a rounded yoke, which is cut to include a pair of ties for the front.

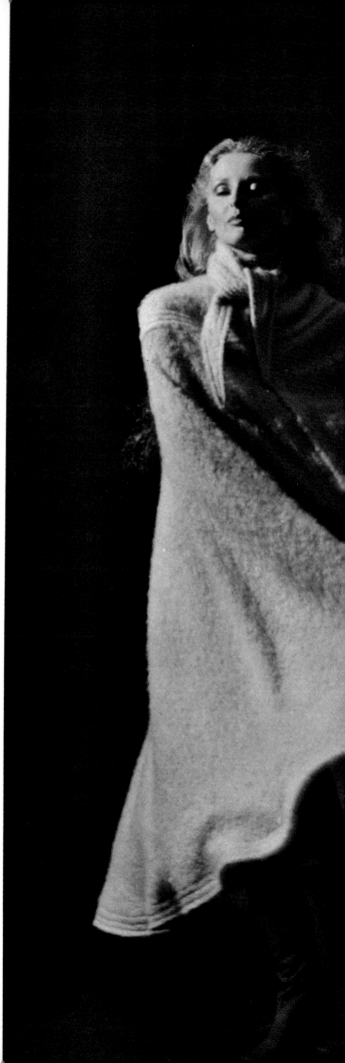

MAKING THE PATTERNS FOR THE CAPE

A MAKING THE YOKE PATTERNS

1. Keeping your arms slightly away from your sides, loosely measure around your body at a point 8 inches below the top of the spine.

2. On your back, measure from the same point to the place on your leg where you want the finished cape to end.

3. Draw a rectangle with a length equal to one fourth of the measurement made in Step 1 and a width of 8 inches. Mark one of the 8-inch sides as the center front.

4. Measure in 4 inches from the center-front edge, and draw a 1-inch line up from the top edge of the rectangle and at right angles to it.

5. Using a curved ruler (Glossary), connect the top of the 1-inch line with the intersection of the top and center-front sides of the rectangle.

6. Measure down 2 inches on the side opposite the center front, and draw a 3-inch horizontal line into the rectangle.

7. Measure up one inch on the same side of the rectangle. Mark.

8. Using the curved ruler, draw an S-shaped line by connecting the ends of the lines drawn in Steps 5 and 6, then the mark made in Step 7.

9. Connect the bottom of the S-shaped line with the lower edge of the center front, with a smoothly curving line. The line should blend into the bottom side of the rectangle about 3 inches from the center front. Label the pattern as the Yoke Front.

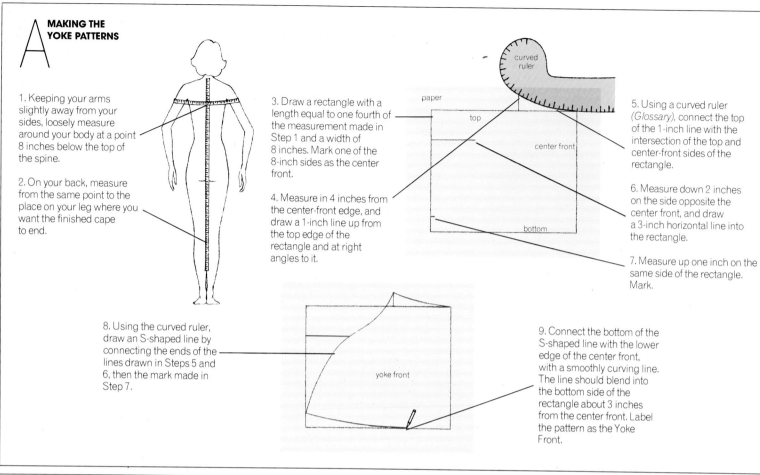

B ADDING THE TIE EXTENSION TO THE PATTERN

10. Tape a piece of paper about 30 inches long to the center-front edge of the pattern.

11. Extend the top edge of the rectangle 28 inches out from the center front.

12. Draw a second 28-inch-long line 3 inches below and parallel to the one drawn in Step 11. Connect the ends of the lines.

13. Measure in 11 inches from the end of the rectangular extension, and mark the top and bottom edges.

14. At the end of the extension, find the center of the line and make a mark 1/4 inch above and below it.

15. Connect the marks made in Step 13 with those made in Step 14, then round off the end, as shown.

16. Mark the line drawn in Step 12 and the center-front edge 3 inches from the point where the two lines intersect.

17. Draw a 1 1/2-inch diagonal line out from the intersection.

18. Connect the marks made in Step 16 with a smooth curve that touches the end of the line drawn in Step 17.

19. Draw a grain-line arrow parallel to the center-front edge.

20. Add cutting lines 5/8 inch outside the seam lines. Cut out the pattern.

21. Pin paper under the pattern and, using a tracing wheel and dressmaker's carbon paper, transfer the seam lines, cutting edge and grain-line arrow to the underside of the paper.

22. Remove the pins, and cut out the duplicate pattern.

23. To make a yoke back pattern repeat Steps 21 and 22, eliminating the tie extension and the grain-line arrow. Label the center edge to be placed on the fold of the fabric.

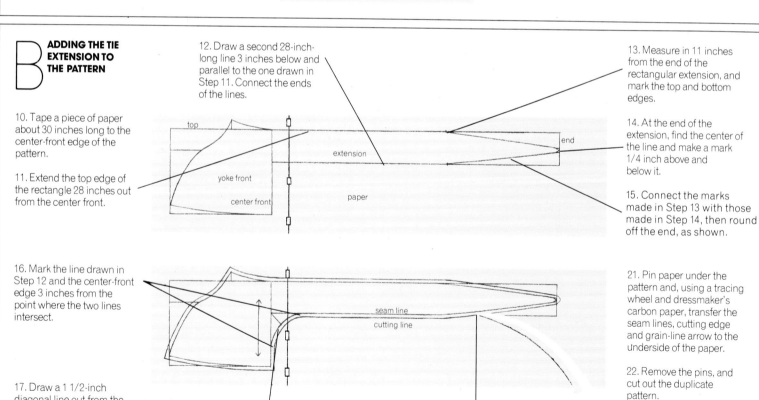

25. Tie one end of a string to a pencil, the other end to a thumbtack. Pulled taut, the length of the string should equal the figure obtained in Step 24. Insert the thumbtack at one corner of a large sheet of paper. Pull the string taut, and draw a quarter circle.

24. Increase the measurement made in Step 1 by 25 per cent; then divide the total by six.

26. Tie another string in the same manner; the length when taut should equal the measurement made in Step 2 plus the figure obtained in Step 24. Then, inserting the thumbtack in the same corner, draw another quarter circle.

27. Cut out the pattern along the quarter-circle lines.

28. Fold the pattern in quarters. Unfold it, and cut off one section along the crease line. Then draw a grain-line arrow parallel to one straight edge.

29. Tape paper under the edges of the pattern. Draw cutting lines 5/8 inch outside the top and side edges. Then draw a hem cutting line 1 1/2 inches outside the bottom edge. Cut out the pattern.

30. Make a duplicate pattern for the cape by repeating Steps 21 and 22.

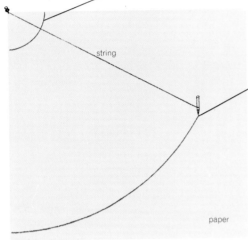

string

paper

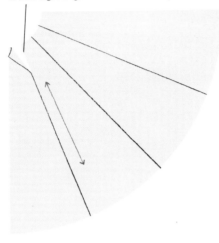

SEWING THE CAPE

A LAYING OUT, CUTTING AND MARKING

3. Arrange the duplicate cape pattern in the same manner near the opposite selvage string, adding string as necessary.

4. Lift the original pattern, and place it below the duplicate pattern, as indicated by the dotted lines. This time, however, the side edge of the pattern should be flush against the selvage string.

5. Repeat Step 4 with the duplicate pattern.

6. Arrange the yoke front pattern below the bottom cape pattern. Then repeat Steps 3-5.

7. Position the yoke back pattern below the bottom yoke front pattern.

8. Replace the bottom string, and measure the length of the box.

1. To determine the amount of fabric you will need, form a string rectangle around the original cape pattern. The side of the pattern that parallels the grain-line arrow should be 1 inch from one of the strings representing the selvage.

2. Measure the distance between the selvage strings to determine the minimum width of the fabric. Increase the width of the rectangle so that it equals the next nearest standard fabric width. Remove the string that parallels the top string.

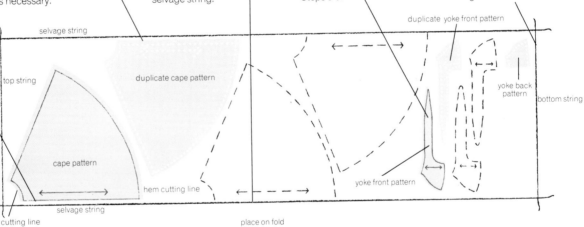

selvage string

top string

duplicate cape pattern

duplicate yoke front pattern

cape pattern

yoke back pattern

bottom string

hem cutting line

yoke front pattern

selvage string

neck cutting line

9. Follow the arrangement determined in Steps 1 and 3 to pin the cape patterns to a single layer of fabric that is wrong side down.

10. Cut around the edges of the patterns, except at the edges that parallel the selvages where the neck and hem cutting lines should extend to the selvage. The extra fabric will serve as a facing for the front of the cape.

11. Using dressmaker's carbon paper and a tracing wheel, transfer the seam lines to the wrong side of the fabric.

12. Remove the patterns, then cut and mark two more cape panels and four yoke front pieces, arranging the patterns on the fabric as you did in the string box.

place on fold

fabric (wrong side)

fold   selvage   selvage   fold

yoke back pattern

13. Fold the remaining fabric, wrong side out, so that the selvages meet in the center. There should be two lengthwise folds.

14. Pin the yoke back pattern to one fold. Cut around the pattern edges and repeat Step 11. Flop the pattern and cut a second yoke back piece from the remaining folded fabric.

continued

B CONSTRUCTING THE YOKE SECTION

15. Place one of the yoke back pieces wrong side down. Over it position a yoke front piece, wrong side up, matching the shoulder seams. Pin.

16. Baste and remove the pins; then machine stitch and remove the basting.

17. Make clips in the seam allowance, perpendicular to the seam. Press the seam open.

18. Repeat Steps 15-17 to attach a yoke front piece to the yoke back at the other shoulder seam.

19. Sew the remaining yoke back and yoke fronts together at the shoulders in the same manner.

20. Place the two yokes together, wrong sides out. Pin.

21. Starting and ending at the bottom of the center-front edge, baste the yokes together just outside the stitching lines. Leave the bottom edge open.

22. Machine stitch along the seam lines, and remove the basting.

23. Trim the seam allowance to 1/4 inch, and make clips, perpendicular to the seam, at the curves.

24. Turn the yoke right side out. Press.

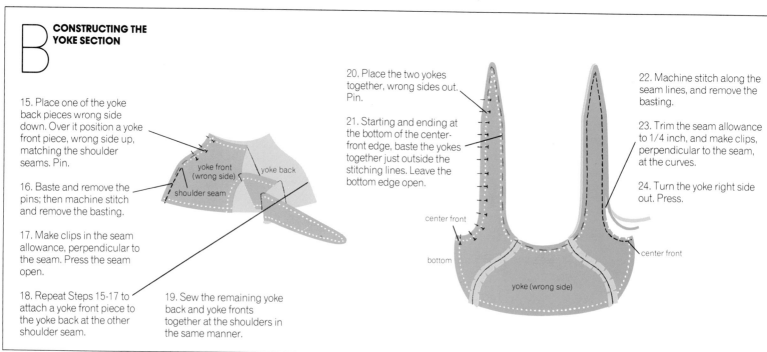

C CONSTRUCTING THE CAPE SECTION

25. On one cape front panel, fold the 1 5/8-inch facing to the wrong side and pin. Baste, and remove the pins. Repeat on the other front panel.

26. Place the two cape back panels together, wrong sides out, and pin along the center-back seam line.

27. Machine stitch and remove the pins. Press the seam allowance open, then zigzag the raw edges.

28. Pin the front panels, wrong sides up, to the back section, wrong side down, along the side seams, then repeat Step 27.

29. Stay stitch (Glossary) the upper edge of the cape just outside the seam line markings.

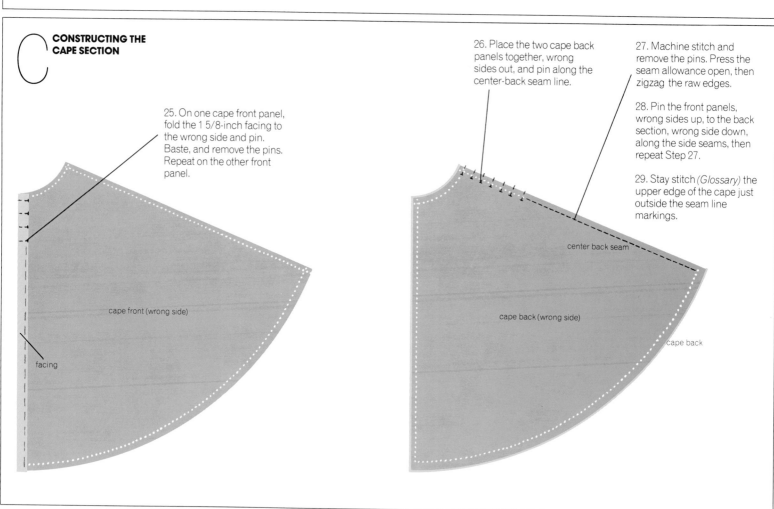

D SEWING THE CAPE TO THE YOKE

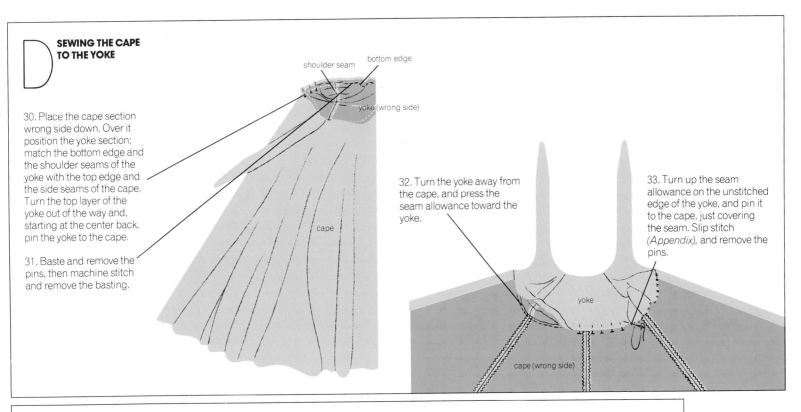

shoulder seam bottom edge

yoke (wrong side)

cape

30. Place the cape section wrong side down. Over it position the yoke section; match the bottom edge and the shoulder seams of the yoke with the top edge and the side seams of the cape. Turn the top layer of the yoke out of the way and, starting at the center back, pin the yoke to the cape.

31. Baste and remove the pins, then machine stitch and remove the basting.

32. Turn the yoke away from the cape, and press the seam allowance toward the yoke.

33. Turn up the seam allowance on the unstitched edge of the yoke, and pin it to the cape, just covering the seam. Slip stitch (*Appendix*), and remove the pins.

yoke

cape (wrong side)

E FINISHING THE CAPE

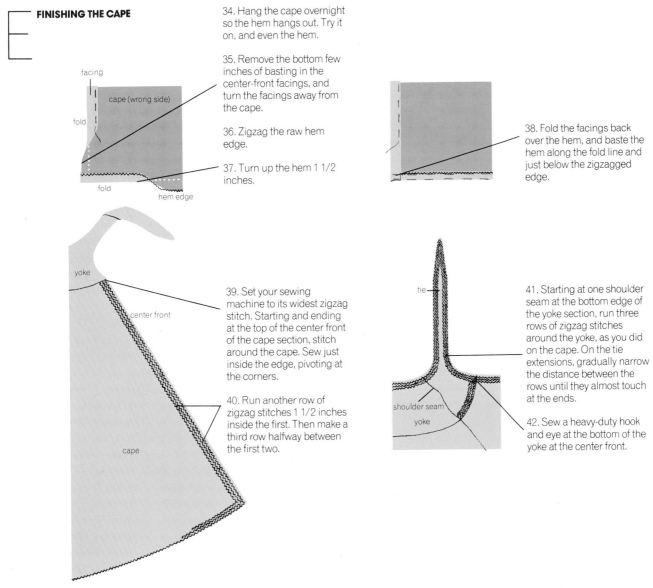

facing

cape (wrong side)

fold

fold

hem edge

34. Hang the cape overnight so the hem hangs out. Try it on, and even the hem.

35. Remove the bottom few inches of basting in the center-front facings, and turn the facings away from the cape.

36. Zigzag the raw hem edge.

37. Turn up the hem 1 1/2 inches.

38. Fold the facings back over the hem, and baste the hem along the fold line and just below the zigzagged edge.

yoke

center front

cape

39. Set your sewing machine to its widest zigzag stitch. Starting and ending at the top of the center front of the cape section, stitch around the cape. Sew just inside the edge, pivoting at the corners.

40. Run another row of zigzag stitches 1 1/2 inches inside the first. Then make a third row halfway between the first two.

tie

shoulder seam

yoke

41. Starting at one shoulder seam at the bottom edge of the yoke section, run three rows of zigzag stitches around the yoke, as you did on the cape. On the tie extensions, gradually narrow the distance between the rows until they almost touch at the ends.

42. Sew a heavy-duty hook and eye at the bottom of the yoke at the center front.

Glamor enfolded in a tunic

Two squares of cloth are all you need for the glamorous, fully lined tunic shown in two views at right. This chiffon version is aglitter with ripples of sequins, but its shape would be just as flattering executed in any other supple, lightweight fabric, and it could be decorated with such flourishes as hand-painted or stenciled designs or ribbon trim.

One size fits all, and the sewing, which is diagramed below and detailed overleaf, is quite simple. In fact, the trickiest part is turning the garment inside and right side out for seaming—a process that is much easier than it looks.

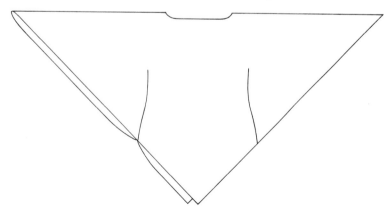

Fabric squares, folded diagonally, form the tunic and lining. The neck opening is centered on the fold; side seams create sleeves.

THE TUNIC

A DRAFTING THE PATTERN

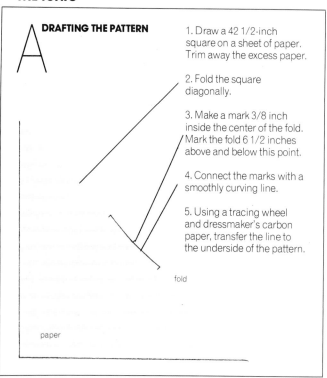

1. Draw a 42 1/2-inch square on a sheet of paper. Trim away the excess paper.

2. Fold the square diagonally.

3. Make a mark 3/8 inch inside the center of the fold. Mark the fold 6 1/2 inches above and below this point.

4. Connect the marks with a smoothly curving line.

5. Using a tracing wheel and dressmaker's carbon paper, transfer the line to the underside of the pattern.

fold

paper

B LAYING OUT, CUTTING AND MARKING

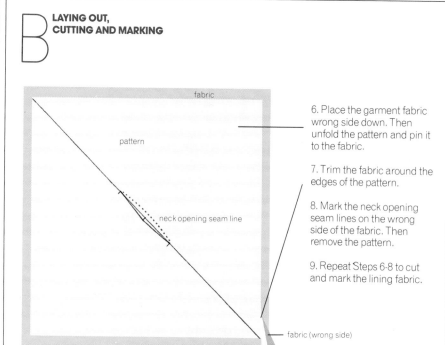

fabric

pattern

neck opening seam line

fabric (wrong side)

6. Place the garment fabric wrong side down. Then unfold the pattern and pin it to the fabric.

7. Trim the fabric around the edges of the pattern.

8. Mark the neck opening seam lines on the wrong side of the fabric. Then remove the pattern.

9. Repeat Steps 6-8 to cut and mark the lining fabric.

C MAKING THE NECK OPENING

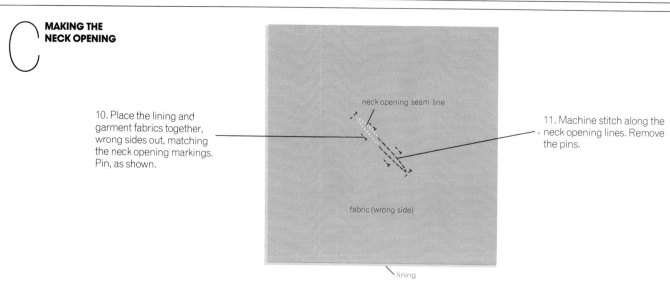

neck opening seam line

fabric (wrong side)

lining

10. Place the lining and garment fabrics together, wrong sides out, matching the neck opening markings. Pin, as shown.

11. Machine stitch along the neck opening lines. Remove the pins.

12. Trim the neck opening 1/4 inch inside the stitching. At the corners, slash up to, but not through, the stitches.

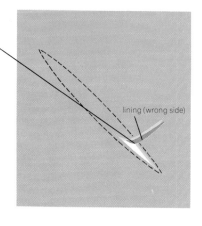

lining (wrong side)

13. Turn the top layer of fabric through the neck opening, so that the wrong sides are together.

14. Roll the neck seam between your fingers, turning the seam slightly to the underside of the garment. Press.

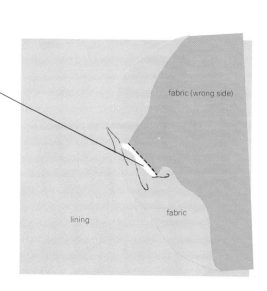

fabric (wrong side)

lining

fabric

D ‖ HEMMING THE GARMENT

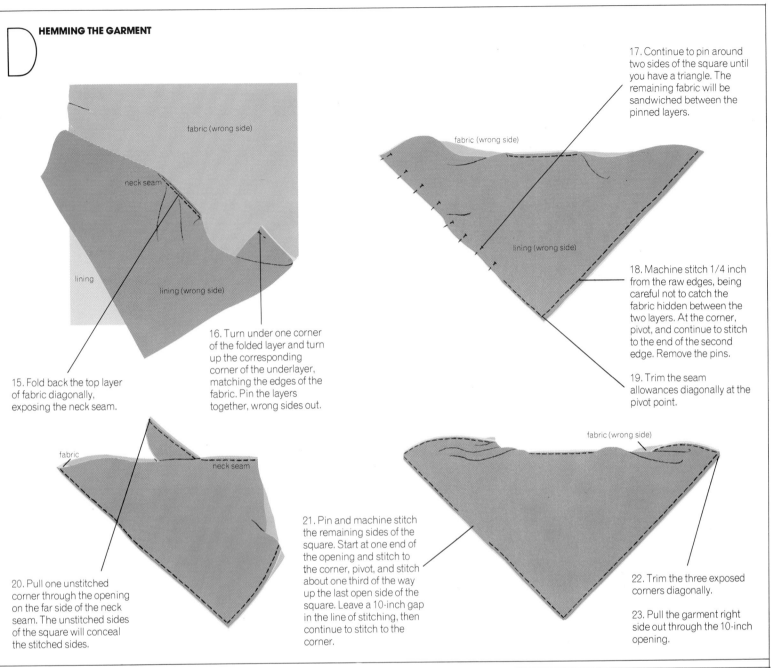

17. Continue to pin around two sides of the square until you have a triangle. The remaining fabric will be sandwiched between the pinned layers.

fabric (wrong side)

lining (wrong side)

18. Machine stitch 1/4 inch from the raw edges, being careful not to catch the fabric hidden between the two layers. At the corner, pivot, and continue to stitch to the end of the second edge. Remove the pins.

19. Trim the seam allowances diagonally at the pivot point.

fabric (wrong side)

neck seam

lining

lining (wrong side)

15. Fold back the top layer of fabric diagonally, exposing the neck seam.

16. Turn under one corner of the folded layer and turn up the corresponding corner of the underlayer, matching the edges of the fabric. Pin the layers together, wrong sides out.

fabric

neck seam

20. Pull one unstitched corner through the opening on the far side of the neck seam. The unstitched sides of the square will conceal the stitched sides.

21. Pin and machine stitch the remaining sides of the square. Start at one end of the opening and stitch to the corner, pivot, and stitch about one third of the way up the last open side of the square. Leave a 10-inch gap in the line of stitching, then continue to stitch to the corner.

22. Trim the three exposed corners diagonally.

23. Pull the garment right side out through the 10-inch opening.

E ‖ COMPLETING THE GARMENT

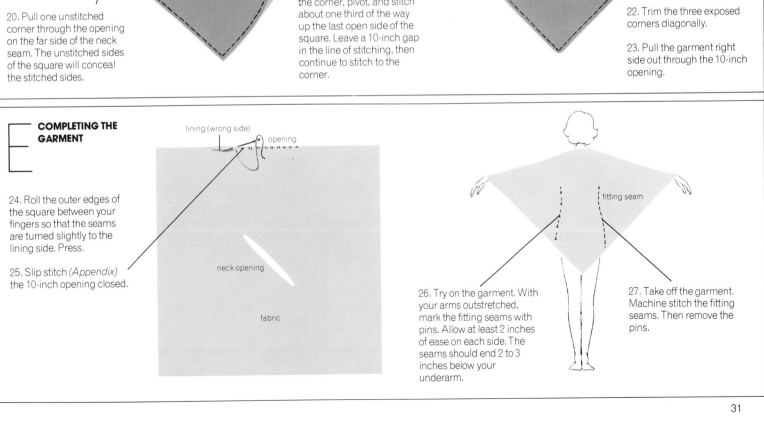

lining (wrong side)

opening

24. Roll the outer edges of the square between your fingers so that the seams are turned slightly to the lining side. Press.

25. Slip stitch (*Appendix*) the 10-inch opening closed.

neck opening

fabric

fitting seam

26. Try on the garment. With your arms outstretched, mark the fitting seams with pins. Allow at least 2 inches of ease on each side. The seams should end 2 to 3 inches below your underarm.

27. Take off the garment. Machine stitch the fitting seams. Then remove the pins.

A grand gesture of an overblouse

With its fluid folds and slinky sleeves, this overblouse could make you feel like Ingrid Bergman on a rendezvous with Humphrey Bogart. Begun as a simple rectangle *(below),* the overblouse dispenses with all but a minimum of seams to allow the fabric natural play.

In this theatrical version, crepe capitalizes on the freedom of the style, but any other soft, drapable fabric would flow just as dramatically. Bands of color accentuate the flowing sleeves shown here, but for added interest, you could decorate the blouse with trimmings—rhinestones, sequins or beads, for example—that are light enough to move with the cloth.

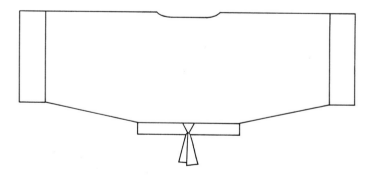

A fabric rectangle, folded in half and opened at the neck *(above),* forms the overblouse. Rectangular strips band the sleeves and waist.

THE OVERBLOUSE

A MAKING THE PATTERN FOR THE OVERBLOUSE

1. Measure from the top of your spine over the shoulder to a point 5 inches above the wristbone. Multiply by two.

2. Draw a rectangle that is the length determined in Step 1, and 17 inches wide. Divide the rectangle in half widthwise, and mark arrows on the center line, designating it as the grain line.

3. At the top of the rectangle, measure out 5 1/2 inches on each side of the center point, and draw 1-inch lines at right angles to the edge. Connect the ends of the lines.

4. To round off the neck opening, first draw 5/8-inch-long diagonal lines from the corners into the opening. Then draw a smoothly curved line that touches the tips of the diagonal lines.

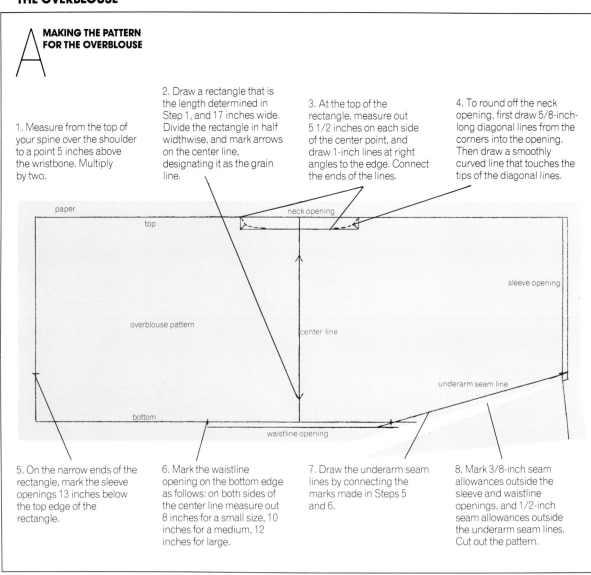

5. On the narrow ends of the rectangle, mark the sleeve openings 13 inches below the top edge of the rectangle.

6. Mark the waistline opening on the bottom edge as follows: on both sides of the center line measure out 8 inches for a small size, 10 inches for a medium, 12 inches for large.

7. Draw the underarm seam lines by connecting the marks made in Steps 5 and 6.

8. Mark 3/8-inch seam allowances outside the sleeve and waistline openings, and 1/2-inch seam allowances outside the underarm seam lines. Cut out the pattern.

B MAKING PATTERNS FOR THE BANDS, WAISTBAND AND TIE

9. To make the band pattern, draw a rectangle 13 inches long and 9 inches wide. Mark one narrow side to be placed on the fold.

11. For the waistband, draw a rectangle that is 32 inches long and 3 inches wide.

12. Measure in 8 inches from one end and 1/4 inch down from the top edge. Mark a 1-inch buttonhole placement line parallel to the ends.

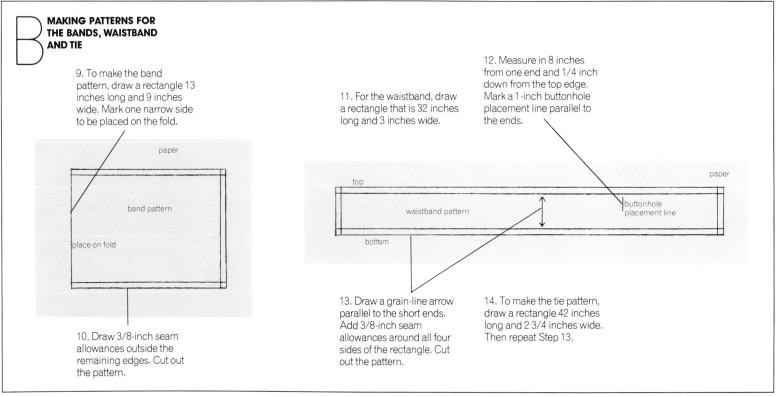

10. Draw 3/8-inch seam allowances outside the remaining edges. Cut out the pattern.

13. Draw a grain-line arrow parallel to the short ends. Add 3/8-inch seam allowances around all four sides of the rectangle. Cut out the pattern.

14. To make the tie pattern, draw a rectangle 42 inches long and 2 3/4 inches wide. Then repeat Step 13.

C LAYING OUT, CUTTING AND MARKING

15. Fold 2 yards of fabric widthwise, wrong side out, so that the double layer measures 18 inches.

16. Pin the overblouse pattern to the fabric so that the shoulder edges are aligned with the fold.

17. Pin the waistband and tie patterns to the single layer of fabric.

18. Cut around the edges of the patterns. Then, using dressmaker's carbon paper and a tracing wheel, transfer all pattern markings to the wrong side of the fabric.

19. Fold the remaining fabric in half lengthwise, wrong side out.

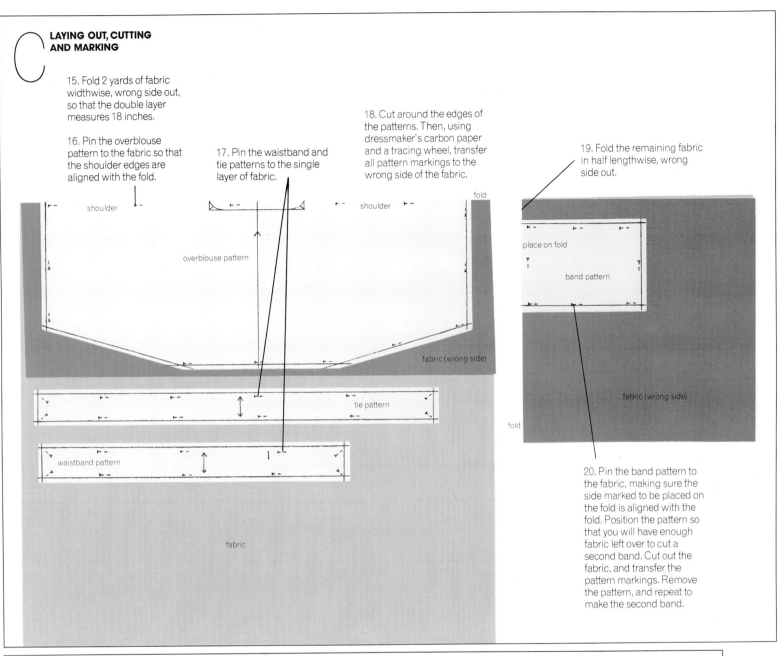

20. Pin the band pattern to the fabric, making sure the side marked to be placed on the fold is aligned with the fold. Position the pattern so that you will have enough fabric left over to cut a second band. Cut out the fabric, and transfer the pattern markings. Remove the pattern, and repeat to make the second band.

D FINISHING THE NECKLINE SEAM

21. With the overblouse piece wrong side out, fold a few inches of the neck edge 1/8 inch. Fold again 1/8 inch, enclosing the raw edge inside the second fold.

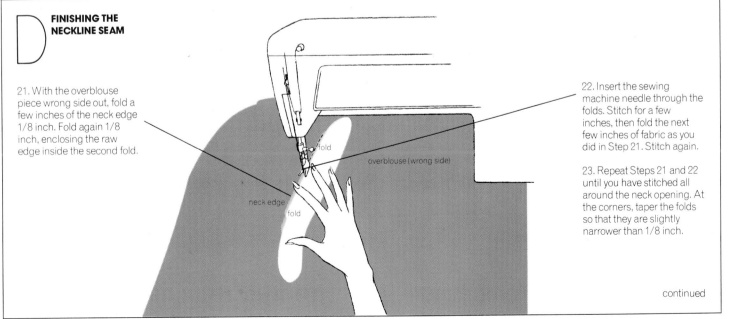

22. Insert the sewing machine needle through the folds. Stitch for a few inches, then fold the next few inches of fabric as you did in Step 21. Stitch again.

23. Repeat Steps 21 and 22 until you have stitched all around the neck opening. At the corners, taper the folds so that they are slightly narrower than 1/8 inch.

continued

FINISHING THE UNDERARM SEAMS

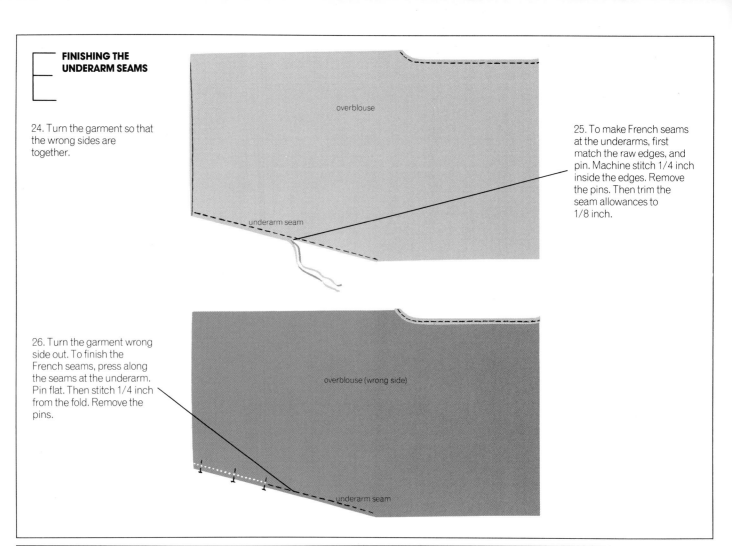

24. Turn the garment so that the wrong sides are together.

25. To make French seams at the underarms, first match the raw edges, and pin. Machine stitch 1/4 inch inside the edges. Remove the pins. Then trim the seam allowances to 1/8 inch.

26. Turn the garment wrong side out. To finish the French seams, press along the seams at the underarm. Pin flat. Then stitch 1/4 inch from the fold. Remove the pins.

ATTACHING THE SLEEVE BANDS

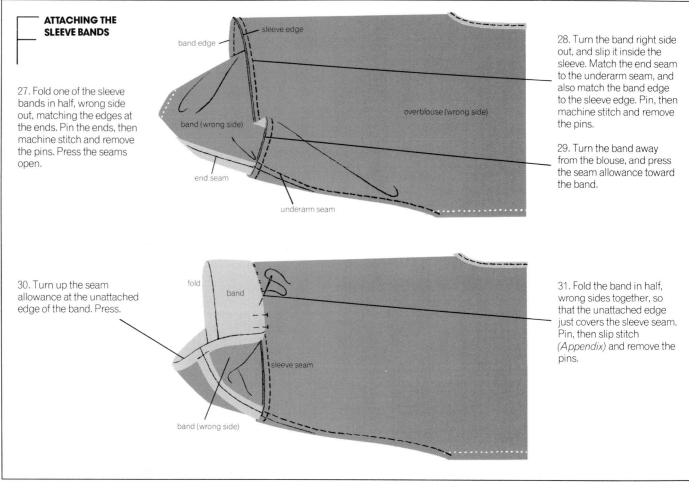

27. Fold one of the sleeve bands in half, wrong side out, matching the edges at the ends. Pin the ends, then machine stitch and remove the pins. Press the seams open.

28. Turn the band right side out, and slip it inside the sleeve. Match the end seam to the underarm seam, and also match the band edge to the sleeve edge. Pin, then machine stitch and remove the pins.

29. Turn the band away from the blouse, and press the seam allowance toward the band.

30. Turn up the seam allowance at the unattached edge of the band. Press.

31. Fold the band in half, wrong sides together, so that the unattached edge just covers the sleeve seam. Pin, then slip stitch (*Appendix*) and remove the pins.

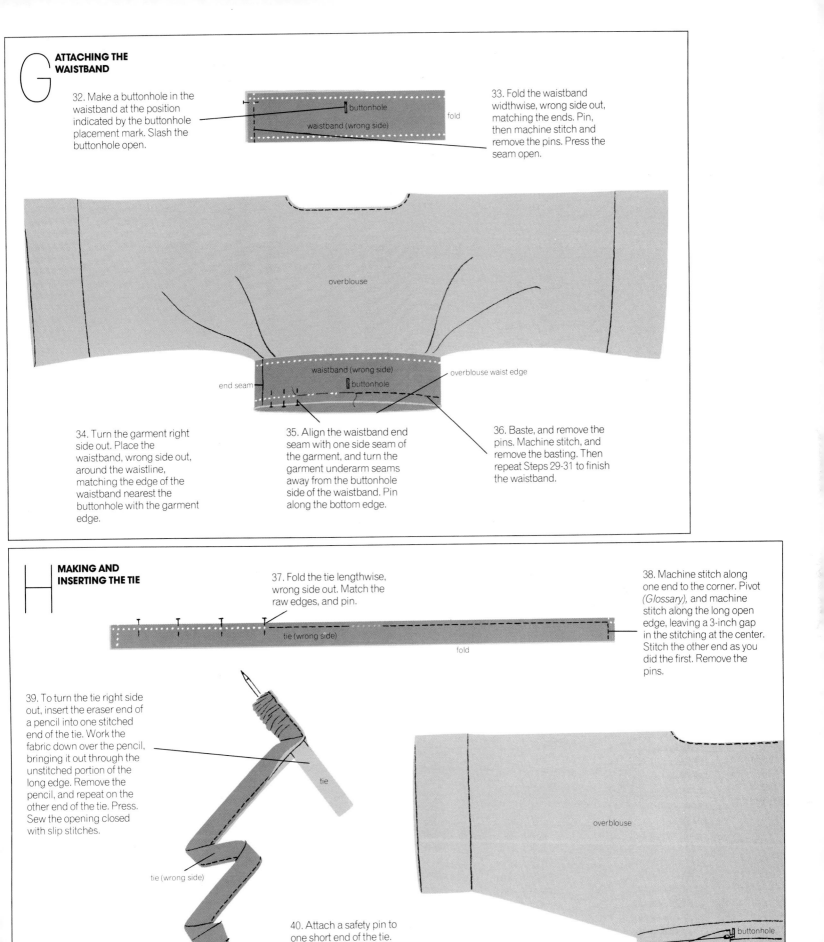

G ATTACHING THE WAISTBAND

32. Make a buttonhole in the waistband at the position indicated by the buttonhole placement mark. Slash the buttonhole open.

buttonhole
waistband (wrong side)
fold

33. Fold the waistband widthwise, wrong side out, matching the ends. Pin, then machine stitch and remove the pins. Press the seam open.

overblouse

waistband (wrong side)
overblouse waist edge
end seam
buttonhole

34. Turn the garment right side out. Place the waistband, wrong side out, around the waistline, matching the edge of the waistband nearest the buttonhole with the garment edge.

35. Align the waistband end seam with one side seam of the garment, and turn the garment underarm seams away from the buttonhole side of the waistband. Pin along the bottom edge.

36. Baste, and remove the pins. Machine stitch, and remove the basting. Then repeat Steps 29-31 to finish the waistband.

H MAKING AND INSERTING THE TIE

37. Fold the tie lengthwise, wrong side out. Match the raw edges, and pin.

tie (wrong side)
fold

38. Machine stitch along one end to the corner. Pivot (Glossary), and machine stitch along the long open edge, leaving a 3-inch gap in the stitching at the center. Stitch the other end as you did the first. Remove the pins.

39. To turn the tie right side out, insert the eraser end of a pencil into one stitched end of the tie. Work the fabric down over the pencil, bringing it out through the unstitched portion of the long edge. Remove the pencil, and repeat on the other end of the tie. Press. Sew the opening closed with slip stitches.

tie

tie (wrong side)

overblouse

40. Attach a safety pin to one short end of the tie. Insert the pin in the buttonhole, and thread the tie through the waistband. Remove the safety pin.

buttonhole

tie

A versatile wraparound jumper

What starts out like an apron becomes a multipurpose jumper that changes mood with the fabric it's made from. In corduroy, as shown here, or in calico or denim, it adds homespun casualness to blouse or sweater. In velveteen or satin, worn alone, it goes seductively to a party.

Since bib and skirt are simple geometric cuts of cloth *(below),* they make fine surfaces for displaying batik or the tie-dyed stripes here. Three yards of 45-inch fabric are needed, and one size fits all.

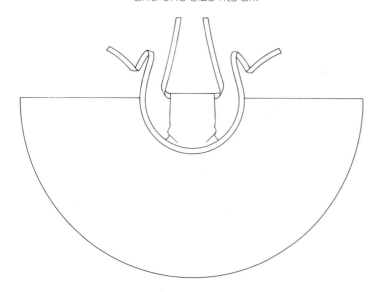

A half circle of fabric forms the jumper skirt while a slightly tapered square forms the bib. The ties are strips of the same fabric.

THE JUMPER

A DRAFTING THE PATTERNS

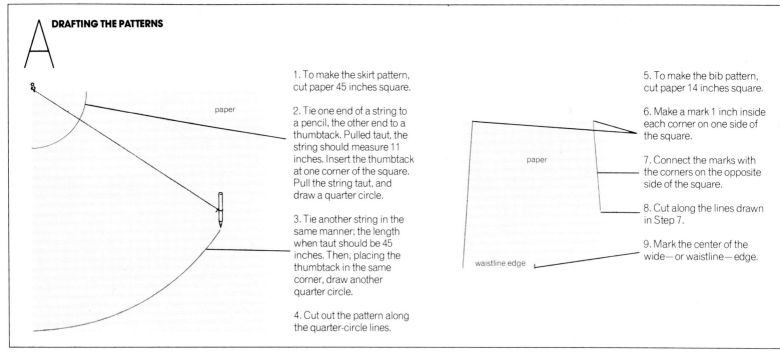

1. To make the skirt pattern, cut paper 45 inches square.

2. Tie one end of a string to a pencil, the other end to a thumbtack. Pulled taut, the string should measure 11 inches. Insert the thumbtack at one corner of the square. Pull the string taut, and draw a quarter circle.

3. Tie another string in the same manner; the length when taut should be 45 inches. Then, placing the thumbtack in the same corner, draw another quarter circle.

4. Cut out the pattern along the quarter-circle lines.

5. To make the bib pattern, cut paper 14 inches square.

6. Make a mark 1 inch inside each corner on one side of the square.

7. Connect the marks with the corners on the opposite side of the square.

8. Cut along the lines drawn in Step 7.

9. Mark the center of the wide—or waistline—edge.

B LAYING OUT, CUTTING AND MARKING

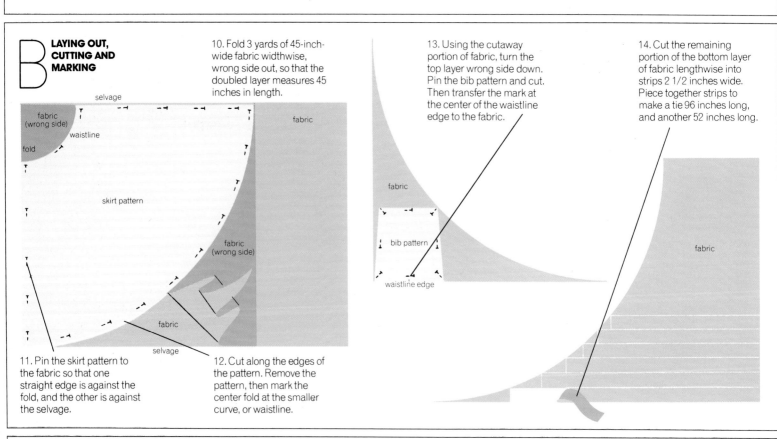

10. Fold 3 yards of 45-inch-wide fabric widthwise, wrong side out, so that the doubled layer measures 45 inches in length.

11. Pin the skirt pattern to the fabric so that one straight edge is against the fold, and the other is against the selvage.

12. Cut along the edges of the pattern. Remove the pattern, then mark the center fold at the smaller curve, or waistline.

13. Using the cutaway portion of fabric, turn the top layer wrong side down. Pin the bib pattern and cut. Then transfer the mark at the center of the waistline edge to the fabric.

14. Cut the remaining portion of the bottom layer of fabric lengthwise into strips 2 1/2 inches wide. Piece together strips to make a tie 96 inches long, and another 52 inches long.

C PREPARING THE BIB

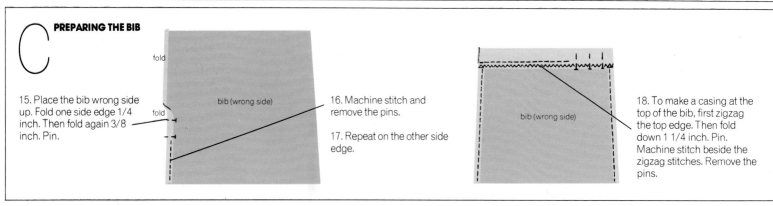

15. Place the bib wrong side up. Fold one side edge 1/4 inch. Then fold again 3/8 inch. Pin.

16. Machine stitch and remove the pins.

17. Repeat on the other side edge.

18. To make a casing at the top of the bib, first zigzag the top edge. Then fold down 1 1/4 inch. Pin. Machine stitch beside the zigzag stitches. Remove the pins.

D | PREPARING THE SKIRT

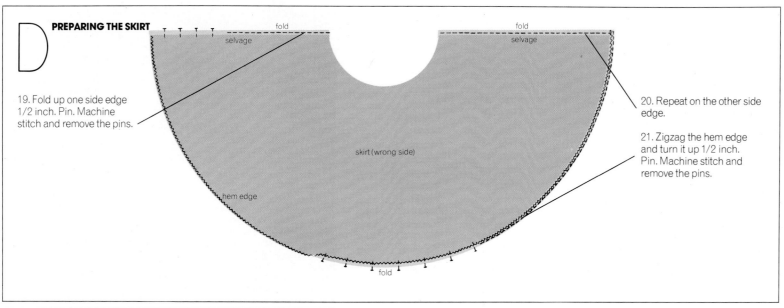

fold
selvage
fold
selvage

19. Fold up one side edge 1/2 inch. Pin. Machine stitch and remove the pins.

20. Repeat on the other side edge.

21. Zigzag the hem edge and turn it up 1/2 inch. Pin. Machine stitch and remove the pins.

skirt (wrong side)

hem edge

fold

E | PREPARING THE TIES

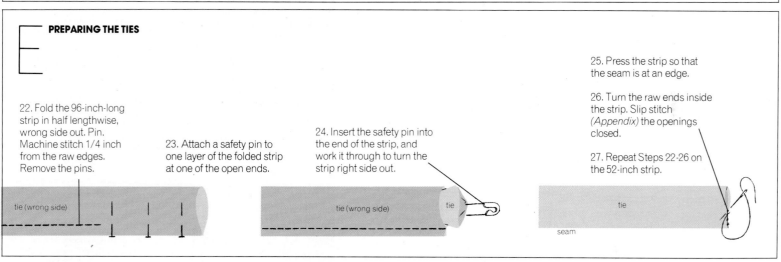

22. Fold the 96-inch-long strip in half lengthwise, wrong side out. Pin. Machine stitch 1/4 inch from the raw edges. Remove the pins.

23. Attach a safety pin to one layer of the folded strip at one of the open ends.

24. Insert the safety pin into the end of the strip, and work it through to turn the strip right side out.

25. Press the strip so that the seam is at an edge.

26. Turn the raw ends inside the strip. Slip stitch (*Appendix*) the openings closed.

27. Repeat Steps 22-26 on the 52-inch strip.

tie (wrong side)

tie (wrong side)

tie

tie

seam

F | ASSEMBLING THE GARMENT

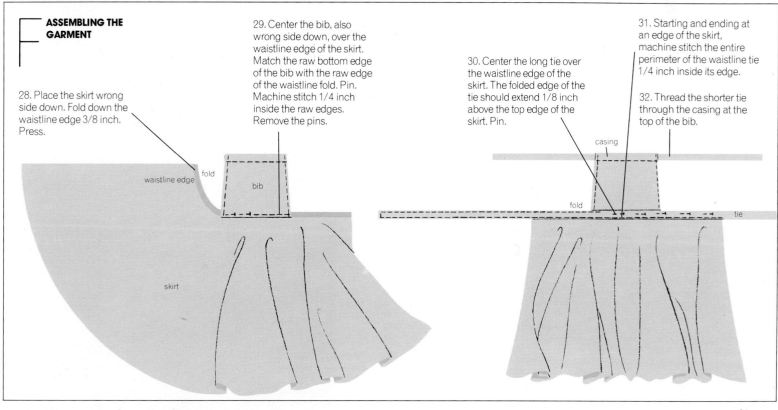

28. Place the skirt wrong side down. Fold down the waistline edge 3/8 inch. Press.

29. Center the bib, also wrong side down, over the waistline edge of the skirt. Match the raw bottom edge of the bib with the raw edge of the waistline fold. Pin. Machine stitch 1/4 inch inside the raw edges. Remove the pins.

30. Center the long tie over the waistline edge of the skirt. The folded edge of the tie should extend 1/8 inch above the top edge of the skirt. Pin.

31. Starting and ending at an edge of the skirt, machine stitch the entire perimeter of the waistline tie 1/4 inch inside its edge.

32. Thread the shorter tie through the casing at the top of the bib.

waistline edge
fold
bib
skirt

casing
fold
tie
skirt

A swirling capelet for a collar

The gentle fullness of this capelet collar accents the sinuous grace of a fabric like the satin crepe shown here. At the same time, the capelet provides an elegant background for such handcrafted decorations as the stenciled flowers that cascade from its shoulders.

The capelet itself is an oval of cloth *(below)* designed to turn a standard wraparound blouse pattern into a dramatic topper for evening. Directions for drawing the oval and stitching it to the blouse appear overleaf.

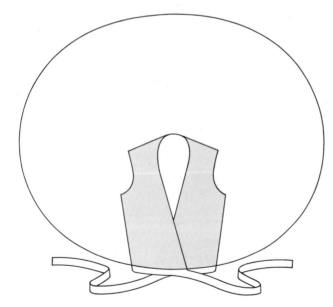

The fabric oval that forms a capelet collar *(above)* is cut out at the center to conform to the blouse neckline and wrap at the waist.

A DRAFTING THE PATTERN

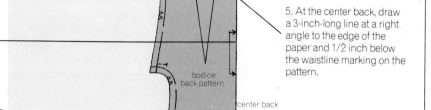

1. Pin the bodice back pattern to a large sheet of paper. Align the center-back edge of the pattern with one long edge of the paper.

2. Arrange the bodice front pattern on the paper so that its neck-shoulder seam line intersection matches that of the bodice back pattern.

3. Align the center-front edge of the front pattern with the long edge of the paper at the mark indicating the waistline closure attachment point. Pin the pattern in place.

4. Measure from the base of your neck over the shoulder to a point 2 inches below your elbow.

5. At the center back, draw a 3-inch-long line at a right angle to the edge of the paper and 1/2 inch below the waistline marking on the pattern.

6. Measure out from the neck-shoulder seam intersections on the patterns a distance equal to the measurement made in Step 4. Mark.

7. Draw a line similar to the one drawn in Step 5 at the mark indicating the attachment point for the waistline closure on the front pattern.

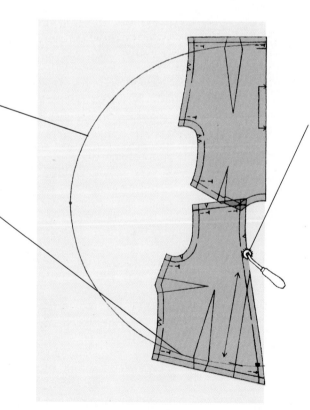

8. Connect the ends of the lines to the mark made in Step 6 with a smoothly curving arch.

9. With dressmaker's carbon paper and a tracing wheel, transfer to the paper any portions of the arched line that are drawn on the pattern pieces.

10. Transfer the neck seam and cutting lines to the paper, and make a mark at the shoulder seam.

11. Remove the patterns from the paper.

12. Draw a cutting line 1/2 inch outside of and parallel to the arched line.

13. Trim away the excess paper along the cutting lines.

B DETERMINING THE FABRIC REQUIREMENTS

14. Lay the collar pattern on a flat surface. Align a length of string with the center-back edge and the bottom point of the center-front edge.

15. Arrange two more lengths of string so they form a right triangle around the pattern piece.

16. Measure the strings that form the right angle. They should be equal in length. This measurement represents the length and minimum width of the fabric required.

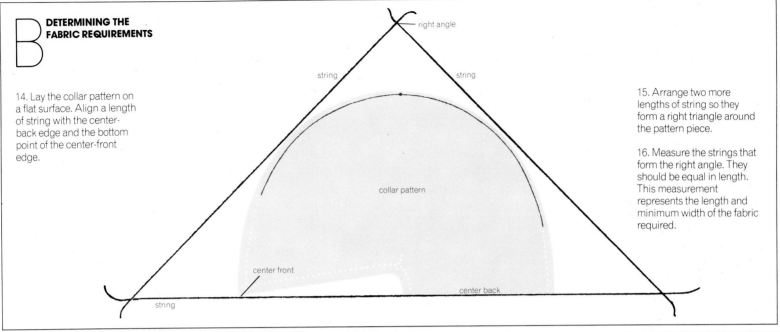

C LAYING OUT, CUTTING AND MARKING

17. To find the bias of the fabric, fold it diagonally so the raw widthwise edge aligns with one selvage.

18. Pin the collar pattern to the fabric with the center-back edge and the bottom center-front point flush against the fold.

19. Cut out the collar. Transfer all pattern markings. Then fold the remaining fabric in half lengthwise, and lay out the remaining pattern pieces according to your pattern instructions.

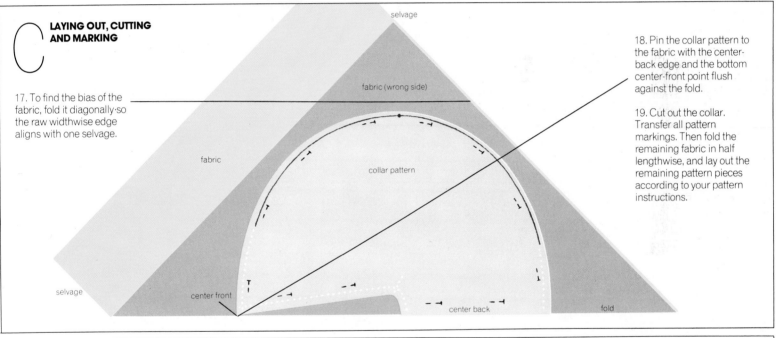

D ASSEMBLING THE GARMENT

20. Assemble the garment according to your pattern instructions, up to the point where you would put on the neck facing. Turn the garment right side out.

21. On the collar piece, cut a 1/4-inch notch in the neckline seam allowance at the center back.

22. Make a hem at the bottom edge of the collar as desired.

23. Position the collar, wrong side down, over the garment. Match the shoulder seam markings on both pieces. Pin.

24. Baste, and remove the pins.

25. Machine stitch, and remove the basting.

26. Attach the facing, and complete the garment according to your pattern instructions.

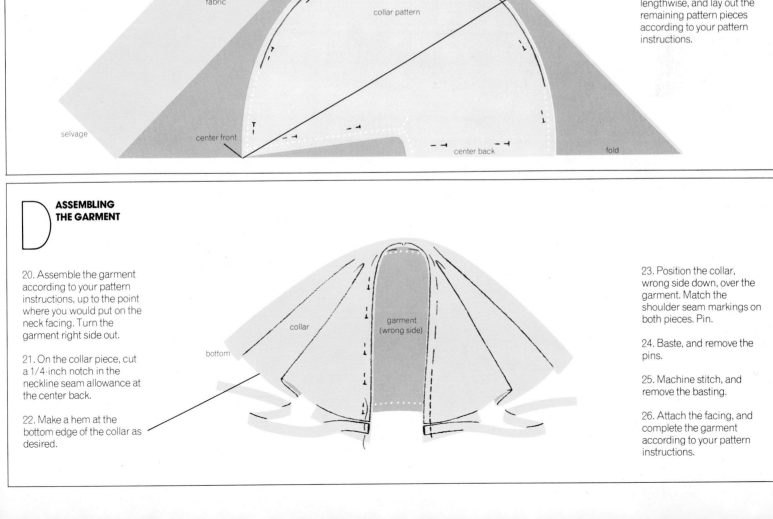

3
MAGIC IN A
MIX OF DYES

Some of the most striking boutique clothes gain their distinction from some of the world's oldest techniques for fabric decoration. Batiking, tie dyeing, stenciling, stamping and freehand painting—effects that are synonymous with the boutique look—are crafts that have been around since the dawn of history. Egyptian wall paintings show women pressing wood blocks onto cloth 2,000 years before the birth of Christ.

THE FASCINATION OF COLORING FABRIC BY HAND

In India, 5,000 years ago, some form of batik was apparently in use—the records tell of a fabric painted with a dye-resistant material before color was added. And the people of Japan, according to archeological evidence, knew about tie dyeing and stenciling when they were still in the Stone Age.

Generations of skilled craftsmen elaborated these ancient methods of decorating cloth until they eventually acquired unbelievable finesse. Six months and a staggering amount of waxing and rewaxing, dyeing and drying, can go into the creation of a single sarong-length piece of Javanese batik, and the Japanese government has bestowed the accolade of National Treasure on at least one tie-dyed kimono.

Yet the basic techniques remain simple; the processes, after all, derive from a time when all tools were hand tools, all fabrics were natural fibers, and dyes were extractions of berries, bugs, shells, roots, bark, wild flowers and nuts. Batik, for instance, is still made by coating fabric with dye-resistant wax in order to block color from certain areas of the fabric. And the wax is often applied with the age-old Indonesian tjanting, a curious spouted device that directs a stream of melted wax onto the cloth, much as the cone of a pastry tube swirls icing onto a cake—indeed, like the pastry tube, the tjanting comes in a variety of spout sizes for creating special effects.

Similarly, stenciling is still done by brushing color through a cutout design—although today the brush is more likely to be a paint roller or an airbrush, a 20th Century invention that permits the stenciled pattern to be shaded. And stamping is still done with wood blocks, although such unconventional stamps as napkin rings or gear wheels are now sometimes employed.

Least changed of all among the ancient crafts is tie dyeing—an array of related techniques that uses nothing more than pressure, simply applied, to bar dye from selected portions of the fabric during the dipping process. The fabric could be tied into knots, wrapped with string, gathered into clusters with rows of tiny running stitches, or pressed into folds with clamps. Each variant creates a distinctive type of pattern in the dyed cloth, but even a single procedure can produce a great range of effects, for they depend on where the pressure is applied and how tightly.

Because these classic methods of decorating fabrics are so simple, requiring a minimal amount of equipment—most of it easily come by—they are well within the competence of anyone with a fair degree of manual dexterity. The results will vary from person to person. But this is precisely what has endeared hand-dyed fabrics to designers of boutique clothing. "There is a marvelous linkup between what you are and what will come out of you," observes tie-dye expert Fay Halpern. "Two people with the same expertise can use the same materials and come out with different designs just because they are different people."

Beyond that, hand-dyed designs offer boundless freedom of expression. "Each time you do a batik garment you can have a new experience—by changing the design, working with new colors or fabrics, using the batik in another form," says Laura Adasko, known for her batik clothes. This freedom to experiment with the technique, to meld design with a vision of the finished garment, is open to anyone who wants to try. At its more inspired it can produce clothes of astonishing beauty. Overleaf, a consummate artist, Reiko Ehrman, combines color sense, innate style and an easy familiarity with the age-old techniques of hand dyeing to create grande luxe gowns to order.

The elegant art of painting a dress design

The word *tsuru* in Japanese means crane and the crane in Japan is a good luck symbol. But for Japanese-born fabric designer Reiko Ehrman, co-owner of the New York boutique called Tsuru, luck is not the operative word. Talent, taste and an easy familiarity with ancient ways of decorating fabric by hand have made her small shop a magnet for women who want very special gowns —and can afford to pay for them.

Reiko's forte is dyeing, using techniques she was taught in Japan—where such skills as tie dyeing, resist dyeing and hand painting on fabric were part of a young girl's preparation for marriage. In fact, Reiko began Tsuru out of a belief that the most beautiful clothes were classic in line—like the kimono—and derived their splendor from the fabric decoration. When customers like Serena Rhinelander come to see her, she shows them examples of her work, and together they discuss color and style, even the occasion for which the gown will be worn. Reiko sketches a design, and when it is approved, it disappears into her workroom. There, aided by a staff of 11 artists and artisans, all Japanese, she converts the sketch into a length of fabric that eventually becomes a striking gown like the one worn by Miss Rhinelander *(overleaf)*.

Reiko shows Serena a hand-painted creation.

For Serena she sketches a design of colored streamers cascading down a black gown.

Reiko's design is sketched out in advance on paper before being transferred onto white nylon fabric.

Reiko colors a streamer while her assistant wields a drier.

Strips of fabric for shoulder straps are painted to match.

Reiko checks the design before the dress is made.

Reiko fits Serena's finished gown, a blend of ancient art form and contemporary style.

A guide to dyes for special effects

The individualistic color patterns of batik, dye painting and tie dyeing are created with standard chemical dyes sold in craft stores. But since the effects desired are different from those of regular dyeing—in tie dyeing, for example, even coloring is not so important as fast action to keep dye out of tied areas—the package instructions may not apply. The procedures here are designed to suit the coloring methods outlined on the pages that follow. The dyeing vessel should be large enough to hold the fabric without crowding; for simmering dye baths it should be of enamel or stainless steel, never aluminum, which reacts with dye chemicals. A plastic dishpan is ideal for the lukewarm dye bath used for batik.

Since the color of cloth affects the result, begin with a white or off-white fabric—one without a permanent press or soil-resistant finish (which may hinder coloring). Wash to remove any sizing and straighten the grain (*Appendix*). Test the dye on a fabric scrap, remembering that colors look darker when wet, and that dye lots may vary. If you are dyeing with several colors, rinse thoroughly between each dye bath—until the water runs clear. Always dry fabric in a flat position on old newspaper. To prevent staining, wear rubber gloves and an apron, and cover work surfaces with newspapers.

	DIRECT DYES
DESCRIPTION OF DYE	To identify a direct dye, read the label. It will stipulate that the dye is suitable for cotton and requires the addition of salt to help dye penetrate fabric. Dyes are sold at craft stores under such brand names as Dick Blick, Fezan, Miyako, Keco and Aljo (Batik Cotton).
SUITABLE FABRICS	Direct dyes can be used for cotton, linen and viscose rayon.
COLOR QUALITY AND COLOR FASTNESS	When used for tie dyeing and painting, direct dyes give deep, intense colors; when used for batik, the colors are subdued. Direct dyes gradually fade if washed. Dry-cleaning is recommended.
PROCEDURE FOR TIE DYEING	**Preparing concentrate:** In a small amount of warm water, make a paste of dye powder, using 1 tablespoon for a pale shade, 2 for a medium shade, and up to 5 for darker shades. Make a concentrate by mixing the paste in a cup or two of hot water and dissolving in it 1 tablespoon of salt for each tablespoon of dye. **Making dye bath:** Stir the concentrate into 2 1/2 gallons of simmering water (180° F.). **Dyeing:** Immerse fabric in dye bath for 15 to 30 minutes; stir occasionally. Rinse in warm water after each dyeing. **Finishing:** To set dye, hold a steam iron above each area for a minute; press with a medium-hot dry iron for 5 minutes under a constantly redampened cloth.
PROCEDURE FOR BATIK DYEING	**Preparing concentrate:** For a dye bath, make concentrate as for tie dyeing (*above*). For brush-on dye, make a paste of 2 teaspoons dye powder in a little warm water; dissolve the paste and 2 teaspoons of salt in 1/2 cup lukewarm water. **Making dye bath:** Stir the concentrate into 2 1/2 gallons of lukewarm water (105° F.). **Dyeing:** When using dye bath, immerse fabric for 15 to 30 minutes, stirring gently so as not to damage the waxed surface. Brush-on dye is applied like paint. Rinse in cool water after dyeing all colors. **Finishing:** The ironing procedure for removing the wax (*page 69*) also sets the dye.
PROCEDURE FOR DYE PAINTING	**Preparing thickener:** Stir 1/2 teaspoon of gum thickener, available at craft stores, into 1 cup of hot water. Let stand several hours or overnight. **Making paint:** Dissolve 1 teaspoon of dye powder and 1 teaspoon of salt in 2 tablespoons of water and mix into the thickener. The thickened dye should be the consistency of honey. If it is too thick, add water. **Finishing:** When dye paint is dry, set dye by holding a steam iron above each area for a minute; then press with a medium-hot dry iron for 5 minutes under a constantly redampened cloth. Rinse and wash.

ACID DYES	HOUSEHOLD DYES	FIBER-REACTIVE DYES
To identify an acid dye, carefully read the label. It will stipulate that the dye is suitable for silk and wool, and requires the addition of acetic acid or vinegar. Dyes are sold at craft stores under such brand names as Keco, Fezan, Miyako and Aljo (Batik Silk and Wool).	Most household dyes are so marked. Typical brand names are Rit, Tintex and Putnam All-Purpose.	To identify this dye, carefully read the label. It will call for salt, to aid penetration, and washing soda, to bond pigment to fabric. Dyes work in lukewarm water, making them suited for batik. They are sold at craft stores under such brand names as Pylam, Fibrac and Dylon.
Acid dyes can be used for silk, nylon and wool.	Household dyes can be used for natural fibers, nylon, acetate and rayon—but not polyester and acrylic.	Fiber-reactive dyes can be used on silk, cotton, linen and viscose rayon.
When used for tie dyeing and painting, acid dyes give bright, intense colors; when used for batik, colors are subdued. Acid dyes are relatively resistant to fading from light, but gradually fade if washed. Dry-cleaning is recommended.	Because these dyes are designed to work with many fabrics, the color range is limited. Dyes work well for batik and painting. In the lukewarm dye bath of batik, colors are much paler. The dyes tend to fade after repeated washings; dry-cleaning is recommended.	Colors are intense and deep, and since they form a chemical bond with the fiber itself, they are extremely colorfast. They will not fade, and can be washed in hot water.
Preparing concentrate: In a small amount of warm water, make a paste of 1 tablespoon of dye powder for a pale shade, 2 for a medium shade, and up to 5 for darker shades. Dissolve the paste in a cup or two of hot water and mix in 1/2 cup of distilled white vinegar for each tablespoon of dye powder. **Making dye bath:** Stir the concentrate into 2 1/2 gallons of simmering water (180° F.). Use boiling water for nylon (212° F.). **Dyeing:** Immerse fabric in dye bath for 45 minutes; stir occasionally. Rinse in warm water after dyeing each color. **Finishing:** Use the method given for tie dyeing with direct dyes *(left)*.	**Preparing concentrate:** Make a paste of powdered dye, using 1/4 packet for a pale shade, 1/2 for a medium shade, and up to 1 packet for darker shades; dissolve paste in a cup or two of hot water. With liquid dye, equivalent amounts for pale, medium and darker shades are 1/8, 1/4 and 1/2 cup. **Making the dye bath:** Mix concentrate in 2 1/2 gallons of water, simmering (180° F.) for cottons, barely simmering (160° F.) for silk and synthetics, and boiling (212°F.) for nylon. **Dyeing:** Put fabric in dye bath for 25 minutes, stirring gently. Rinse in warm water after dyeing each color. **Finishing:** Use the method given for tie dyeing with direct dyes *(far left)*.	**Preparing concentrate:** In a little water, make a paste of 1/2 teaspoon for a pale shade, 1 for a medium shade, up to 3 for dark shades. Dissolve paste in a cup or two of water. **Making dye bath:** Stir concentrate into 2 1/2 gallons of lukewarm water (105° F.), and dissolve 12 tablespoons of salt for each teaspoon of dye. **Dyeing:** Immerse fabric in dye bath for 10 to 15 minutes, stirring frequently. Remove fabric and add 3 tablespoons of washing soda dissolved in a cup of water. Reimmerse fabric for 30 to 40 minutes, stirring occasionally. Rinse in warm water between each color. **Finishing:** Wash in hot water using soap or detergent; set dye by dry pressing with iron on steam setting.
Preparing concentrate: For a dye bath, make concentrate as for tie dyeing *(above)*. For brush-on dye, make a paste of 2 teaspoons of dye powder in a little warm water; dissolve the paste in 1/4 cup of lukewarm water and add 1/4 cup of distilled white vinegar. **Making dye bath:** Stir concentrate into 2 1/2 gallons of lukewarm water (105° F.). **Dyeing and finishing:** Use the methods given for batiking with direct dyes *(left)*.	**Preparing concentrate:** For a dye bath, make concentrate as for tie dyeing *(above)*. For brush-on dye, use liquid dye undiluted, or make a paste of dye powder by mixing 1/2 tablespoon in a little warm water and then dissolve the paste in 1/2 cup of lukewarm water. **Dyeing and Finishing:** Use the methods given for batiking with direct dyes *(far left)*.	**Preparing concentrate:** For a dye bath, make concentrate as for tie dyeing *(above)*. For brush-on dye, make a paste of 1/2 teaspoon of dye in a little cold water; then dissolve paste and 1/2 teaspoon of salt in 1/2 cup of warm water. **Making dye bath:** Stir concentrate into 2 1/2 gallons of lukewarm water (105° F.). **Dyeing:** For dye bath, follow directions for tie dyeing. Stir without damaging the waxed surface. For brush-on dye, coat the cloth with 1 1/2 teaspoons of washing soda dissolved in a cup of water. When dry, apply dye like paint. Rinse in warm water after each dyeing. **Finishing:** The ironing procedure for removing the wax *(page 69)* also sets the dye.
Preparing thickener: Use the method given for direct dyes *(left)*. **Making paint:** Dissolve 1 teaspoon of dye powder in a tablespoon of water, add to a cup of thickener and mix in 2 tablespoons of distilled white vinegar. The thickened dye should be the consistency of honey. If it is too thick, add water. **Finishing:** When dye paint is completely dry, steam and press exactly as for tie dyeing with direct dyes *(above, left)*. Rinse and wash in mild detergent and warm water.	**Preparing thickener:** Use the method given for direct dyes *(far left)*. **Making paint:** Into a cup of thickener, mix 2 teaspoons of liquid dye, or 4 teaspoons of dye powder dissolved in 2 tablespoons of water—the thickened dye should be the consistency of honey. If it is too thick, add water. **Finishing:** When dye paint is completely dry, set dye by holding a steam iron above each area of fabric for a minute; then press for 5 minutes with a medium-hot dry iron under a constantly redampened cloth. Rinse and wash in mild detergent and warm water.	**Preparing thickened dye:** Stir 2 teaspoons of thickener into a cup of water, and let stand several hours. If fixer is separate, stir in 1 teaspoon with powder. **Making paint:** Into each cup of thickening, stir 1/2 teaspoon of dye powder. Thickened dye should be the consistency of honey. If too thick, add warm water. **Finishing:** When dye paint is dry, set by holding a steam iron above each area for a minute; press for 5 minutes with a medium-hot dry iron under a constantly redampened cloth. Rinse and wash in mild detergent in warm water.

A random look from tie-dye

Wrapping fabric with string or tying it in knots, then dipping it in dye, is such an easy way to achieve startlingly colorful patterns that for a while almost every teenager sported home-tie-dyed jeans. These kitchen-counter experiments only hinted at the potential. For the designs shown here, fabric was stitched *(left),* tied with string *(center)* or folded and clamped *(right)* for partial resistance to dye baths. The colors seep and mingle, creating the rich shading that is one of tie dyeing's charms.

Only a minimum of equipment beyond ordinary sewing gear is needed for tie dyeing: string, C clamps, blocks for clamping and dye pots.

Dipping into the delights of tie dyeing

Of the many ways of decorating fabric by compressing certain areas to control dye penetration, the simplest involves nothing more than a few knots. This kind of tie dyeing is also the least predictable. When you untie the knots that bind the dyed fabric into clumps, you never know quite what you will get. The weight of the fabric, the manner in which it is bundled, and the winding of string can result in patterns ranging from simple circles to splendid sunbursts, from filigreed borders to zigzags.

Variants on the basic tie-dyeing method are more controllable, gaining in form what they lose in surprise. In one, blocks of plastic or wood are clamped over fabric that has been folded into rectangles, squares or triangles; the result is an allover pattern. In another, the fabric is rolled and tied around a cylinder *(here, a soft-drink can),* producing zebra stripes. Still a third uses running stitches to outline a shape or form a pointillist border.

Cotton twine or thread should be used for tying and stitching since cotton does not stretch and thus can be pulled tight. It should be left in place through the rinsing process to prevent any excess dye from blurring the design, and then should be cut. Take care when cutting, so that you do not nick the fabric that lies against the cord.

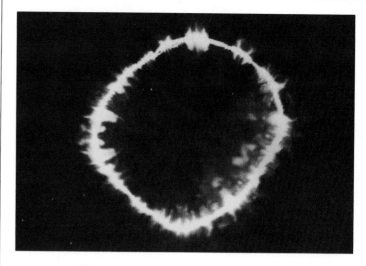

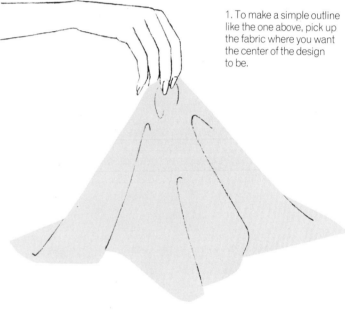

1. To make a simple outline like the one above, pick up the fabric where you want the center of the design to be.

2. Gather the fabric where you want the outline to be.

3. Wind string around the neck of the gathered fabric, crossing the loose end to lock the string as you continue winding.

4. Wind the string around the neck several more times, keeping it tight. Do not leave space between coils.

5. Knot the loose ends.

6. To make several outlines, repeat Steps 1-5.

7. Wet the fabric, dip it in dye and rinse *(pages 54-55).*

8. Cut the string, and spread out the fabric to dry.

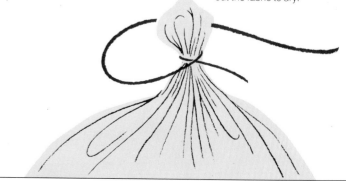

TYING WITH STRING FOR STRIPES

1. Fold a single layer of fabric into accordion pleats, folding at right angles to the direction in which you want the stripes to fall. Pleat evenly.

2. Gather the pleated fabric where you want the first stripe to appear.

3. Wind string around the gathered fabric, locking the string as in tying with string for an outline (Step 3, opposite). Wind up and back. Knot the two loose ends of the string.

4. Repeat Steps 2 and 3 for as many stripes as desired. The larger each gathered-and-tied section, the wider the stripe. For a fairly uniform stripe (above left), wrap the string closely; for a lacy effect (middle), space the coils slightly; for a stripe within a stripe (right), wrap solidly, then leave some fabric untied, and wrap solidly again.

5. Wet the fabric, dip it in dye and rinse (pages 54-55).

6. Cut the string and dry the fabric.

TYING WITH STRING FOR A CHEVRON

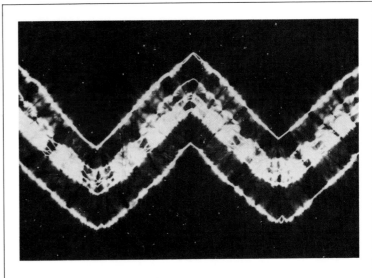

1. Fold a single layer of fabric into accordion pleats, as in tying with string for stripes (Step 1, left), but make the pleats wider.

2. Gather the fabric on a slant.

3. Wind string around the gathered fabric, as in tying with string for stripes (Step 3, left).

4. Wet the fabric, dip it in dye and rinse (pages 54-55).

5. Cut the string and dry the fabric.

KNOTTING FOR A SUNBURST

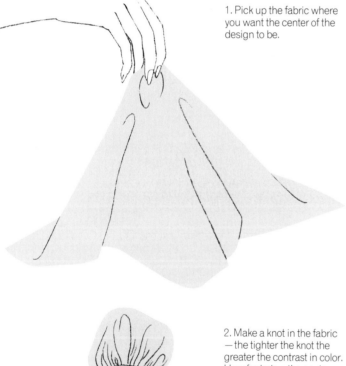

1. Pick up the fabric where you want the center of the design to be.

2. Make a knot in the fabric — the tighter the knot the greater the contrast in color. How far below the center the knot is will determine the size of the sunburst.

3. Wet the fabric, dip it in dye and rinse (*pages 54-55*).

4. Untie the fabric and dry.

KNOTTING FOR A CORNER DESIGN

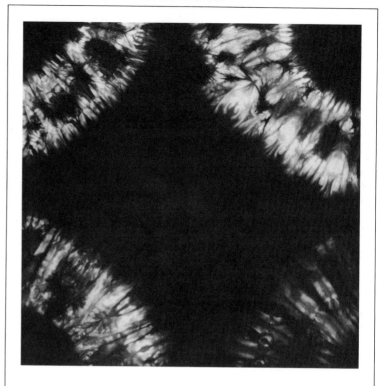

1. Make a knot in each corner of the fabric — the tighter the knot the more color contrast, the farther from the corner the larger the pattern.

2. Wet the fabric, dip it in dye and rinse (*pages 54-55*).

3. Untie the fabric and dry.

CLAMPING FOR SHADED STRIPES

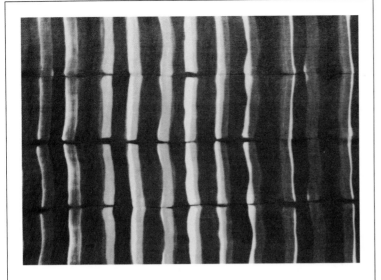

1. Fold a single layer of fabric into lengthwise accordion pleats, as in tying with string for stripes (page 59, Step 1). The width of the folded fabric should equal the length of the blocks you plan to use.

2. Fold the pleated fabric into crosswise accordion pleats. Each of these folds should equal the width of the blocks.

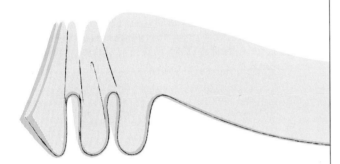

3. Place one block on top of the folded fabric. Place the other below the fabric, aligning them.

4. Secure the blocks and fabric with two or more clamps—you need one at least every 3 inches.

5. Wet the fabric, dip it in light-colored dye and rinse (pages 54-55).

6. Remove the clamps.

7. While the fabric is still wet, unfold the crosswise pleats made in Step 2. Do not unfold the lengthwise pleats.

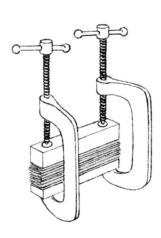

8. Refold the pleated fabric into crosswise accordion pleats, letting the new folds fall irregularly close to, but not on, the previous folds.

9. Repeat Steps 3-8, then repeat Steps 3-6, darkening the dye mixture each time. Then unfold the fabric completely and dry.

BINDING TWINE AROUND A CAN FOR STRIPES

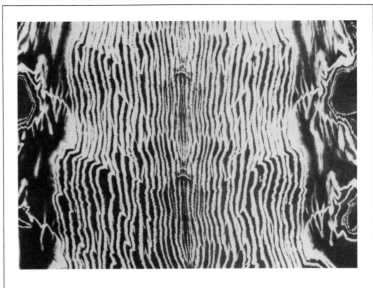

1. Fold a single layer of sheer fabric into accordion pleats, as in tying with string for stripes (page 59, Step 1). The folded fabric should be 7 or 8 inches wide.

2. Place one end of an empty soft-drink can along one of the folded edges of the fabric, then roll the can up in the fabric. The fabric will extend beyond the other end of the can.

3. Wind a piece of twine tightly around the fabric, starting at the edge of the fabric that is aligned with the can edge. Knot the twine. Continue to wind tightly, leaving about 1/4 inch of space between coils.

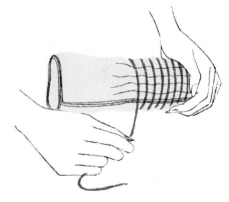

4. After 2 inches or so of winding, stand the can on its end (the end near the wound area) on a firm flat surface, and push downward on the twine to bring the coils close together. Some of the fabric will be squeezed out between the coils.

5. When the entire can has been bound, lock the loose end of the twine by slipping it through the final coil and pulling it tight.

6. Wet the wrapped can, dip it in dye and rinse (pages 54-55) while the fabric is still wrapped around the can.

7. Untie the fabric, unwrap it and dry.

STITCHING FOR DOTS AND LINES

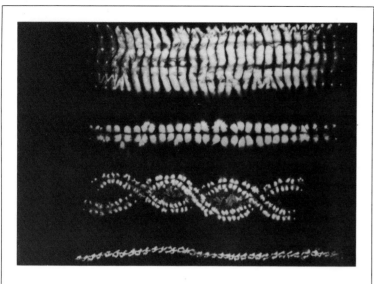

1. To create a shirred effect *(top row, above),* make parallel rows of medium-length running stitches *(Appendix)* across the fabric with a knotted double strand of white cotton thread; leave 3 inches of loose thread at the end of each row. Make the stitches 1/4 inch long for lightweight fabric, longer for heavier fabric.

2. For a double-dot effect *(second row),* fold the fabric and make a tuck, using medium-length running stitches—1/4 inch long for lightweight fabric, longer for heavier fabric.

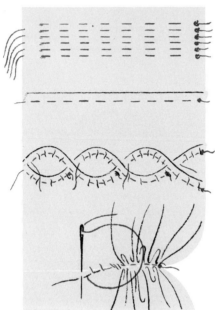

3. To create a braided pattern *(third row),* draw two crisscrossing S curves on the fabric with a soft pencil. Fold the fabric along these guide lines and make two curving tucks, using small running stitches—about 1/8 inch long for lightweight fabric, longer for heavier fabric. Wherever the tucks cross, cut the thread, leaving about 3 inches loose at the end; start again with freshly knotted thread.

4. To create a chain pattern *(bottom row),* draw a guide line with a soft pencil across the fabric. Then, using a knotted double strand of white thread, make overcast stitches *(Appendix)* along the guide line, pulling the thread tight after several stitches.

5. When you have finished stitching, pull the loose end of the thread or threads gradually but firmly until the fabric is tightly gathered. For the shirred effect in Step 1, pull all 6 rows at once. Distribute the fabric as equally as possible above and below the stitching.

6. Knot the loose ends tightly.

7. Wet the fabric, dip it in dye and rinse *(pages 54-55).*

8. Remove the stitches and dry.

STITCHING FOR A DOTTED OUTLINE

1. Draw a design on the fabric with a soft pencil. Or draw it on paper and transfer it *(Appendix),* using light-colored dressmaker's carbon paper.

2. Make a line of running stitches *(Appendix)* along the guide line with a knotted double strand of white cotton thread. For a simple design, use a medium-length stitch—about 1/4 inch long for lightweight fabric, longer for heavier fabric. For a more intricate design, use a small stitch.

3. To make it easier to pull the thread in a large or extremely intricate design, cut the thread several times along the way, leaving about 3 inches of loose thread and starting again with freshly knotted thread.

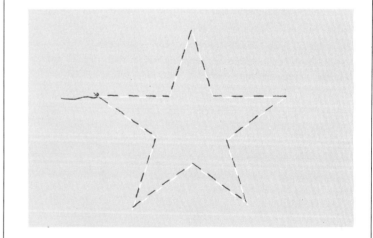

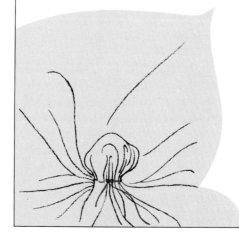

4. Gather the fabric by pulling threads and then dye it, following the directions in stitching for dots and lines *(left, Steps 5-8).*

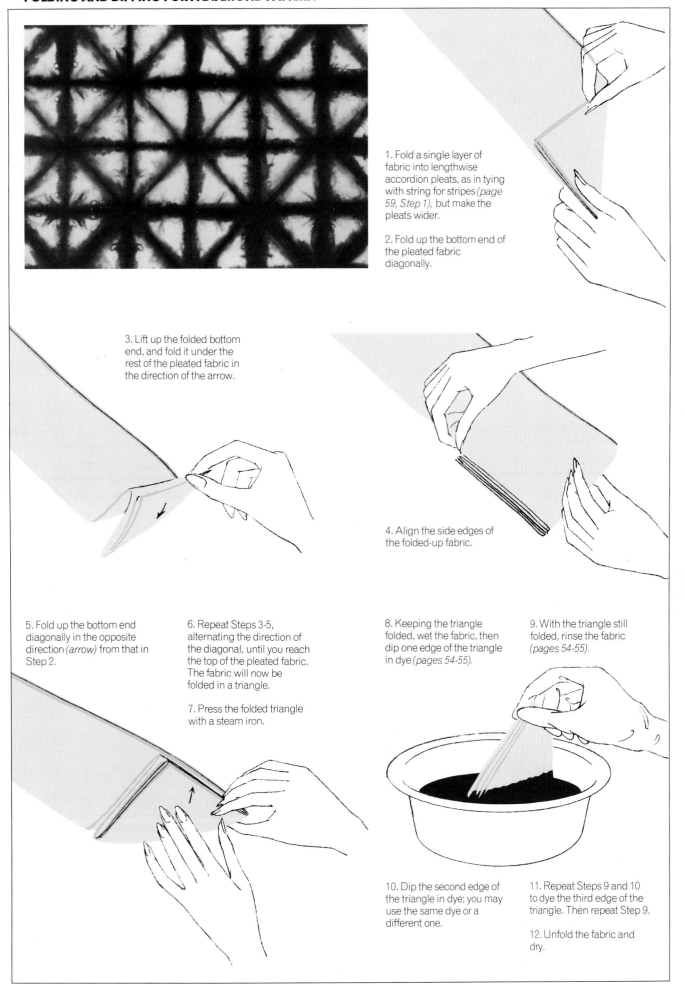

1. Fold a single layer of fabric into lengthwise accordion pleats, as in tying with string for stripes *(page 59, Step 1)*, but make the pleats wider.

2. Fold up the bottom end of the pleated fabric diagonally.

3. Lift up the folded bottom end, and fold it under the rest of the pleated fabric in the direction of the arrow.

4. Align the side edges of the folded-up fabric.

5. Fold up the bottom end diagonally in the opposite direction *(arrow)* from that in Step 2.

6. Repeat Steps 3-5, alternating the direction of the diagonal, until you reach the top of the pleated fabric. The fabric will now be folded in a triangle.

7. Press the folded triangle with a steam iron.

8. Keeping the triangle folded, wet the fabric, then dip one edge of the triangle in dye *(pages 54-55)*.

9. With the triangle still folded, rinse the fabric *(pages 54-55)*.

10. Dip the second edge of the triangle in dye; you may use the same dye or a different one.

11. Repeat Steps 9 and 10 to dye the third edge of the triangle. Then repeat Step 9.

12. Unfold the fabric and dry.

Batik: hot wax and cool dye

The art of batiking, in which a pattern painted in wax resists dyes that color the rest of the cloth, has one advantage to counter the effort involved: the results are not only various and beautiful but easily controlled. The crackling in the fabric here comes from crushing the cloth in the hand after the wax hardens, then dipping it in dye. The stained-glass look comes from drawing a wax outline to contain the colors as they are applied. For the stenciled flight of doves, the design is filled solidly with wax before dyeing.

Batiking fabrics like the ones shown here requires a frame for stretching fabric, a tjanting (Indonesian wax pen, below frame), brushes for wax and dyes, a thermometer to regulate the melting of paraffin and beeswax, and enamel and plastic containers for holding dyes.

Waxing and dyeing batiks

Batik offers a wide range of effects — from broad, hazy ombrés to finely etched lines — largely because there are so many ways to apply the wax that affects the color design. The wax can be painted onto cloth with a natural-bristle brush, drawn on with an Indonesian waxing pen called a tjanting (sold in craft-supply stores) or stamped on. Crackling the wax surface makes a crisscross pattern; the wax can also be scratched with a point. The frame on which the fabric is stretched can be a picture frame, a canvas or curtain stretcher, even a dresser drawer — anything to keep the cloth taut, to prevent it from touching the work surface.

When using more than one color, dye lighter colors first, since each dye affects the color already present.

Precautions must be taken in handling the wax (preferably a flammable, 50-50 mixture of beeswax and paraffin). It should be melted in a double boiler over a hot plate, never a gas flame, and never left unattended. Drips or splatters can cause painful burns. Keep your hair covered; do not allow the ends to swish into the melted wax. Finally, the newspapers used for removing the wax should be at least two weeks old so that the ink is dry and will not rub off on the fabric. The papers should be disposed of with care, for the wax makes them highly flammable.

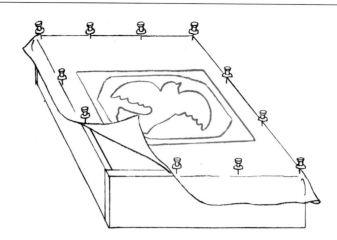

1. If you want to work from a design, draw or copy it on a sheet of paper, outlining the areas to be waxed. Transfer the design to the fabric (*Appendix*), using light-colored dressmaker's carbon paper.

2. Stretch the fabric taut over the frame, centering the design, and attach with pushpins. Keep the grain of the fabric aligned with two sides of the frame.

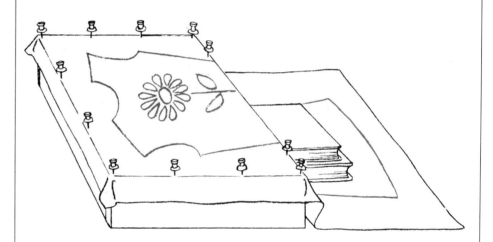

3. If the shape of the garment or wall hanging you are making is larger than the frame, outline the shape on the fabric with a soft pencil.

4. Cut the fabric, making sure to leave enough fabric all around the outline to cover the frame.

5. Attach the fabric as in Step 2, but pin only outside the outline — otherwise there will be holes in the finished work — and secure the unpinned areas with a heavy weight such as an iron or several books. Apply wax to the framed part, then move the fabric and repin as necessary to complete the design.

MELTING THE WAX

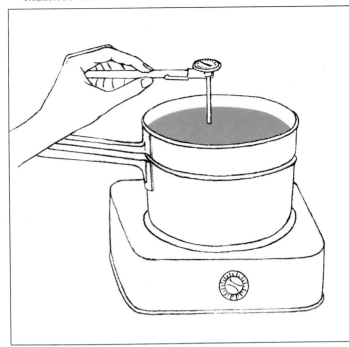

Melt the wax in a double boiler on a hot plate (not a gas flame), checking the temperature with a thermometer that has a holder, such as the one in the drawing, or a clip. The temperature should be approximately 180°. Do not let the wax overheat, and do not leave it unattended. If the wax begins to smoke, turn off the heat immediately.

APPLYING WAX WITH A TJANTING

1. To draw lines, such as the veins, stems and outlines of the leaves shown below right, first hold the tjanting in the melted wax for a few minutes to heat the metal tip and remove any wax left from previous use.

2. Dip the tjanting in the wax. The cone or bowl of the tjanting will fill with wax.

3. To keep wax from dripping on the fabric accidentally as you work, hold a piece of cloth or paper under the tjanting except when you are actually applying wax. If drops fall on the fabric by mistake, modify the design to include the spots; do not try to remove the wax.

4. Place the tip of the tjanting on the fabric and draw with it as you would with a pen. The wax should flow smoothly, penetrating to the back of the fabric. If the wax does not spread easily, increase the heat slightly; if it spreads too fast, decrease the heat.

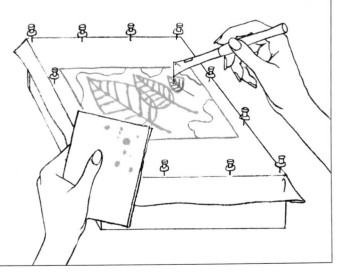

APPLYING WAX WITH A BRUSH

1. If you are using a new brush, dip it in the melting wax before the wax gets hot; direct exposure to very hot wax tends to curl new bristles. If the brush is old, soak it in the wax until the old wax on it softens.

2. Hold a piece of cloth or paper under the brush except when you are actually applying wax.

3. Brush wax on those areas of the design where you want to retain the color of the fabric. If the design is drawn on the fabric, apply the wax sufficiently away from the guide line to allow for the wax to spread to, but not over, the guide line.

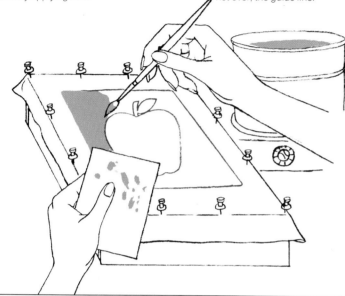

STAMPING WITH WAX

1. Ready-made tools for stamping wax onto batik are available at craft stores. But interesting patterns can be created with any wood or metal object that you can grasp firmly or add a handle to, such as this small gear.

2. Spread the fabric on several sheets of old newspaper on a hard, flat surface.

3. Immerse the stamping tool in the wax for a minute to heat it.

4. Apply the stamp firmly to the fabric. To get gradations in tone, stamp 2 or 3 times before dipping again. For a more defined pattern, dip the tool into the wax before each stamping.

CRACKLING WAX FOR A LINE PATTERN

1. Remove the waxed fabric from the frame.

2. Hold the fabric in cold water to make the wax brittle. For especially sharp and clear crackling, put the fabric in a plastic bag in the refrigerator for about ten minutes.

3. Gather each area of the fabric to be crackled, and gently crush it.

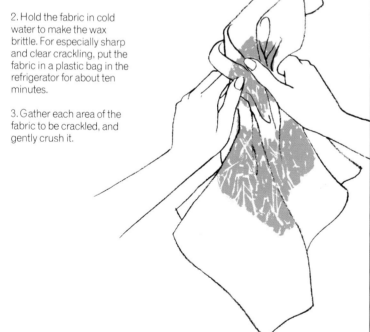

ETCHING WAX FOR A LINEAR DESIGN

1. Spread the fabric on several sheets of old newspaper on a hard, flat surface.

2. Using any sharp-pointed instrument—an etching tool, nut pick, pushpin or nail—scratch through the wax along the design, making sure to penetrate to the fabric.

3. When mixing the dye, add a few drops of liquid detergent to help it penetrate the scratched lines.

COLORING THE FABRIC BY DIPPING IT IN THE DYE

1. After removing the fabric from the frame, wet it and dip it in the lightest dye you will be using, then rinse and dry (*pages 54-55*). All of the fabric will be colored, except for the areas that were covered with wax.

2. For each color to be added, wax the areas where you want to retain the color achieved by the previous dipping. Then wet the fabric, dip it in dye, rinse and dry.

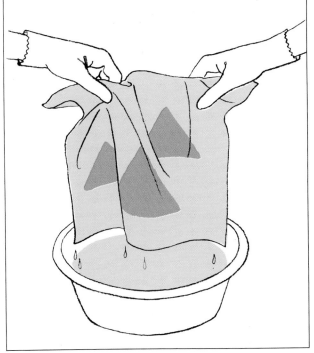

COLORING THE FABRIC BY PAINTING ON THE DYE

1. Mix the dye in a small cup (*pages 54-55*).

2. Place a separate cup of clear water nearby for rinsing the brush.

3. With the fabric still on the frame, paint over the desired area with a medium-sized pointed brush (do not use a brush that has been used for waxing). Use a nylon brush for fiber-reactive dyes (*pages 54-55*); use either a nylon or natural-bristle brush for other dyes. Work fast for an even effect, brushing up to and over the edges of the adjoining wax.

4. Wipe off excess paint from the surface of the wax with a cloth or paper towel; otherwise the dye will be transferred to the fabric when you remove the wax.

5. If other colors are to be brushed on, mix additional dye, and apply to the design as desired.

6. Dry the fabric (*pages 54-55*).

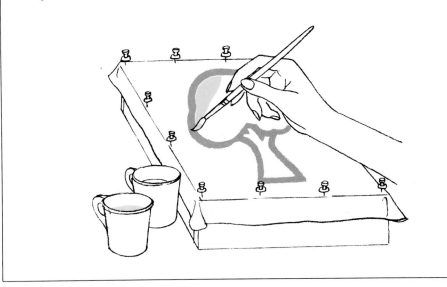

REMOVING THE WAX

1. After the fabric has been completely dyed and dried, spread it on several layers of old newspaper.

2. Cover the fabric with several more layers of newspaper.

3. Run a hot iron over the top layer; the wax will melt, and the paper will absorb it.

4. When the newspaper becomes yellow with wax, replace the paper with fresh sheets, and press again. Continue pressing until the newspaper no longer shows any sign of wax.

5. To remove the last traces of wax— some will still be left on the fabric— have the fabric dry-cleaned.

Artistry with a free hand

For maximum freedom of expression in applying decoration to fabric, nothing beats a paintbrush. The ultimate is freehand painting, which created these anemones on silk, but stenciling does repetitive designs like the wisteria quickly and easily.

The anemones and wisteria are obviously the work of skilled artisans, but even a naïve daisy can be the start of a lovely design. For painting or stenciling, dyes must be thickened to keep them from spreading.

The equipment used for stenciling or painting fabrics includes plastic to cut into stencils *(left),* dye cups, grains of thickener *(pages 54-55),* brushes for painting and a roller for stenciling.

Painting and stenciling with dyes

Painting cloth with thickened dye is not only the freest way to color fabric—it is also the most directly controlled. The technique uses no external substance, such as wax or string, to make the dye go one place and not another. Rather, the dye itself—thickened with gum or paste—is placed only where you want it to be.

Prepare the thickener according to the chart on pages 54-55, making enough for all dye colors you intend to use. Test the consistency, which should be that of honey, on a scrap of fabric. Divide the mixture into separate cups for each dye; add dye until you achieve the shade you want.

A medium-sized (No. 18) pointed brush is the most versatile for painting with dye—it can create a range of effects from broad strokes to fine lines. Use nylon-bristled brushes for fiber-reactive dyes, either nylon- or natural-bristled ones for other dyes.

Although stenciling is not as free-wheeling as painting, it can attain a blitheness of its own through random repetition on a fabric. Cut the stencil from acetate plastic sheeting (sold in craft stores); so-called 5-point sheeting is the best weight. Test the dye to be sure it is thick enough not to seep under the stencil. To apply the dye, use a rubber ink roller or napped paint roller, preferably in a size wide enough to encompass the whole design.

PAINTING FREEHAND WITH THICKENED DYE

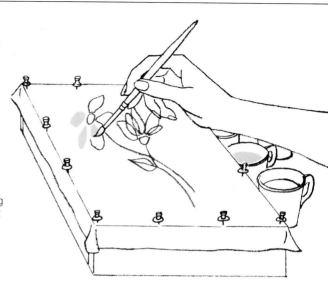

1. Prepare the design and frame, following the instructions for batik dyeing (*page 66*).

2. Brush the desired areas with dye, mixed and thickened as described on pages 54-55. If you are using a less-than-average amount of thickener for a softer effect, stay inside the guide lines far enough to prevent dye from spreading outside the design.

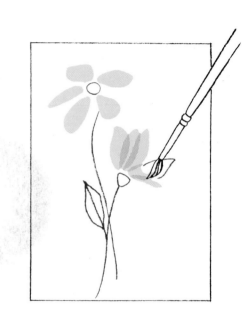

3. To achieve a darker tone of the same color in adjoining areas, let the first application dry, then brush on more dye.

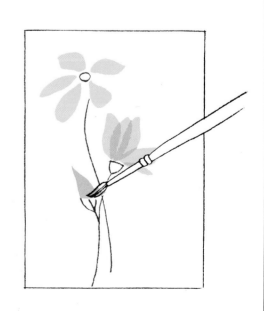

4. If you are applying several colors, work first in areas that do not touch; otherwise the two dyes may run together.

5. Fill in skipped areas after an adjoining color has dried.

6. Let the final color dry (*pages 54-55*).

STENCILING WITH THICKENED DYE

A CUTTING THE STENCIL

1. Cut a piece of acetate plastic sheeting large enough to allow at least a 2-inch margin all around the design. The acetate should be at least 4 inches wider than the roller.

2. Transfer the design (*Appendix*) to the acetate.

3. Place the acetate on cardboard on a hard, flat surface, and cut out the design with a stencil knife or other sharp-bladed instrument.

B SECURING THE FABRIC

4. Cut the fabric slightly larger than the size needed.

5. Spread out the fabric on fresh cardboard. (Do not use the cardboard employed in cutting the stencil.)

6. Stretch the fabric taut, and secure the edges to the cardboard with masking tape. Tape only on the excess parts of the fabric.

7. Place the stencil on the fabric where you want the design to go.

8. If the project you are making is larger than the cardboard, follow the instructions for batik dyeing (*page 66, Steps 3-5*), but secure the fabric to cardboard with masking tape instead of using a frame and pushpins.

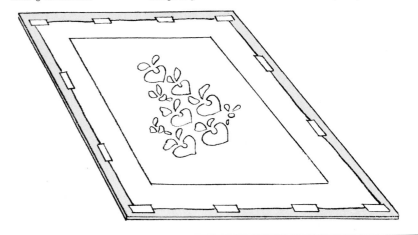

C APPLYING DYE

9. Pour dye, prepared and thickened as described on pages 54-55, into a household paint tray. (Since most of these trays are aluminum, which may affect the dye, use a disposable plastic tray liner.)

10. Saturate the roller in the thickened dye, rolling off any excess.

11. Hold the stencil firmly on the fabric with one hand, and place the roller on the stencil just above the design. Roll down over the design, then roll up.

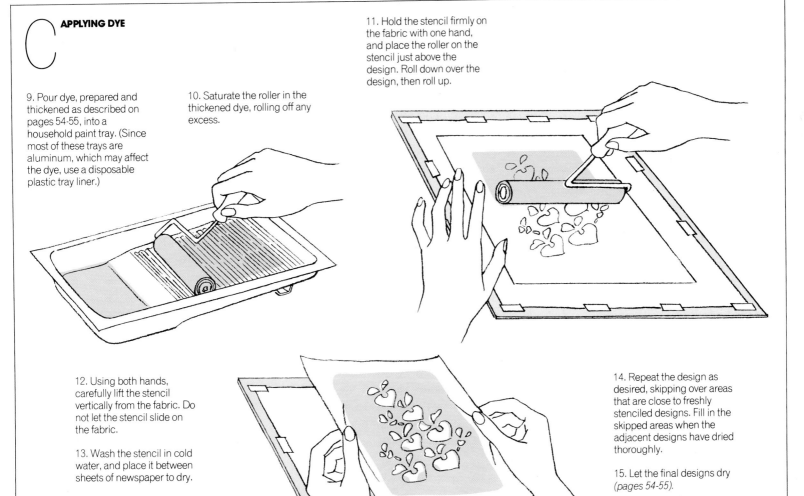

12. Using both hands, carefully lift the stencil vertically from the fabric. Do not let the stencil slide on the fabric.

13. Wash the stencil in cold water, and place it between sheets of newspaper to dry.

14. Repeat the design as desired, skipping over areas that are close to freshly stenciled designs. Fill in the skipped areas when the adjacent designs have dried thoroughly.

15. Let the final designs dry (*pages 54-55*).

4

TOUCHES
THAT MAKE
A DIFFERENCE

During the early 1970s, gallerygoers at the openings of certain Manhattan art shows sometimes found the works on display less startling than the clothing on one of the guests. That was the case if graphics designer Mario Rivoli turned up—parading in a jacket that was an outrageous mix of Pop Art and Junk Shop.

Sewed, pinned, buckled, laced and glued onto Rivoli's bulky garment were just under

DETAILS THAT TURN CLOTHES INTO ART

35 pounds' worth of beaded and feathered appliqués, crocheted tidbits, rhinestone pins, political campaign buttons, a strip of exposed film, a coil of red telephone wire, Girl Scout badges, cloth patches (one of which read "Campbell's Quality"), miniature plastic soldiers, an empty cigarette pack and a bedraggled baby shoe. It was, said Rivoli, "wonderful. People were devastated, awestruck by my jacket."

Boutique fashion designers are just as

enthusiastic about trimmings as Rivoli is. But the decorative devices they use, such as the rhinestone studding and quilting on the preceding pages, are much more wearable than old film or wire and considerably more tempting for a home project.

The velveteen jacket pictured on page 14, a design by California's Constance Rivemale, shows how appealing such trims can be. The bodice is plain muslin, overlaid with pieces of giddily colored fabrics that themselves are adorned with braid, rhinestones and sequins. Any of these embellishments could be used alone to create a boutique effect. Combined, they produce a garment so singular that Rivemale's jacket ceases to be merely clothing and becomes what she calls wearable art.

Applying what she had learned as an art student in San Francisco and Paris, Rivemale treats the piecing of scraps like the assembly of a fabric collage. She sees each work as an abstract picture—of a desert, perhaps, or a forest—and cuts the scraps to form such shapes as dunes or trees. She picks metallic cloth like lamé to suggest sparkling water, napped cloth like velvet for shade. This interplay of fabrics not only supplies texture, but also gives the assemblage a sense of third dimension. To add highlights, she squiggles sequins or glittery paste gems on top of the piecing.

In adapting Constance Rivemale's technique the home seamstress too might work from a mental picture or—as a precautionary step—make a rough sketch of the design she wants to piece. Rivemale's choicest fabrics and gewgaws come from a collection of old opera costumes she found years ago; a home seamstress might rely on her rag bag and remnants counters, or rescue snippets from old clothes out of the attic or a flea market.

Whoever the artist, and whatever the materials, however, the secret in using trims to produce clothing-as-art or art-as-clothing is to give imagination free rein. The designs for some kinds of trimmings—elaborate braids or metallic studs—might be sketched out on the garment ahead of time with dressmaker's chalk. Even the simple crisscrossing lines of plain quilting may need some forethought. But finicky planning is unnecessary and even undesirable in boutique styles. Unlike more serious clothing, in which colors and patterns must match and textures harmonize, boutique fashions thrive on dissonance and extravagant innovation; accidental effects are often the best.

If one ribbon is good, two—or 20—are better for the boutique look. Where braid outlining a seam would seem conventional, braids used like fabric crayons to form ornate arabesques would not. Sequins are standard trim for a chiffon dress, but surprising on a gray flannel one—and a chiffon blouse takes on unexpected glamor when it is adorned with pheasant plumage.

Breaking old rules and setting up new, personal ones is what makes boutique fashions fun to produce. And trimmings like ribbons or sequins that are a traditional part of a seamstress' stock in trade can furnish all the ingredients she needs to make her own artistic statement.

Fashions from bits and pieces

Cotton handkerchiefs from the five-and-dime and denim strips from worn-out jeans are stitched together for this wraparound skirt—a simple but smart example of the versatile technique of piecing. It gives you a chance to design original material by assembling it from scraps.

Not even a pattern is needed for the skirt, but most garments require the procedure outlined at right, which shows how to arrange and assemble pieces for a vest. The materials also make a difference. Leather pieces are glued together before the final topstitching, and a mixture of fabrics, old with new, fragile with strong, may require piecing and patching over a muslin base. For crazy-quilt designs, hand stitching is not only necessary but can add an extra dimension if the stitching is decorative embroidery.

PIECING BY FOLLOWING A GRID

A CUTTING OUT THE PATCHES

1. Preshrink (Glossary) any new fabrics, and clean any remnants to be used. Press. Determine the size of the patches, adding 1/2 inch to the length and width for a 1/4-inch seam allowance.

2. Place one piece of fabric wrong side up. Follow a lengthwise and a crosswise grain to draw lines the length and width of the scrap. The lines should be at right angles to each other, intersecting near one corner.

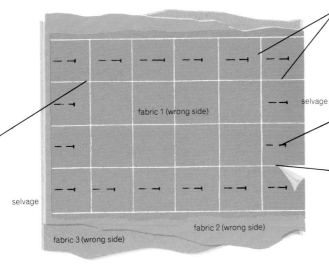

3. Draw a grid on the fabric, making its rectangles the length and width determined in Step 1.

4. Place two other fabrics, wrong side up, under the marked fabric. Align the grains.

5. Pin the fabrics together, being careful not to pin on the grid lines.

6. Cut through all fabric thicknesses along the lines in one direction, making strips. Then cut the strips into patches. Remove the pins.

7. If you are using more than three fabrics for the piecing, mark and cut the remaining fabrics by repeating Steps 2-6.

B ARRANGING THE PATCHES ON THE PATTERN

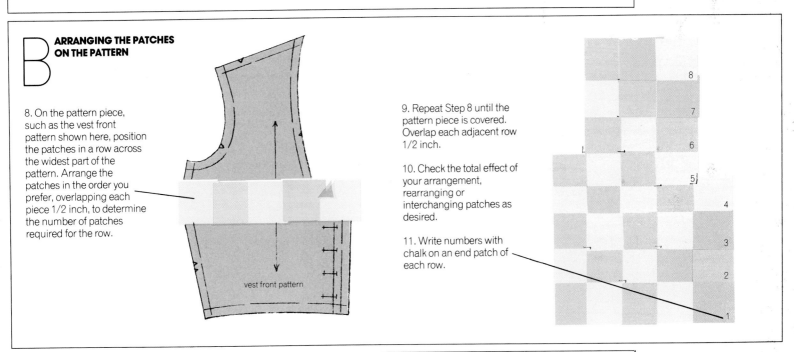

8. On the pattern piece, such as the vest front pattern shown here, position the patches in a row across the widest part of the pattern. Arrange the patches in the order you prefer, overlapping each piece 1/2 inch, to determine the number of patches required for the row.

9. Repeat Step 8 until the pattern piece is covered. Overlap each adjacent row 1/2 inch.

10. Check the total effect of your arrangement, rearranging or interchanging patches as desired.

11. Write numbers with chalk on an end patch of each row.

C JOINING THE PATCHES INTO A STRIP

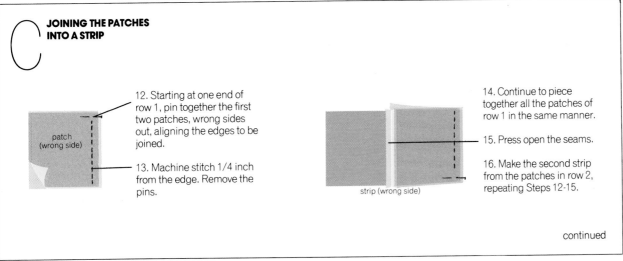

12. Starting at one end of row 1, pin together the first two patches, wrong sides out, aligning the edges to be joined.

13. Machine stitch 1/4 inch from the edge. Remove the pins.

14. Continue to piece together all the patches of row 1 in the same manner.

15. Press open the seams.

16. Make the second strip from the patches in row 2, repeating Steps 12-15.

continued

JOINING THE STRIPS INTO PATCHWORK FABRIC

17. Place strips 1 and 2 together, wrong sides out, aligning the edges to be joined and matching the seams carefully. Pin at each seam and at the corners.

18. Baste 3/16 inch from the edge. Remove the pins.

19. Machine stitch 1/4 inch from the edge. Remove the basting.

22. Check the pattern against the patchwork fabric to be sure the fabric is large enough to accommodate the pattern.

23. Repeat Steps 8-22 to make patchwork fabric for any remaining pattern pieces. If you need two patchwork fabric pieces to cut out a pattern, such as the vest front pattern here, flop the pattern before you make the second piece.

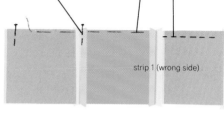
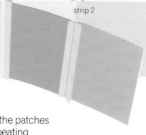

strip 1 (wrong side)

strip 2

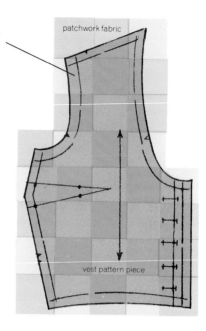

patchwork fabric

vest pattern piece

20. Press open the seam, then turn the piece over and press on the other side.

21. Join row 3 of the patches into a strip by repeating Steps 12-15. Then attach strip 3 to strip 2, following Steps 17-20. Repeat these steps to complete the patchwork fabric.

E

CUTTING OUT THE PATTERN

24. If the pattern piece is designed to be cut from a single thickness of fabric, cut as you would any fabric. For pattern pieces designed to be cut from a double thickness, place the two patchwork pieces together, wrong sides out. Match the seams. Pin the fabrics together near the edges.

25. Place the pinned-together fabrics on a flat surface. Position the pattern over it, aligning the grain-line arrow with the nearest parallel seaming. If the pattern has buttonhole markings, shift the pattern up or down to avoid placing the markings on thick seam allowances. Pin. Cut along the pattern.

patchwork fabric (wrong side)

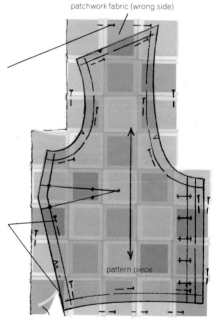

pattern piece

26. Finish the garment according to the pattern instructions.

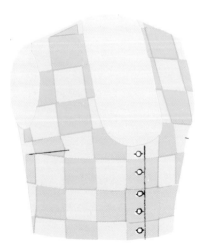

PIECING BY DESIGN

A DIVIDING THE PATTERN

1. Draw the design you want for the patchwork on the appropriate patterns, avoiding buttonholes and dart markings. The straighter the lines, the easier it will be to sew the fabrics together.

2. Number each pattern segment.

3. Draw grain-line arrows on all segments.

4. Cut the pattern segments apart along the lines drawn in Step 1.

5. Pin the pattern segments to paper along the cut edges.

6. Add 5/8-inch seam allowances to the edges.

7. Trim away the excess paper along the newly drawn seam allowances.

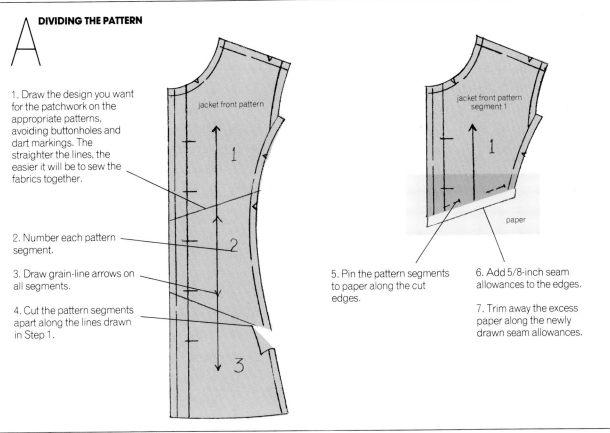

B CUTTING AND MARKING THE FABRICS

8. Pin each pattern segment to the fabric selected for it, making sure to align the grain-line arrows with the grain of selvage edges. Cut out the segments.

9. Using a tracing wheel and dressmaker's carbon paper, transfer the pattern markings onto the fabrics. Do not remove the patterns.

10. Cut and mark any patterns that have not been divided into segments.

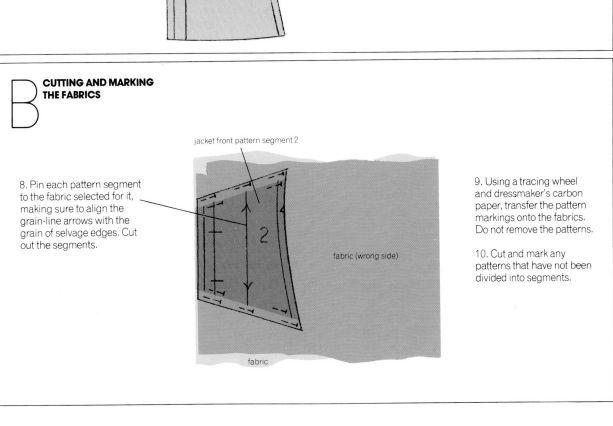

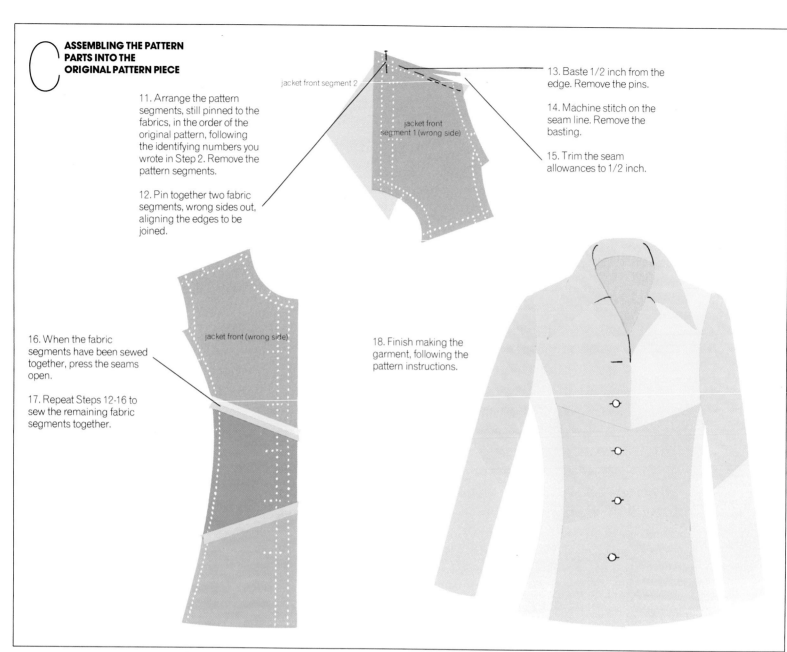

C ASSEMBLING THE PATTERN PARTS INTO THE ORIGINAL PATTERN PIECE

11. Arrange the pattern segments, still pinned to the fabrics, in the order of the original pattern, following the identifying numbers you wrote in Step 2. Remove the pattern segments.

12. Pin together two fabric segments, wrong sides out, aligning the edges to be joined.

jacket front segment 2

jacket front segment 1 (wrong side)

13. Baste 1/2 inch from the edge. Remove the pins.

14. Machine stitch on the seam line. Remove the basting.

15. Trim the seam allowances to 1/2 inch.

16. When the fabric segments have been sewed together, press the seams open.

17. Repeat Steps 12-16 to sew the remaining fabric segments together.

jacket front (wrong side)

18. Finish making the garment, following the pattern instructions.

CRAZY-QUILT PIECING

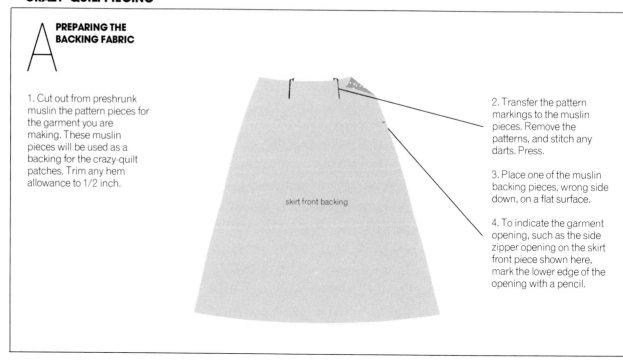

A PREPARING THE BACKING FABRIC

1. Cut out from preshrunk muslin the pattern pieces for the garment you are making. These muslin pieces will be used as a backing for the crazy-quilt patches. Trim any hem allowance to 1/2 inch.

skirt front backing

2. Transfer the pattern markings to the muslin pieces. Remove the patterns, and stitch any darts. Press.

3. Place one of the muslin backing pieces, wrong side down, on a flat surface.

4. To indicate the garment opening, such as the side zipper opening on the skirt front piece shown here, mark the lower edge of the opening with a pencil.

B ATTACHING PATCHES TO THE TOP EDGE OF THE BACKING FABRIC

patch

skirt front backing

5. Preshrink any new fabrics, and clean any remnants to be used.

6. Cut out an irregularly shaped patch about the size you desire from the fabric you chose for the top left-hand corner of the garment.

7. If you want to conceal a garment seam—such as the side seams of the skirt —with overlapping patches, position the patch so that it extends beyond the edge of the backing.

8. Trim off any other edge of the patch that extends beyond the edge of the backing. Pin.

9. If there is a dart nearby, lift the patch, and trim it near the dart—or, if there is a pair of darts, in between the darts—to break the flat surface of the patch.

10. Baste 1/2 inch from the top of the backing edge, and 1 1/2 inches from the edge of the seam to be concealed. Remove the pins.

11. Cut out the next patch, varying the size and shape from the first patch.

12. Place the second patch wrong side up on the first patch, overlapping it as desired.

13. Pin 1/4 inch in from, and parallel to, the edge to be stitched.

14. Turn the patch over the pins and toward the backing to check the position.

15. Return the patch to its original position, and machine stitch 1/4 inch from the edge, removing the pins as you sew.

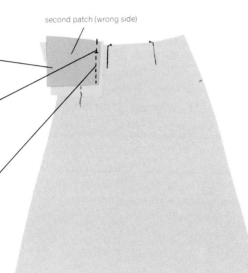

second patch (wrong side)

16. Turn the patch over at the seam, and press.

17. Trim and baste the patch along the top edge of the backing.

18. Repeat Steps 11-17 to attach other patches along the top edge of the backing. Trim any patches at the edge of the garment opening.

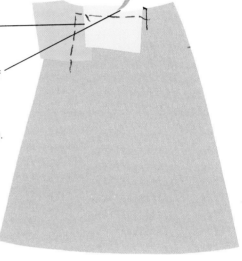

C ATTACHING PATCHES BELOW THE TOP ROW

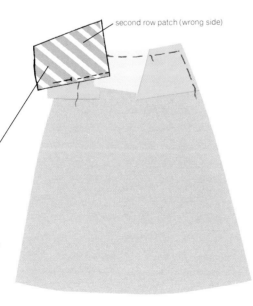

second row patch (wrong side)

19. Cut out the patch to be used for the beginning of the second row.

20. Place the patch, wrong side up, on the patch in the row above, overlapping the patches as desired. Make sure to position the new patch so that it will extend beyond the seam to be concealed.

21. Attach the new patch by repeating Steps 13-16. Baste 1 1/2 inches from the edge of the seam to be concealed.

22. Cut each new patch and position it, wrong side up, on the preceding patch, so that the new patch overlaps the preceding one and the patch above.

23. Attach each patch by repeating Steps 13-16, leaving the top 1/4 inch unstitched. Then turn under the top and side edges 1/4 inch, and slip stitch (Appendix) it to the patch above and the backing.

24. For a more decorative effect, use embroidery thread of a contrasting color and attach the patch with a catch stitch or embroidery stitch (Appendix). Keep the fabric on a flat surface so that the stitches will not pucker the fabric.

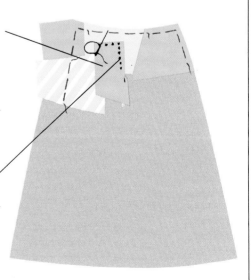

continued

D ATTACHING CURVED PATCHES

25. To attach a patch with rounded edges, fold the raw edge under 1/4 inch. Baste. Turn the patch wrong side down and press.

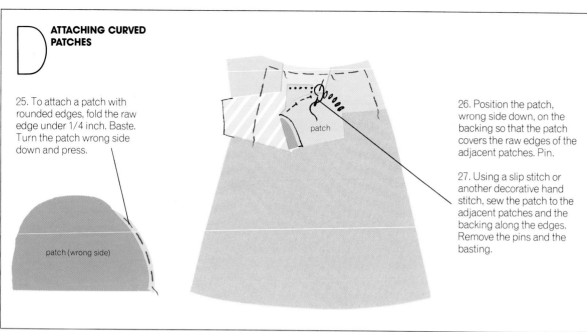

patch (wrong side)

patch

26. Position the patch, wrong side down, on the backing so that the patch covers the raw edges of the adjacent patches. Pin.

27. Using a slip stitch or another decorative hand stitch, sew the patch to the adjacent patches and the backing along the edges. Remove the pins and the basting.

E CONCEALING THE GARMENT SEAMS WITH THE PATCHES

28. Place the crazy-quilted pieces wrong sides together. Turn aside the loose ends of the patches and pin the seams to be joined.

29. Baste 1/2 inch from the edges. Remove the pins. Machine stitch 5/8 inch from the edges. Remove the basting.

30. Trim the seam allowances to 1/4 inch. Crease the seams open with your fingers.

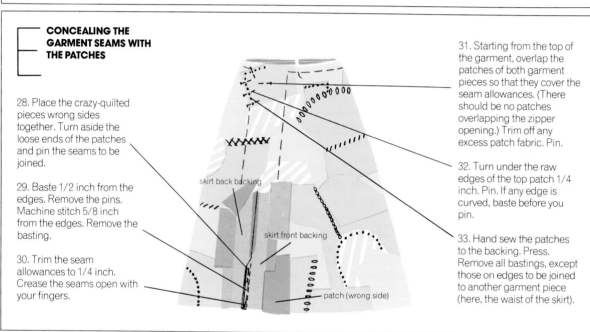

skirt back backing

skirt front backing

patch (wrong side)

31. Starting from the top of the garment, overlap the patches of both garment pieces so that they cover the seam allowances. (There should be no patches overlapping the zipper opening.) Trim off any excess patch fabric. Pin.

32. Turn under the raw edges of the top patch 1/4 inch. Pin. If any edge is curved, baste before you pin.

33. Hand sew the patches to the backing. Press. Remove all bastings, except those on edges to be joined to another garment piece (here, the waist of the skirt).

PIECING LEATHER

A PREPARING THE PATTERN

1. Make any necessary pattern adjustment and remove the hem, if any, at the length you desire.

2. If a pattern is a half-section designed to be cut on the fold of a fabric, such as the skirt front shown here, use it to make a complete pattern. Pin the pattern to a folded piece of paper, and transfer the pattern markings with a saw-toothed tracing wheel. Make sure the tracing wheel perforates both layers of the paper. Remove the pattern.

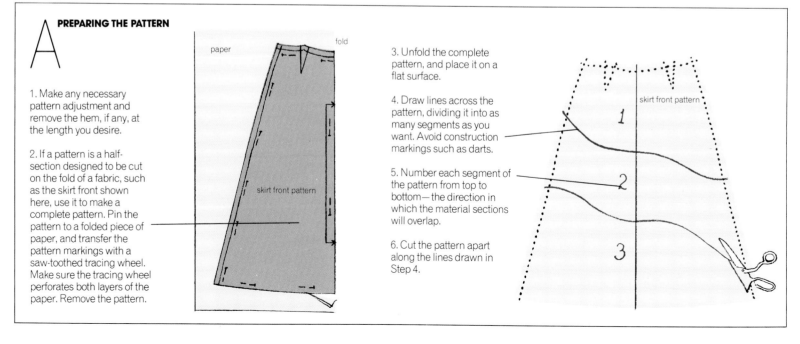

paper

fold

skirt front pattern

skirt front pattern

1

2

3

3. Unfold the complete pattern, and place it on a flat surface.

4. Draw lines across the pattern, dividing it into as many segments as you want. Avoid construction markings such as darts.

5. Number each segment of the pattern from top to bottom—the direction in which the material sections will overlap.

6. Cut the pattern apart along the lines drawn in Step 4.

7. Determine the arrangement you want for the different pieces.

8. Check for flawed spots on the side that will be visible in the finished garment, and mark these areas on the wrong side with a washable felt-tipped pen.

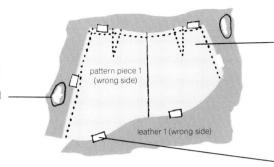

9. Place the material you chose for pattern segment 1 wrong side up on a flat surface. Position the pattern, marked side down, avoiding any flawed areas.

10. Secure the pattern with masking tape rather than pins, since it is difficult to pierce leather with pins. (If you are using imitation suede, use pins and pin only in the seam allowances so that the pin marks will not show on the finished garment.) Cut along the outline.

11. To transfer construction markings, such as darts, place a ruler on the pattern line to be transferred—the perforations from the tracing wheel will be visible on the wrong side of the pattern.

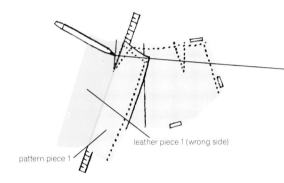

12. Fold the pattern over the ruler. With a washable felt-tipped pen, draw the line on the leather along the folded edge of the pattern. Remove the pattern, and mark the material as piece 1. (Mark imitation suede like cloth, using a smooth-edged tracing wheel.)

13. Position and secure the material for piece 2, repeating Steps 8-10, but do not cut along the outline.

14. To provide a seam allowance when connecting the pieces, use a dressmaker's pencil to draw a line 1/2 inch above and parallel to the top of the pattern.

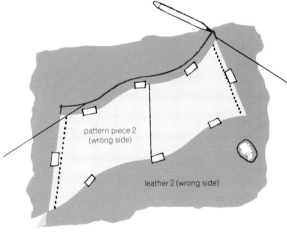

15. Extend the side lines to the ends of the line drawn in Step 14. Cut along the outline, mark the material as you did in Steps 11 and 12 and remove the pattern.

16. Turn the material wrong side down. Position the pattern, marked side up, on the material.

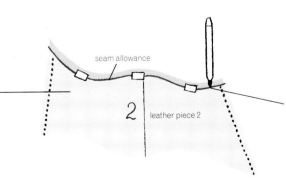

17. Lightly mark the seam line by drawing a line along the top of the pattern. Remove the pattern.

18. Cut and mark the remaining material by repeating Steps 13-17.

continued

C ASSEMBLING THE PIECES

19. Position the first two pieces, wrong sides down, on a flat surface, with the edges to be joined next to each other.

20. Apply rubber cement to the seam allowance at the top of piece number 2, and to the wrong side of the bottom edge of piece number 1. Align the pieces, and press together with your fingers. (If you are working with imitation suede, tape the seam near the edges and at regular intervals in between.)

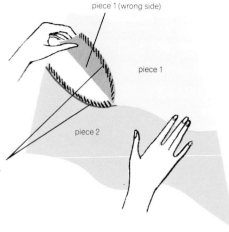

piece 1 (wrong side)

piece 1

piece 2

21. Set the sewing machine gauge to 6 to 8 stitches to the inch. Test the tension on a scrap of material. Then topstitch close to the raw overlapped edge. (If you are working with imitation suede, remove the tape as you stitch.)

22. Make a second row of topstitching 1/4 inch inside the first row, using the pressure foot as a guide.

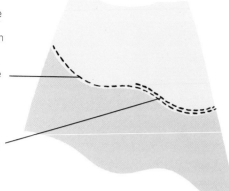

23. Join the remaining pieces in the same manner.

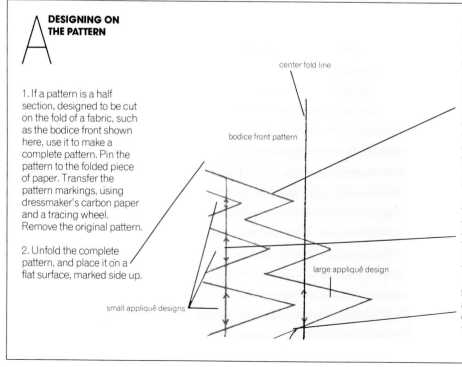

piece 3

24. After completing the garment, finish the raw hem edge by making two rows of topstitching as you did in Steps 21 and 22.

LAYERED APPLIQUÉ

A DESIGNING ON THE PATTERN

1. If a pattern is a half section, designed to be cut on the fold of a fabric, such as the bodice front shown here, use it to make a complete pattern. Pin the pattern to the folded piece of paper. Transfer the pattern markings, using dressmaker's carbon paper and a tracing wheel. Remove the original pattern.

2. Unfold the complete pattern, and place it on a flat surface, marked side up.

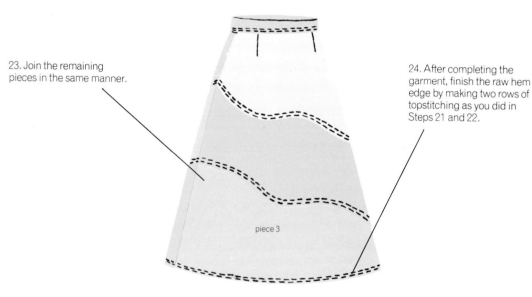

center fold line

bodice front pattern

small appliqué designs

large appliqué design

3. Draw the design for the large appliqué on the pattern, avoiding construction markings, such as darts. To make the layered appliqué, draw smaller designs within the large design. In this example, the zigzag design will be appliquéd to the garment fabric. Then the triangular designs will be sewed on top of the large appliqué.

4. If the pattern grain-line arrow does not pass through all the appliqué forms, draw them on each design, keeping the lines parallel to the center fold line.

5. Cut apart the pattern along the large appliqué outline—the zigzag line in this example.

B CUTTING OUT THE APPLIQUÉ FABRIC PIECES

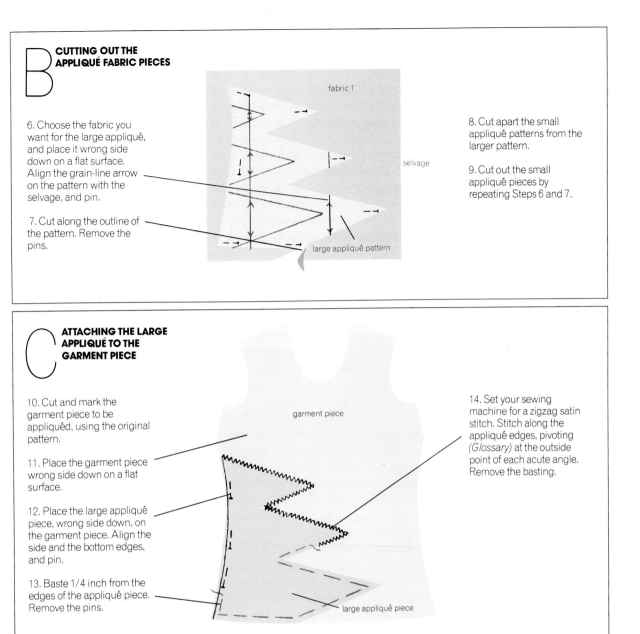

fabric 1

selvage

large appliqué pattern

6. Choose the fabric you want for the large appliqué, and place it wrong side down on a flat surface. Align the grain-line arrow on the pattern with the selvage, and pin.

7. Cut along the outline of the pattern. Remove the pins.

8. Cut apart the small appliqué patterns from the larger pattern.

9. Cut out the small appliqué pieces by repeating Steps 6 and 7.

C ATTACHING THE LARGE APPLIQUÉ TO THE GARMENT PIECE

garment piece

large appliqué piece

10. Cut and mark the garment piece to be appliquéd, using the original pattern.

11. Place the garment piece wrong side down on a flat surface.

12. Place the large appliqué piece, wrong side down, on the garment piece. Align the side and the bottom edges, and pin.

13. Baste 1/4 inch from the edges of the appliqué piece. Remove the pins.

14. Set your sewing machine for a zigzag satin stitch. Stitch along the appliqué edges, pivoting (Glossary) at the outside point of each acute angle. Remove the basting.

D ATTACHING THE SMALL APPLIQUÉS TO THE LARGE APPLIQUÉ

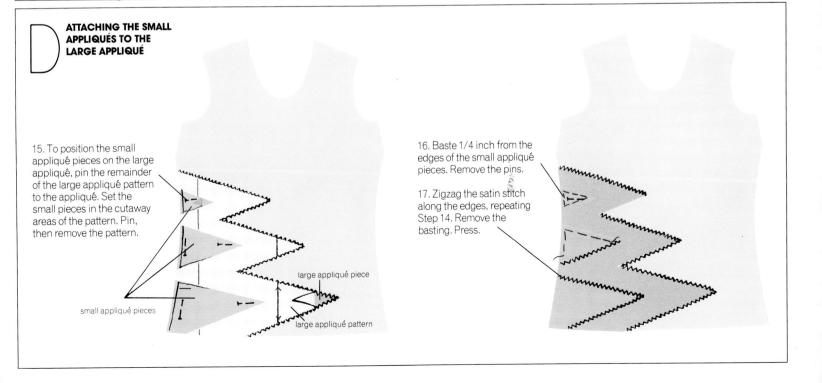

small appliqué pieces

large appliqué piece

large appliqué pattern

15. To position the small appliqué pieces on the large appliqué, pin the remainder of the large appliqué pattern to the appliqué. Set the small pieces in the cutaway areas of the pattern. Pin, then remove the pattern.

16. Baste 1/4 inch from the edges of the small appliqué pieces. Remove the pins.

17. Zigzag the satin stitch along the edges, repeating Step 14. Remove the basting. Press.

A galaxy of quilted pufferies

Once limited to cozy bedcovers, the traditional craft of quilting is now often used to adorn garments like the pieced jacket here. The apparent complexity of its quilting lines, which run in all directions, is deceiving; the design is achieved by quilting each piece before assembling. This method works since the jacket was made from a pattern with no darts and few seams; the edges were bound instead of hemmed.

For more venturesome quilters there are variations on this basic technique. Biscuit quilting, which gets its name from its resemblance to puffy pastries, is actually a patchwork soufflé of tiny, muslin-backed squares of fabric, individually stuffed and then sewed together. Trapunto, perhaps the most intricate form of quilting, gets its elegantly embossed patterns from cording and batting, which are stuffed through slits in the muslin backing after the design has been stitched. A lining hides construction details.

QUILTING A GARMENT

A PREPARING TO QUILT

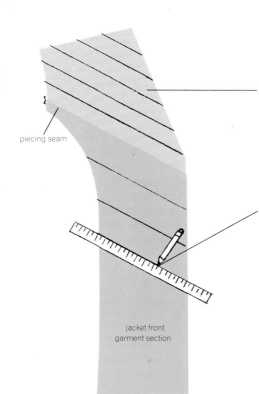

piecing seam

jacket front
garment section

1. Use your pattern pieces to cut the polyester fleece interlining and muslin backing pieces you will need to quilt the garment. Leave a 1-inch seam allowance to allow for the contraction that will occur as you quilt.

2. Cut out the garment pieces as usual, but do not transfer the pattern markings. For a pieced garment, like the jacket at left, follow the instructions for piecing by design (pages 81-82, Steps 1-17).

3. Place one garment section on a flat surface, wrong side down.

4. Using a ruler and pencil, draw quilting lines to create the design you desire. If the garment section has been pieced—such as the jacket front shown here—you can use the piecing seams as quilting lines, and space other lines parallel to them.

5. Plan quilting lines to avoid buttonholes. Check against the pattern and correct lines as necessary.

B ASSEMBLING THE GARMENT, INTERLINING AND BACKING PIECES

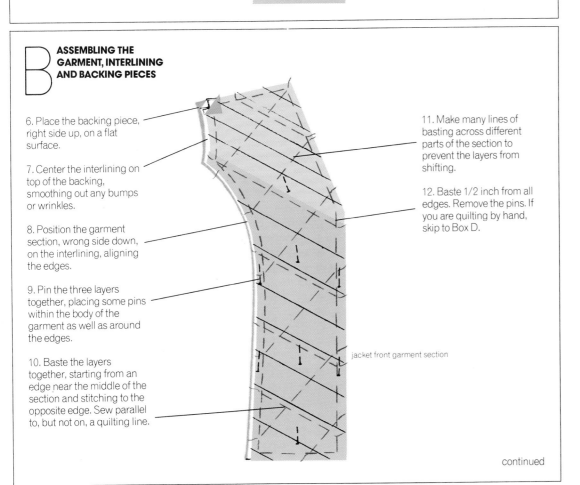

jacket front garment section

6. Place the backing piece, right side up, on a flat surface.

7. Center the interlining on top of the backing, smoothing out any bumps or wrinkles.

8. Position the garment section, wrong side down, on the interlining, aligning the edges.

9. Pin the three layers together, placing some pins within the body of the garment as well as around the edges.

10. Baste the layers together, starting from an edge near the middle of the section and stitching to the opposite edge. Sew parallel to, but not on, a quilting line.

11. Make many lines of basting across different parts of the section to prevent the layers from shifting.

12. Baste 1/2 inch from all edges. Remove the pins. If you are quilting by hand, skip to Box D.

continued

C QUILTING BY MACHINE

13. Thread your sewing machine with mercerized cotton or polyester-coated cotton thread, and set the gauge at 8 to 10 stitches to the inch. Test the tension on scraps of materials.

14. Starting at the center quilting line, or the piecing seam near the center, machine stitch along the line from one edge of the garment section to the other. As you stitch, press down the layers on each side of the needle, pulling the garment fabric somewhat to the sides to keep the fabric from slipping.

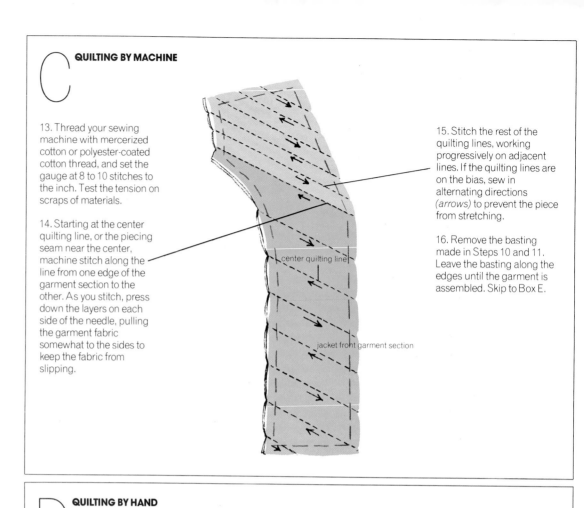

center quilting line

jacket front garment section

15. Stitch the rest of the quilting lines, working progressively on adjacent lines. If the quilting lines are on the bias, sew in alternating directions (arrows) to prevent the piece from stretching.

16. Remove the basting made in Steps 10 and 11. Leave the basting along the edges until the garment is assembled. Skip to Box E.

D QUILTING BY HAND

17. Center the quilting piece inside an embroidery hoop that has an adjustable screw. Tighten the hoop.

18. Thread your needle with quilting thread, or mercerized cotton thread coated with beeswax. Knot the thread.

19. Insert the needle 1/2 inch from one end of the center quilting line; take 2 or 3 small running stitches (Appendix) through all layers, then pull the needle through. As you sew, flatten the fabric just ahead of the stitches with your thumb.

center quilting line

jacket front garment section

20. Repeat along the quilting line, making 5 to 8 stitches to the inch.

21. If the hoop is wider than the fabric so that the ends of a line of quilting are inside it, unclamped, go over the stitching with your fingers on a flat surface to keep the thread from puckering the fabric.

22. End the stitches with a fastening stitch (Appendix), 1/2 inch from the edge.

23. Working progressively on adjacent lines, stitch all lines in the same way. Remove the hoop and bastings made in Steps 10 and 11.

MARKING AND TRIMMING THE QUILTED GARMENT SECTION

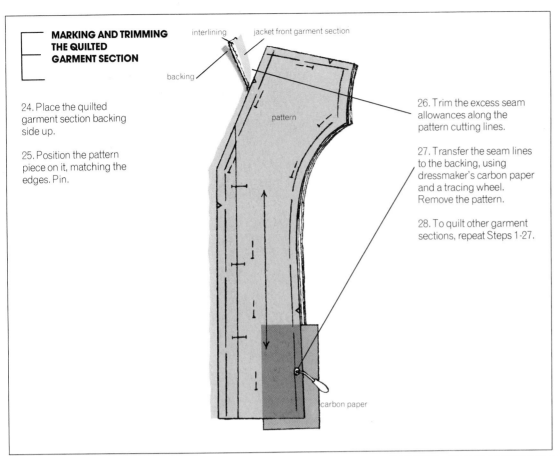

interlining

jacket front garment section

backing

pattern

carbon paper

24. Place the quilted garment section backing side up.

25. Position the pattern piece on it, matching the edges. Pin.

26. Trim the excess seam allowances along the pattern cutting lines.

27. Transfer the seam lines to the backing, using dressmaker's carbon paper and a tracing wheel. Remove the pattern.

28. To quilt other garment sections, repeat Steps 1-27.

ASSEMBLING THE QUILTED GARMENT SECTIONS

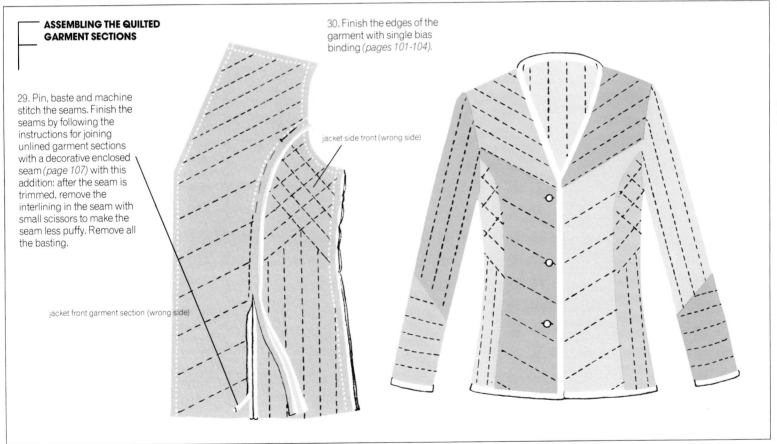

jacket side front (wrong side)

jacket front garment section (wrong side)

29. Pin, baste and machine stitch the seams. Finish the seams by following the instructions for joining unlined garment sections with a decorative enclosed seam (page 107) with this addition: after the seam is trimmed, remove the interlining in the seam with small scissors to make the seam less puffy. Remove all the basting.

30. Finish the edges of the garment with single bias binding (pages 101-104).

BISCUIT QUILTING

A DETERMINING THE SIZE OF THE BACKING SQUARE

1. To make a garment from biscuit quilting, select a pattern that has no darts and is designed for stretch fabrics.

2. Measure the widest part of a pattern piece, measuring between the seam lines— not the cutting lines— of the pattern.

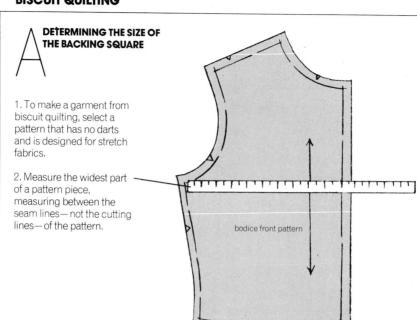

bodice front pattern

3. Divide the measurement by the number of biscuits, or patches, you want for the row. (Smaller patches are easier to fit into the pattern's shape, and also make the garment less bulky.) This measurement will be the finished length and width of the square of muslin backing fabric needed for the patch.

4. To provide a 1/4-inch seam allowance on all sides of the square, add 1/2 inch to the measurement obtained in Step 3.

B MAKING THE GRID PATTERN

5. Draw a grid at least as large as the pattern on a piece of tracing paper. The distance between the lines should be equal to the backing square measurement determined in Step 3.

6. Position the tracing paper on the pattern, aligning one outer vertical line with the vertical edge of the pattern and the other outer line with the widest point of the pattern.

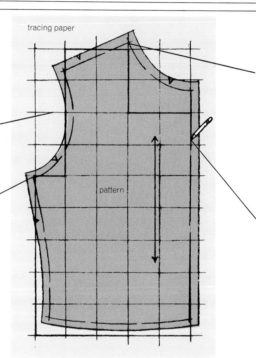

tracing paper

pattern

7. Fit as many squares of the grid as possible into the shape of the pattern, moving the tracing paper up or down. Watch a few crucial points— here, the top of the neckline, the end of the shoulder line, and the bottom of the armhole curve. When the squares are as close as possible to the seam lines at these points, pin the paper to the pattern.

8. Using a soft lead pencil, go over the grid lines closest to the outer seam line of the pattern. At the neckline, trace over only grid lines inside the neckline seam line. Remove the pins.

9. Cut out the tracing paper along the traced lines. This will be the pattern for making the biscuit patches and lining.

C CUTTING OUT THE FABRIC SQUARES

10. Draw a grid on the wrong side of the muslin backing, following a lengthwise and a crosswise grain. The distance between the lines should be equal to the measurement determined in Step 4.

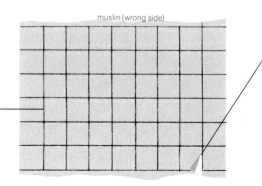

muslin (wrong side)

11. Cut along the lines in one direction making strips. Then cut the strips into patches.

12. To cut out the covering fabric squares, follow the instructions for piecing by following a grid (page 79, Steps 1-7). The measurement for the patch should be 3/4 inch larger than the backing patch cut out in Steps 10 and 11.

D ⎤ MAKING THE BISCUIT PATCH

13. Pin a covering square to a backing square at two corners, wrong sides together.

14. Midway between the pinned corners, fold the extra 3/4 inch of the covering square into a right-to-left pleat, and pin it to the backing square.

17. Insert polyester batting through the opening. Insert just enough stuffing to puff the covering square, yet keep the backing square relatively flat.

15. Pin together the remaining corners, and make pleats at two more sides, repeating Step 14. Do not make a pleat on the fourth side.

16. Baste the three pleated sides 3/16 inch from the edges. If you are machine basting, use the zipper foot. Remove the pins.

18. Make a pleat on the fourth side by repeating Step 14.

19. Baste 3/16 inch from the fourth edge. Remove the pin.

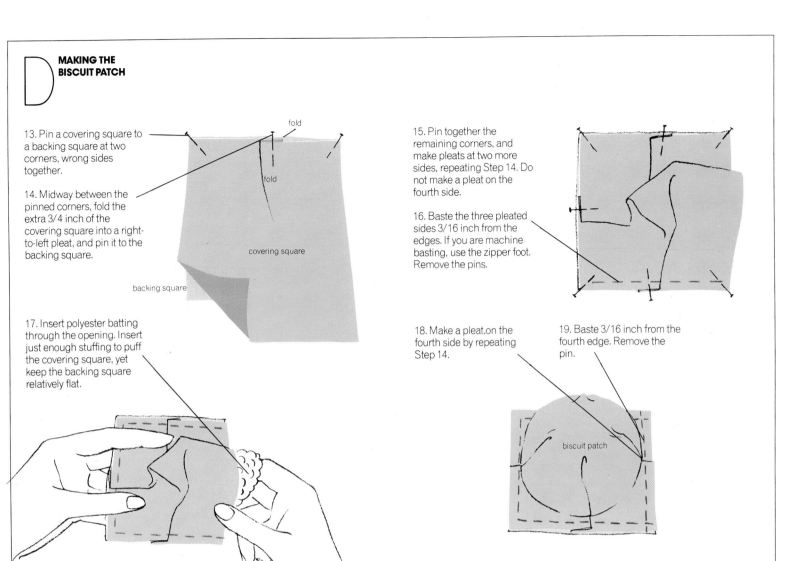

E ⎤ JOINING THE PATCHES INTO THE GARMENT PIECE

20. On a flat surface, arrange the patches into the shape of the grid pattern made in Step 9.

21. Starting with the bottom row, join the patches into a strip, and the strips into the patchwork garment piece, following the instructions for piecing by following a grid (pages 79-80, Steps 12-21). Remove any basting that is unnecessary.

F ⎤ FINISHING A GARMENT

22. Make other garment pieces following Steps 1-21.

23. Seam the garment pieces the same way you joined the strips.

24. Cut out the lining from the grid patterns, adding 1/4-inch seam allowance on all edges. Then line the garment.

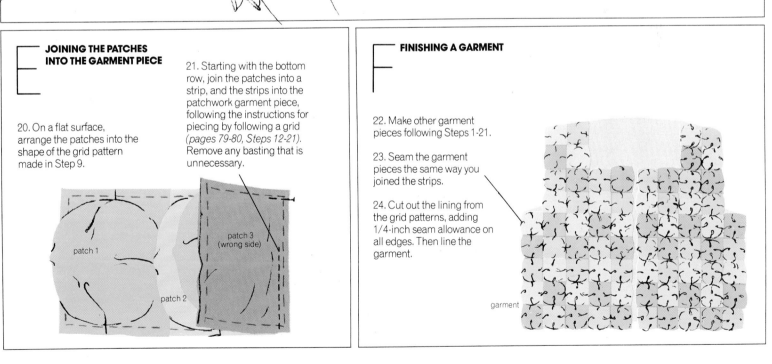

TRAPUNTO QUILTING

A PREPARING TO QUILT

1. Following the pattern, cut out the garment section to be quilted and the identical muslin backing and lining.

2A. To fill the whole garment section with a trapunto design, make a duplicate pattern on tracing paper. If the original pattern piece is a half section designed to be cut on the fold of a fabric, use it to make a complete pattern by cutting it out from folded tracing paper. Transfer all pattern markings with a tracing wheel and dressmaker's carbon paper.

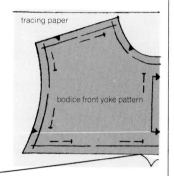

2B. To make a small trapunto design within a garment section, cut a square piece of tracing paper about the size of the design.

3. Draw or trace the outline of the desired design on the tracing paper. If you are covering an entire garment section, arrange the design to avoid darts.

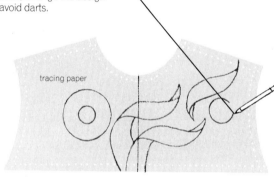

4. Place the backing piece, wrong side up, on a flat surface. Position the tracing paper, design side down, where desired on the backing. Pin at corners.

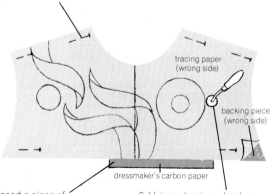

5. Insert a piece of dressmaker's carbon paper, carbon side down, between the tracing paper and the backing.

6. Using a tracing wheel or a hard-lead pencil, trace the design onto the backing piece. Remove the carbon paper and the tracing paper.

B DESIGNING QUILTING LINES

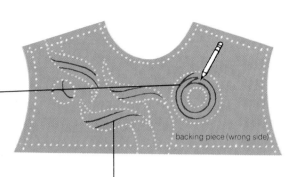

7. To make a circular ridged design, first draw as many concentric circles as you want ridges. The width between each circle should be the width of the cotton cord plus 1/16 inch.

8. Adjust the lines of the inner circles so that there is a continuous channel spiraling inward from the outermost circle.

9. To make a ridged design, pencil in parallel lines to form channels through which to thread a cording. The width between the lines should be the same as in Step 7.

10. To divide part of a design, pencil in the lines where desired.

11. Place the garment piece, wrong side up, on a flat surface. Position the backing piece, marked side up, on it. Pin.

12. Baste from corner to corner and 1/2 inch from the edges. Remove the pins.

13. Wind your machine bobbin with buttonhole twist. Use the same color thread to thread the machine's needle. Set the gauge at 8 to 10 stitches to the inch.

14. Stitch on the design outline and all the penciled-in inner quilting lines.

15. Pull the buttonhole twist ends to the wrong side, and knot. Remove the crisscross basting.

C PADDING WITH BATTING

16. Using a seam ripper or a small scissors, make a tiny opening in the backing within the stitched area to be padded. Be careful not to catch the garment fabric underneath.

17. Using the end of a crochet hook or the blunt end of a blunt needle, stuff batting through the opening. Keep the padding even and smooth. To pad a large area, stuff the batting in small amounts, gradually filling in the area.

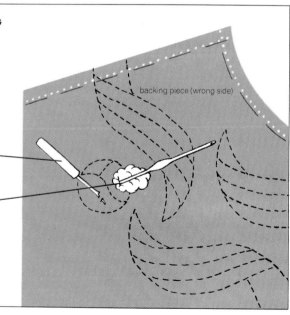

D PADDING WITH CORDING

18. Cut a piece of cotton cord a few inches longer than the length of the channel through which it is to be threaded.

19. Wrap a small piece of masking or cellophane tape around one end of the cording.

20. Attach a safety pin—one that is smaller than the width of the channel—to the taped end of the cord.

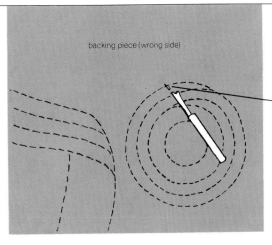

backing piece (wrong side)

21. Make an opening near one end of the continuous channel, repeating Step 16.

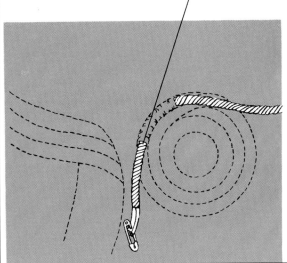

22. Insert the pin, and work the cord as far as it can go through the channel.

23. At curves, the pin may not move through the narrow passageway. Snip open the backing fabric, and pull the pin and the cord through the opening.

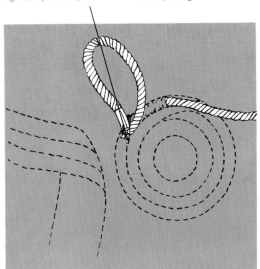

24. Insert the pin again through the same opening, and work it through the next segment of the channel. When the pin will not move again, repeat Step 23.

25. When you have threaded the pin and cord through a little distance, pull them out until 1 inch of the cord remains outside the first opening.

26. Finish threading the pin and cord through the channel, repeating Step 24 as necessary. Pull up the excess length of cord occasionally to make it lie flat inside the channel. Do not pull too tightly.

27. When you reach the end of the channel, make an opening and pull out the pin and the cord. Cut off the excess cord at both ends.

28. If the design does not stand out enough on the garment side, use a tapestry needle to thread a strand of yarn through the same channel in the same way.

29. To fill any ends of the channels that are too narrow, stuff small amounts of batting through the holes nearest the ends.

E COMPLETING THE GARMENT

30. Check the lining against the trapuntoed piece. Trim off any excess lining.

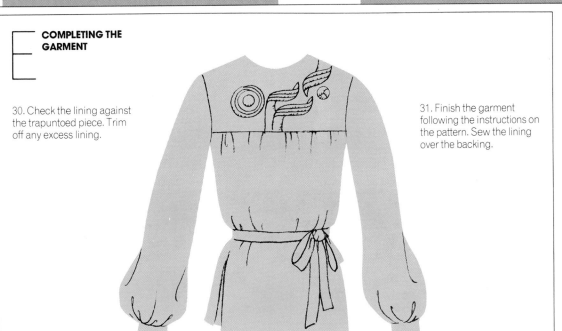

31. Finish the garment following the instructions on the pattern. Sew the lining over the backing.

Decorative
ways to join
the parts

Garment sections must inevitably be joined, and raw edges finished—but you can make the results decorative by using imaginative materials and methods, like the crochet that scallops the edges and joins the seams of the suede outfit at left. It is worked through slits made with a leather cutting tool sold at most craft stores.

Decorative braids, grosgrain ribbon and bias binding (ready-made or cut from your own fabric) are other alternative edgings. One binding particularly suitable for sheer fabrics is the double-folded strip of bias-cut material, whose uniform opacity creates an edge without visible layers. And conventional bias tape also provides an unusual method for finishing seams of unlined garments.

BINDING GARMENT EDGES WITH CROCHET

A — PREPARING THE EDGES

1. Trim the edges to be bound along the seam-line markings.

2. Place the garment wrong side down. Depending on the effect desired, mark a guide line 3/16 to 1/2 inch from the edge for making slits. Mark garments made of leather, suede or imitation suede by lightly scoring a line with a stylus. Use chalk for garments made of felt or nonravelly fabrics.

3. To make slits through which to crochet the binding, place the garment, wrong side down, on a piece of heavy cardboard.

4. Position the cutting edges of the slit cutter on the guide line near one end. Hold the tool at a right angle to the garment and hammer down on the end until you have pierced the material.

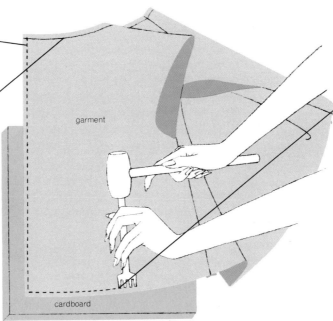

garment

cardboard

5. To punch the next series of slits, position the cutting edges of the tool along the guide line, with the last prong inserted in the last slit punched, and continue along the length of the guide line.

6. At the corners, punch the slits up to, but not beyond, the intersection of the guide lines. If necessary, insert several prongs of the cutter into previously punched slits. On the second side forming the corner, place the cutting edges of the tool on the guide line one slit width away from the intersection.

7. Bind the edges, following the instructions in Boxes B and C for a single crochet binding or Box D for a shell pattern binding.

B — STARTING A BINDING WITH SINGLE CROCHET STITCHES

8. Tie the yarn to the crochet hook as described in Steps 1 and 2 of the chain stitch (Appendix).

9. With the finished side of the garment toward you, make 1 single crochet stitch in each slit along the garment edge. Treat each slit as though it were a stitch in a foundation chain.

garment

10. If you are binding an edge that is not continuous, make the first single crochet stitch at one end of the row of slits. Start to bind a continuous edge at an unobtrusive point along the garment edge, such as at the center back of the collar, neckline or hem.

11. At the corners, make 3 single crochet stitches in the corner slit. Then make 1 single crochet stitch in each slit along the next edge.

12A. If you are binding a continuous edge, continue to make 1 single crochet stitch in each remaining slit in the garment. Repeat Step 11 at corners. Complete the first round by making a slip stitch in the first single crochet stitch of the round, as shown.

garment

12B. If you are working a noncontinuous edge, complete the first row by making 1 single crochet stitch in each remaining hole or slit in the garment. Chain 1, as shown, and turn.

garment

continued

C FINISHING A BINDING WITH SINGLE CROCHET STITCHES

13A. Work a second round by making 1 single crochet stitch in each stitch of the first round. At the corners, make 3 single crochet stitches in the corner stitch of the previous round. Complete the round by making a slip stitch in the first single crochet stitch of the round. Fasten off (Appendix).

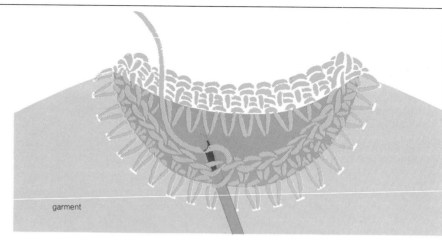

garment

13B. Make a second row of single crochet stitches, and fasten off (Appendix).

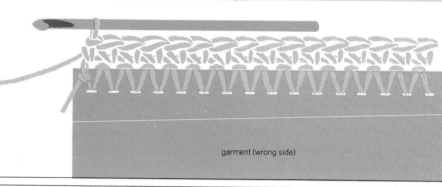

garment (wrong side)

D MAKING A SHELL PATTERN BINDING

14. Make a single crochet binding around the garment edge, following the directions given (page 97 and above), but do not fasten off the yarn.

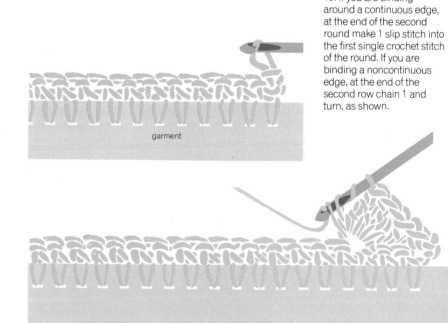

garment

15. If you are binding around a continuous edge, at the end of the second round make 1 slip stitch into the first single crochet stitch of the round. If you are binding a noncontinuous edge, at the end of the second row chain 1 and turn, as shown.

16. Make 1 single crochet stitch in the first stitch of the row or, on a continuous edge, in the next stitch of the round. Skip 2 stitches. Make a shell in the next stitch by making 5 triple crochet stitches (Appendix), as shown.

17. Make the pattern to be followed across the row, or round, in this sequence: Skip 2 stitches, make 1 single crochet stitch in the next stitch, skip 2 stitches, and make a shell in the next stitch. Repeat this sequence across the row or round, ending with 1 single crochet stitch. Fasten off (Appendix).

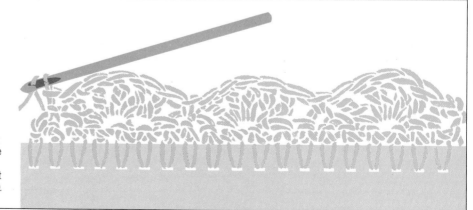

JOINING GARMENT PIECES WITH CROCHET

A DETERMINING THE WIDTH OF THE SEAMS

1. Punch slits along the edge of two swatches of garment fabric, following the directions for binding garment edges with crochet *(page 97, Steps 2-6)*. Be sure to align the holes on both edges.

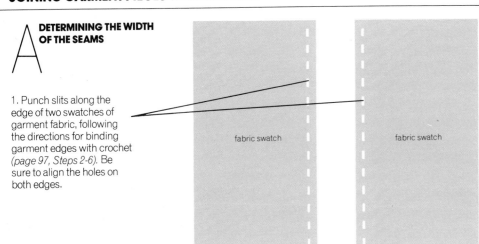

fabric swatch

fabric swatch

2. Join the two swatches, following the instructions in Box B to make a ridged single crochet seam, Box C to make a pebbled single crochet seam or Box D to make a slip stitch crocheted seam.

3. After the swatches are crocheted together, measure the distance between the two edges of the swatches taken up by the crochet work. Divide by two. This figure will be used in adjusting the seam lines on actual garment sections *(BoxD, page 100, Step 16)*.

B MAKING A RIDGED SINGLE CROCHET SEAM

4. Make a loose slip knot on the crochet hook, as shown in Steps 1 and 2 of the chain stitch *(Appendix)*.

5. Working from the finished side, make 1 single crochet stitch in each slit along the edge of one of the sections to be joined. Treat the slits as though they were stitches in a foundation chain. Fasten off *(Appendix)*.

6. Repeat Steps 4 and 5 to make a row of single crochet stitches along the edge of the other section.

7. With the sections to be joined wrong sides together, align the two crocheted edges.

8. Begin to make a single crochet stitch by inserting the crochet hook from front to back through both loops of the first stitch at the end of each section (four loops in all). Place a strand of yarn over the hook, and draw it through all four loops, leaving a loop on the hook.

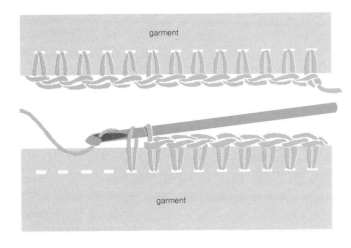

garment

garment

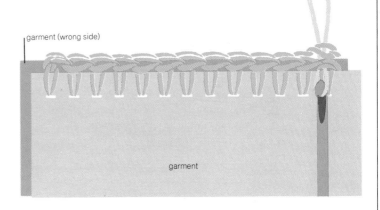

garment (wrong side)

garment

9. Insert the hook through the four loops of the next pair of stitches and bring the yarn over the hook. Then draw it through these four loops, leaving two loops on the hook.

10. Complete the single crochet stitch by bringing the yarn over the hook, and drawing it through both remaining loops on the hook.

11. Repeat Steps 9 and 10 until the sections are joined. Then fasten off *(Appendix)*.

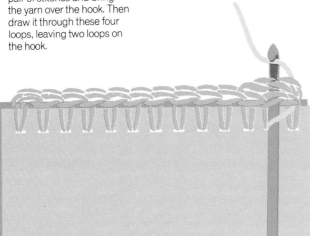

C THE SLIP STITCH CROCHETED SEAM

12. To bind the garment sections to be seamed, follow the directions for the ridged single crochet seam *(Steps 4-6)*.

13. With the garment sections to be joined wrong sides together, align the two crocheted edges.

14. Insert the hook from front to back through both loops of the first stitch at the end of each section (four loops in all). Place a strand of yarn over the hook, and draw it through all-four loops, leaving a loop on the hook.

15. Insert the hook through the four loops of the next pair of stitches. Bring the yarn over the hook and, in one motion, draw it through these stitches as well as through the loop on the hook. Repeat until the pieces are joined. Fasten off *(Appendix)*.

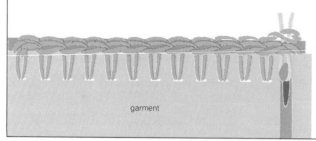

garment

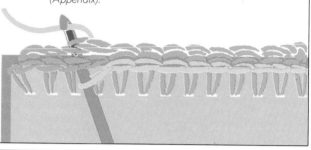

D JOINING THE GARMENT SEAMS

16. To adjust the markings of seams to be crocheted to compensate for the added width of the crocheted work, place the garment sections to be joined wrong side up. Using the figure arrived at in Step 3, draw a chalk line inside of and parallel to each seam line to be joined.

17. Trim off the seam allowances along the adjusted seam lines.

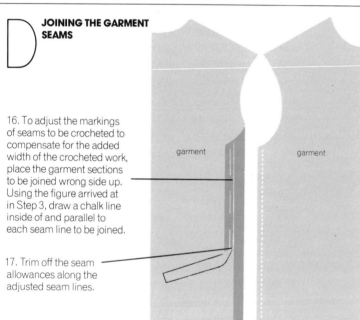

garment

garment

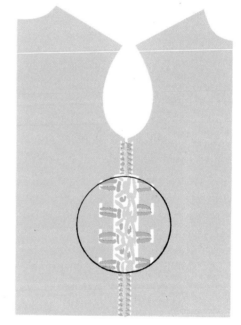

18. Place the garment sections wrong side down. Punch slits as you did on the swatches, along the garment edges to be joined.

19. Join the garment pieces, following the instructions for the crochet pattern chosen *(Box B or C)*.

MAKING BIAS BINDING

A CUTTING THE FABRIC STRIPS FOR THE BINDING

1. To determine the total length of the binding strip you will need, measure all edges to be bound. Add 12 inches to this figure.

2. Fold the fabric diagonally so that a crosswise edge is aligned with a lengthwise (selvage) edge and the wrong sides are together. Pin the edges.

3. Cut along the folded edge. Remove the pins and the top piece of fabric.

4. Determine the number of fabric strips you will need to make the total length of binding required, adding 1/2 inch for seam allowances on every strip.

5. To mark the strips, draw chalk lines parallel to the diagonal edge. For a single bias binding, each strip should be twice the desired finished width, plus 1/2 inch for seam allowances. For a double bias binding, each strip should be six times the desired finished width.

6. Trim off both selvages.

7. Cut out the strips along the chalk lines.

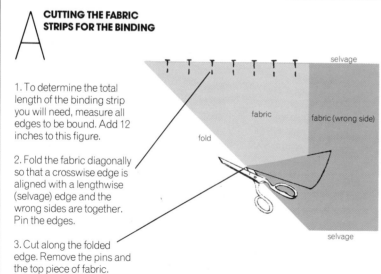

selvage

fabric

fabric (wrong side)

fold

selvage

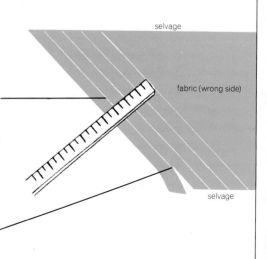

selvage

fabric (wrong side)

selvage

B JOINING THE BIAS STRIPS

8. Mark a 1/4-inch seam allowance with chalk on the ends of each strip.

9. Place two strips together, wrong sides out, so that they form a V. Align the seam lines and pin.

10. Machine stitch and remove the pins.

11. Repeat Steps 8-10 as many times as necessary to make one long strip of the length required.

12. Press open the seams and trim the extended points of the seam allowances.

13. Cut off one end of the strip at a right angle to the sides.

14. Measure the length you determined in Step 1, and cut off the other end of the strip. Again make the cut at a right angle to the sides.

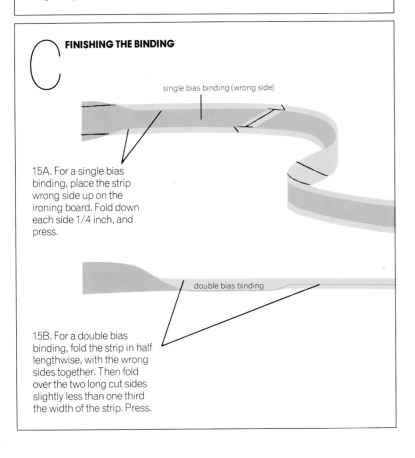

bias strip

bias strip (wrong side)

C FINISHING THE BINDING

single bias binding (wrong side)

15A. For a single bias binding, place the strip wrong side up on the ironing board. Fold down each side 1/4 inch, and press.

double bias binding

15B. For a double bias binding, fold the strip in half lengthwise, with the wrong sides together. Then fold over the two long cut sides slightly less than one third the width of the strip. Press.

ATTACHING SINGLE BIAS BINDING

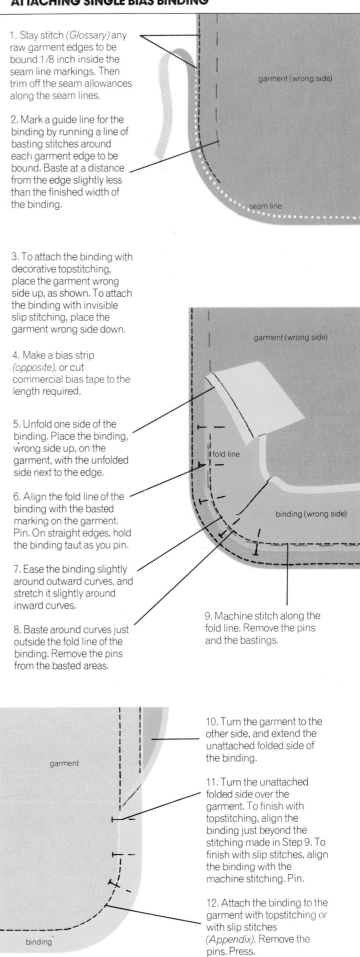

1. Stay stitch (Glossary) any raw garment edges to be bound 1/8 inch inside the seam line markings. Then trim off the seam allowances along the seam lines.

2. Mark a guide line for the binding by running a line of basting stitches around each garment edge to be bound. Baste at a distance from the edge slightly less than the finished width of the binding.

3. To attach the binding with decorative topstitching, place the garment wrong side up, as shown. To attach the binding with invisible slip stitching, place the garment wrong side down.

4. Make a bias strip (opposite), or cut commercial bias tape to the length required.

5. Unfold one side of the binding. Place the binding, wrong side up, on the garment, with the unfolded side next to the edge.

6. Align the fold line of the binding with the basted marking on the garment. Pin. On straight edges, hold the binding taut as you pin.

7. Ease the binding slightly around outward curves, and stretch it slightly around inward curves.

8. Baste around curves just outside the fold line of the binding. Remove the pins from the basted areas.

9. Machine stitch along the fold line. Remove the pins and the bastings.

10. Turn the garment to the other side, and extend the unattached folded side of the binding.

11. Turn the unattached folded side over the garment. To finish with topstitching, align the binding just beyond the stitching made in Step 9. To finish with slip stitches, align the binding with the machine stitching. Pin.

12. Attach the binding to the garment with topstitching or with slip stitches (Appendix). Remove the pins. Press.

garment (wrong side)

seam line

garment (wrong side)

fold line

binding (wrong side)

garment

binding

ATTACHING DOUBLE BIAS BINDING

1. Stay stitch *(Glossary)* any raw garment edges to be bound 1/8 inch inside the seam-line markings. Then trim off the seam allowances along the seam lines.

2. Make a bias strip for the double bias binding *(pages 100-101)*.

3. Place the garment wrong side down. Unfold the cut edges of the binding. Place the binding on the garment, aligning the cut edges with the garment edge.

4. Pin the binding to the garment along the fold line. Along straight edges, hold the binding taut as you pin.

5. Ease the binding around outward curves, and stretch it around inward curves.

6. Baste around the curves. Remove the pins from the basted areas.

7. Machine stitch along the fold line. Remove the pins and the basting.

8. Place the garment wrong side up, and extend the unattached side of the binding.

9. Turn the unattached side of the binding over the garment edge, and align it with the machine stitching made in Step 7. Pin.

10. Attach the binding with a slip stitch *(Appendix)*. Remove the pins. Press.

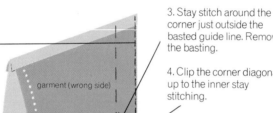

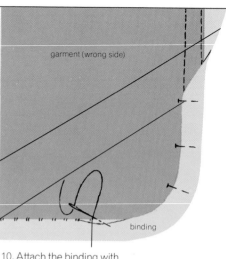

MITERING AN INSIDE CORNER WITH BIAS BINDING

1. To attach bias binding around an inside corner, such as on a square neckline, first stay stitch *(Glossary)* any raw edges 1/8 inch inside the seam-line markings. Then trim off the seam allowances along the seam lines.

2. Baste a guide line around the inside corner. Baste at a distance from the edges slightly less than the finished width of the binding.

3. Stay stitch around the corner just outside the basted guide line. Remove the basting.

4. Clip the corner diagonally up to the inner stay stitching.

5. Spread the fabric so that the two garment edges form a straight line. Attach one side of the binding along the entire edge, following the directions for attaching single or double bias binding, depending on the type selected.

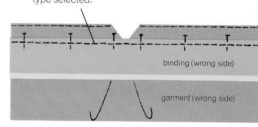

6. At the corner, re-form the garment to its original shape.

7. Turn the binding right side up along one side of the corner, creating a diagonal fold. Press the fold.

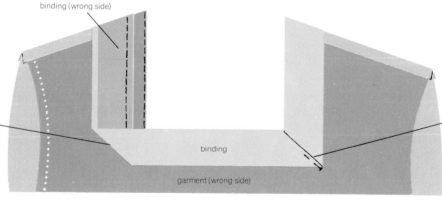

8. To create the miter, turn the binding right side up along the other side of the corner. Insert a pin near the inner stitched edge of the binding to hold the overlapped fabric in place. Do not pin through the garment fabric.

9. Turn the garment to the other side.

10. Pull the excess binding material through the slit in the garment fabric.

11. Fold the unattached edge of the binding over the garment edge. At the corner, re-form the diagonal fold of the miter.

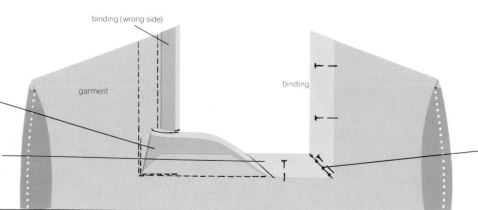

12. Finish attaching the binding to the garment, following the instructions for attaching single or double bias binding.

13. Slip stitch *(Appendix)* the outside and inside folds of the miter, if desired.

MITERING AN OUTSIDE CORNER WITH BIAS BINDING

1. To attach bias binding around an outside corner, such as at the intersection of the hemline and front opening on a jacket, first attach one side of the binding to the garment along one of the sides that forms the corner. Follow the directions for attaching single or double bias binding, depending on the type selected.

2. End the stitching at the basted corner marking or, for double bias binding, at a distance from the corner equal to the finished width of the binding.

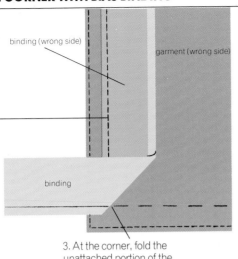

binding (wrong side)

garment (wrong side)

binding

3. At the corner, fold the unattached portion of the binding diagonally up to the end of the machine stitching.

4. Fold the unattached portion of the binding again, aligning the fold with the garment edge.

5. For a single bias binding, line up the fold line of the binding with the basted marking on the garment, as shown. For a double bias binding, line up the outer cut edges of the binding with the other garment edge.

6. Pin the binding to the garment along the binding fold line.

7. Machine stitch along the fold line, beginning at the garment edge. Remove the pins.

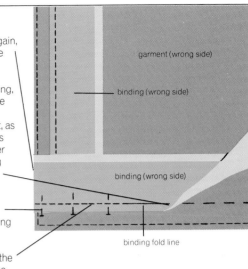

garment (wrong side)

binding (wrong side)

binding (wrong side)

binding fold line

8. Turn the binding right side up to form the miter.

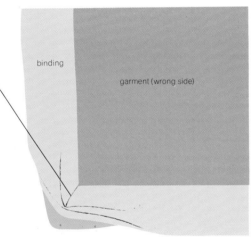

binding

garment (wrong side)

9. Turn the garment to the other side.

10. Fold the unattached edge of the binding over the garment edge. At the corner, re-form the diagonal fold.

11. Finish attaching the binding to the garment, following the instructions for attaching single or double bias binding.

12. Slip stitch (Appendix) the outside and inside folds of the miter, if desired.

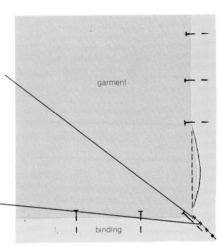

garment

binding

ENDING BIAS BINDING AT A GARMENT OPENING

1. To attach a bias binding that will end at a garment opening, such as a neck opening, attach one side of the binding to the garment, following the instructions for attaching single or double bias binding, depending on the type selected. Be sure to leave 1/2 inch to 5/8 inch of binding extending beyond the garment edges at the opening.

2. Turn the garment to the other side, and fold each extended end of the binding over the garment edge at the opening. Pin.

3. Fold the unattached side of the binding over the garment edge. Finish attaching the binding, following the instructions for attaching single or double bias binding.

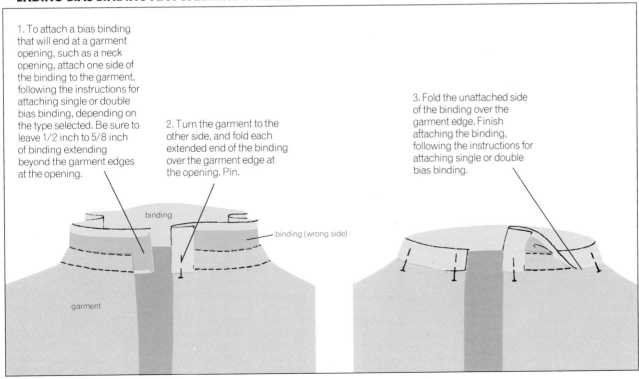

binding

binding (wrong side)

garment

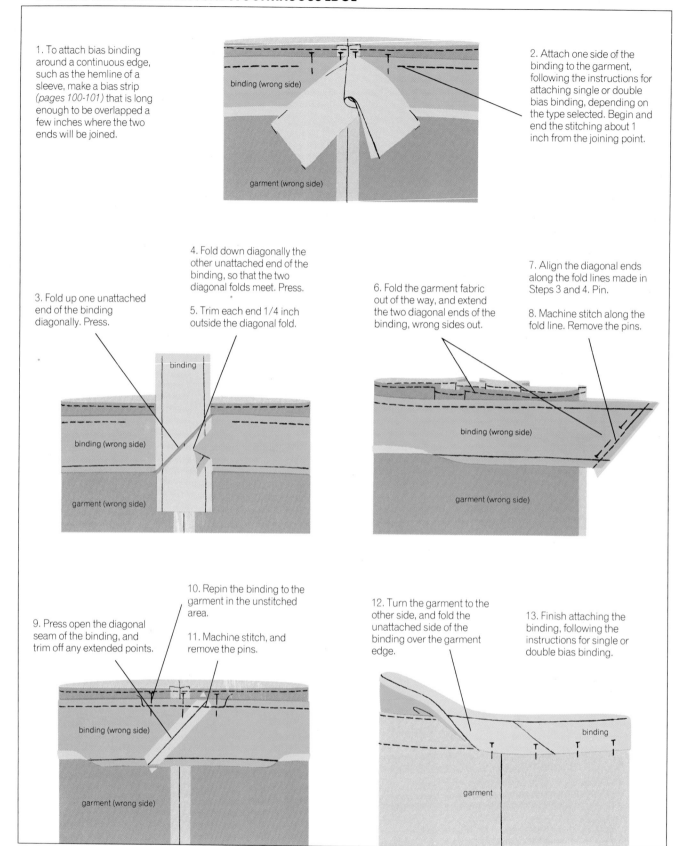

1. To attach bias binding around a continuous edge, such as the hemline of a sleeve, make a bias strip *(pages 100-101)* that is long enough to be overlapped a few inches where the two ends will be joined.

2. Attach one side of the binding to the garment, following the instructions for attaching single or double bias binding, depending on the type selected. Begin and end the stitching about 1 inch from the joining point.

3. Fold up one unattached end of the binding diagonally. Press.

4. Fold down diagonally the other unattached end of the binding, so that the two diagonal folds meet. Press.

5. Trim each end 1/4 inch outside the diagonal fold.

6. Fold the garment fabric out of the way, and extend the two diagonal ends of the binding, wrong sides out.

7. Align the diagonal ends along the fold lines made in Steps 3 and 4. Pin.

8. Machine stitch along the fold line. Remove the pins.

9. Press open the diagonal seam of the binding, and trim off any extended points.

10. Repin the binding to the garment in the unstitched area.

11. Machine stitch, and remove the pins.

12. Turn the garment to the other side, and fold the unattached side of the binding over the garment edge.

13. Finish attaching the binding, following the instructions for single or double bias binding.

BINDING WITH BRAID OR GROSGRAIN RIBBON

1. Stay stitch *(Glossary)* any raw edges to be bound 1/8 inch inside the seam line markings. Then trim off the seam allowances along the seam lines.

2. Fold grosgrain ribbon lengthwise, almost in half, so that one long edge is about 1/16 inch inside the other long edge. Press.

3. To preshape either binding to fit around a garment curve, arrange the folded binding on the ironing board, approximating the curve desired. Dampen the binding if necessary, and press in the curve with a steam iron.

4. Place the garment wrong side up. Open the binding, and place the narrower side, wrong side down, on the garment. Align the fold line of the binding with the garment edge.

5. Pin the binding to the garment edge.

6. Machine stitch close to the inner edge of the binding. Remove the pins.

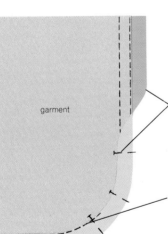

7. Turn the garment wrong side down.

8. Fold the unattached edge of the binding over the garment edge, and align it just beyond the line of stitches made in Step 7. Pin.

9. Sewing from the finished side of the garment, machine stitch close to the inner edge of the binding. Remove the pins. Press.

MITERING AN INSIDE CORNER WITH BRAID OR RIBBON

1. To bind an inside corner, such as a square neckline, stay stitch *(Glossary)* any raw edges 1/8 inch inside the seam lines. Trim off the seam allowances along the seam lines.

2. Mark a guide line around the inside corner with basting stitches. Baste at a distance from the garment edges equal to the finished width of the binding.

3. Stay stitch around the corner just outside the basted guide line. Remove the basting.

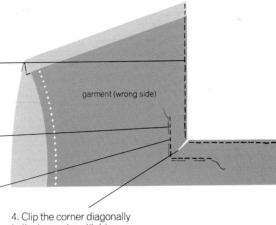

4. Clip the corner diagonally to the inner stay stitching.

5. Spread the fabric so that the two garment edges form a straight line. Then attach the binding to the wrong side of the garment along the entire edge, following the directions for binding with braid or grosgrain ribbon *(left, Steps 2-6)*.

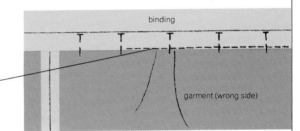

6. At the corner, re-form the garment to its original shape. Fold the binding diagonally to create the miter.

7. Insert a pin between the fold line and the inner stitched edge to hold the overlapped binding in place. Do not pin through the garment fabric.

8. Place the garment wrong side down. Pull the excess binding fabric through the slit in the garment.

9. Fold the unattached side of the binding over the garment edge. At the corner, re-form the diagonal fold.

10. Pin the binding to the garment just beyond the line of machine stitching made in Step 5.

11. Baste the binding to the garment around the corner. Remove the pins from the basted area.

12. Machine stitch from the finished side of the garment close to the edge of the binding. Remove the pins and the basting.

13. At the corner, slip stitch *(Appendix)* the fold of the miter if desired.

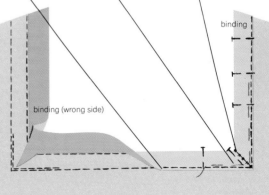

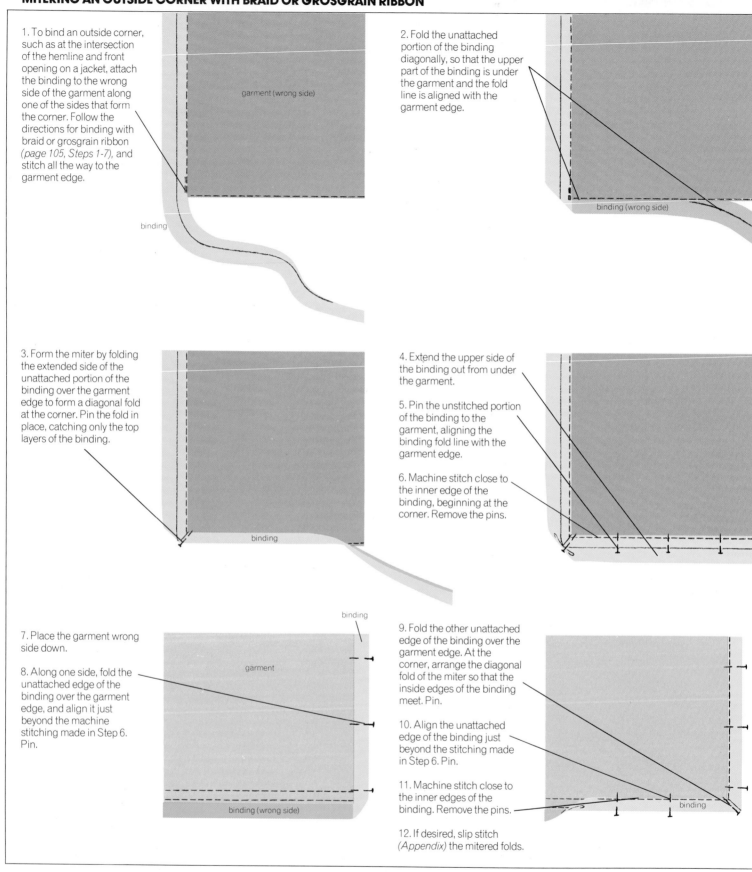

1. To bind an outside corner, such as at the intersection of the hemline and front opening on a jacket, attach the binding to the wrong side of the garment along one of the sides that form the corner. Follow the directions for binding with braid or grosgrain ribbon *(page 105, Steps 1-7),* and stitch all the way to the garment edge.

garment (wrong side)

binding

2. Fold the unattached portion of the binding diagonally, so that the upper part of the binding is under the garment and the fold line is aligned with the garment edge.

binding (wrong side)

3. Form the miter by folding the extended side of the unattached portion of the binding over the garment edge to form a diagonal fold at the corner. Pin the fold in place, catching only the top layers of the binding.

binding

4. Extend the upper side of the binding out from under the garment.

5. Pin the unstitched portion of the binding to the garment, aligning the binding fold line with the garment edge.

6. Machine stitch close to the inner edge of the binding, beginning at the corner. Remove the pins.

7. Place the garment wrong side down.

8. Along one side, fold the unattached edge of the binding over the garment edge, and align it just beyond the machine stitching made in Step 6. Pin.

garment

binding (wrong side)

binding

9. Fold the other unattached edge of the binding over the garment edge. At the corner, arrange the diagonal fold of the miter so that the inside edges of the binding meet. Pin.

10. Align the unattached edge of the binding just beyond the stitching made in Step 6. Pin.

11. Machine stitch close to the inner edges of the binding. Remove the pins.

12. If desired, slip stitch *(Appendix)* the mitered folds.

binding

ENDING BRAID OR GROSGRAIN RIBBON BINDING AT A GARMENT OPENING

1. To attach braid or grosgrain ribbon binding to a garment at an opening, such as the neckline of a dress, attach the binding to the wrong side of the garment, following the instructions for binding with braid or grosgrain ribbon (*page 105, Steps 1-6*). Leave 1/2 to 5/8 inch of binding extending beyond the edges of the garment opening.

2. Turn the garment wrong side down.

3. Fold each binding end over the garment edge at the opening. Pin.

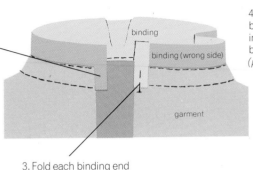

4. Finish attaching the binding, following the instructions for binding with braid or grosgrain ribbon (*page 105, Steps 8 and 9*).

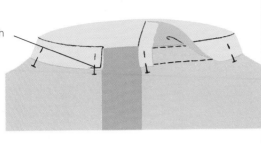

JOINING BRAID OR GROSGRAIN RIBBON BINDING AROUND A CONTINUOUS EDGE

1. To attach the binding around a continuous edge, such as the hem of a sleeve, follow the directions for binding with braid or grosgrain ribbon (*page 105, Steps 1-6*).

2. When you have pinned the binding around the garment edge and have returned to the starting point, overlap the binding 1/2 inch and pin. Then, starting at the last pin, trim off the excess binding diagonally.

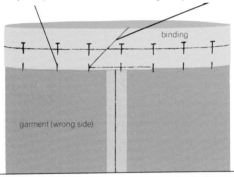

3. Fold under the diagonal edge 1/4 inch, and trim any extended edges.

4. Pin the ends of the binding together along the diagonal edge and attach with a slip stitch (*Appendix*).

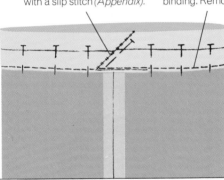

5. Machine stitch the binding to the wrong side of the garment. Stitch close to the inner edge of the binding. Remove the pins.

6. Finish attaching the binding, following the directions for binding with braid or grosgrain ribbon (*page 105, Steps 7-9*).

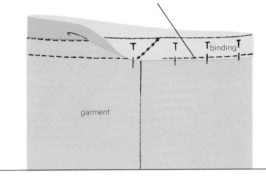

JOINING UNLINED GARMENT SECTIONS WITH A DECORATIVE ENCLOSED SEAM

1. Construct a plain seam on the wrong side of the garment. Press open.

2. Trim each seam allowance to 3/8 inch.

3. Cut a strip of 1-inch-wide commercial single bias tape the length of your seam, or prepare your own 1-inch single bias binding (*pages 100-101, Steps 2-15A*).

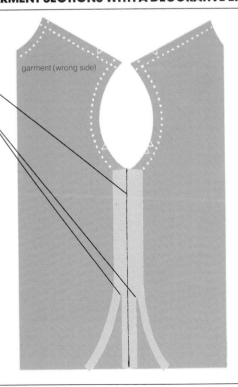

4. Place the garment wrong side up. Position the bias binding, wrong side down, over the seam allowances.

5. Fold the binding seam allowances over the edges of the garment seam allowances, enclosing them.

6. Pin the binding and garment seam allowances to the garment along both edges.

7. Attach the binding to the garment with a slip stitch (*Appendix*). Remove the pins. Press.

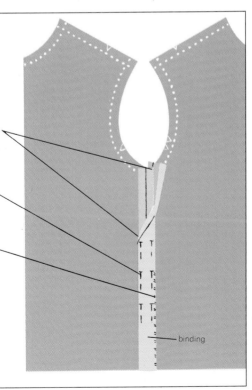

Splurging on fanciful trimming

Not since Victorian times have trims been lavished so extravagantly on so many kinds of garments as in the exuberant clothing of today. A rainbow of ribbons, stitched over the bodice and cascading from the high waistline, transforms a simple style into a glorious evening gown. Even jeans and T-shirts glitter, with rhinestones and studs that have pronged backs to clamp into fabric with a special tool. Dresses shimmer with sequins and beads that must be strung together and hand-stitched, either directly to the garment or to a backing.

The ultimate in turning simplicity into fine feathers are the genuine articles—like those in the pheasant-feathered blouse on pages 124-125. Such feathers, bought in clusters already joined together, are glued to an organza backing, which is hand-stitched to the garment so that it can be removed for dry cleaning.

TRIMMING WITH FLAT RIBBON

A STITCHING RIBBON TO A GARMENT SECTION

1. Stitch any darts on the garment section, but do not stitch the side seams.

2. Measure the garment section from the highest point on the raw edge at the top to the raw edge at the bottom. Cut ribbons to that length.

3. To stitch ribbon to the garment section—as on the bodice of the dress at left—begin by running a row of basting stitches down the center of the garment section.

4. Turn the garment section wrong side down. Pin the center ribbon over the bastings, starting at the top edge. Trim off excess ribbon at the bottom edge.

5. Pin the next ribbon at the top edge, aligning one side with one side of the first ribbon. Do not overlap the edges. Trim off excess ribbon at the bottom edge.

6. Adjust your sewing machine for a wide setting for zigzag stitches. Stitch the ribbons together along the edges from the top to the bottom edge. Hold the ribbons together, and keep the garment spread flat as you stitch. Remove the pins.

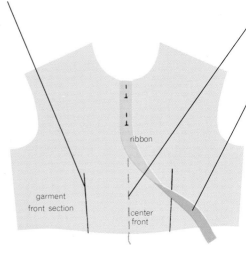

ribbon

garment front section

center front

B SHAPING RIBBON AT A DART

7. When you reach a dart, pin a ribbon down the length of the garment section. It will not lie flat over the dart. Make small running stitches (Appendix) in the area of the ribbon where it stands away from the garment. Begin with a fastening stitch, and end with a loose end of thread.

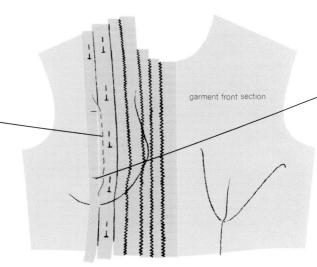

garment front section

8. Pin the next ribbon to the garment section. It, like the one preceding, will not lie flat near the dart. Mark with chalk the area adjacent to the running stitches. Unpin the two ribbons.

9. Place the stitched ribbon on an ironing board. Pull the thread to gather the ribbon.

10. Dampen the ribbon with the steam iron, holding the iron slightly above the ribbon. Then run the iron along the stitched edge to shrink any excess fullness. The edge of the ribbon will curve concavely.

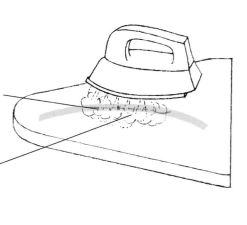

11. To shape the marked ribbon, place it on the ironing board, and dampen the ribbon between the chalk marks with steam. Spread the ribbon taut, place the iron at the lower chalk mark and curve the ribbon so that the marked edge is convex. Run the iron along the marked edge. Then shrink any fullness along the unmarked, concave edge.

12. Pin and stitch the shaped ribbons to the garment as in Steps 5 and 6, making sure they do not pucker in the shaped area.

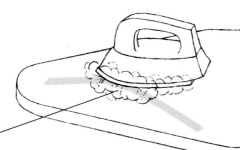

continued

C ATTACHING RIBBON OVER GARMENT SEAMS

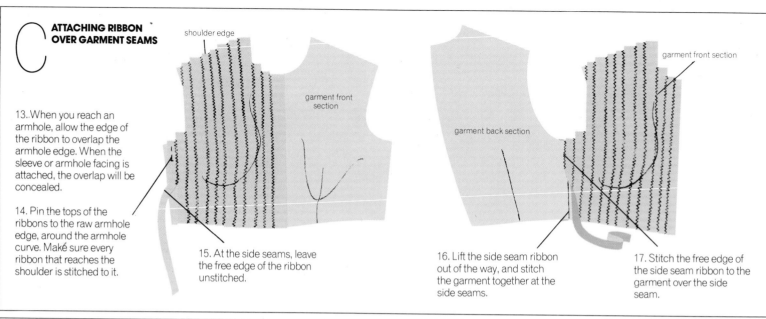

shoulder edge

garment front section

garment front section

garment back section

13..When you reach an armhole, allow the edge of the ribbon to overlap the armhole edge. When the sleeve or armhole facing is attached, the overlap will be concealed.

14. Pin the tops of the ribbons to the raw armhole edge, around the armhole curve. Maké sure every ribbon that reaches the shoulder is stitched to it.

15. At the side seams, leave the free edge of the ribbon unstitched.

16. Lift the side seam ribbon out of the way, and stitch the garment together at the side seams.

17. Stitch the free edge of the side seam ribbon to the garment over the side seam.

D ATTACHING RIBBON TO A GARMENT SECTION AT A SEAM

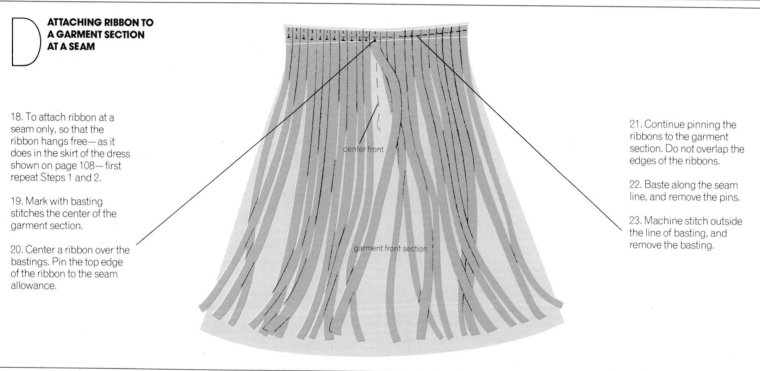

center front

garment front section

18. To attach ribbon at a seam only, so that the ribbon hangs free—as it does in the skirt of the dress shown on page 108—first repeat Steps 1 and 2.

19. Mark with basting stitches the center of the garment section.

20. Center a ribbon over the bastings. Pin the top edge of the ribbon to the seam allowance.

21. Continue pinning the ribbons to the garment section. Do not overlap the edges of the ribbons.

22. Baste along the seam line, and remove the pins.

23. Machine stitch outside the line of basting, and remove the basting.

ATTACHING ROUND BRAID

1. Chalk a guide line for the design on the garment. In creating the design, bear in mind that round braids can be eased around smooth curves but not sharp angles. Plan to conceal the ends of the braid in seams or under a section of the braid design.

2. To determine the amount of braid you will need, lay a string along the design. Measure the string, and add 1 inch for finishing.

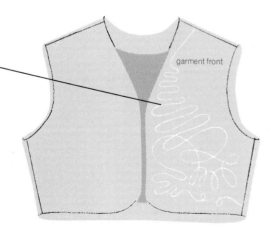

garment front

3. At the beginning of the design, carefully take out several stitches in the seam of the garment. Insert 1/2 inch of the braid. Restitch the seam, catching the braid in the stitching.

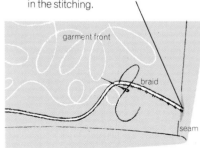

garment front

braid

seam

4. Holding the braid along the guide line, use a slip stitch (Appendix) to sew the braid to the garment. When making the stitches, treat the braid as you would the fold normally held by slip stitching.

5. A more decorative finish is provided by an embroidery couching stitch (Appendix).

6. To end the design, repeat Step 3, or conceal the raw edge under the braid and slip stitch.

APPLYING PRONGED STUDS

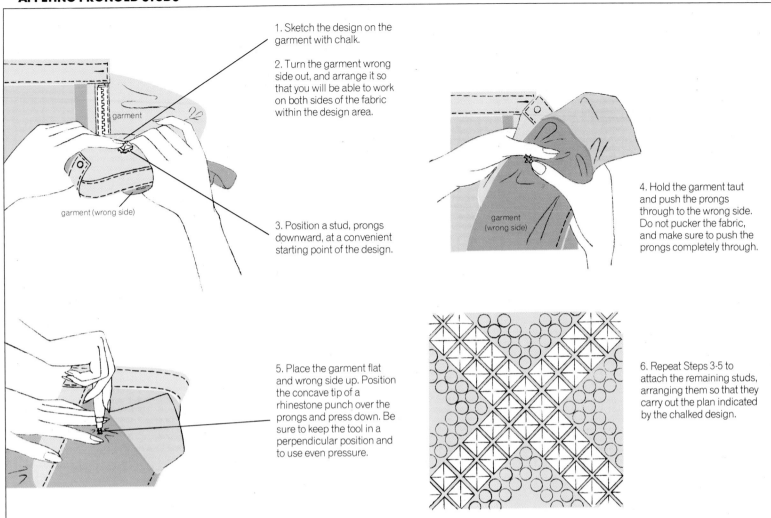

1. Sketch the design on the garment with chalk.

2. Turn the garment wrong side out, and arrange it so that you will be able to work on both sides of the fabric within the design area.

garment

garment (wrong side)

3. Position a stud, prongs downward, at a convenient starting point of the design.

garment (wrong side)

4. Hold the garment taut and push the prongs through to the wrong side. Do not pucker the fabric, and make sure to push the prongs completely through.

5. Place the garment flat and wrong side up. Position the concave tip of a rhinestone punch over the prongs and press down. Be sure to keep the tool in a perpendicular position and to use even pressure.

6. Repeat Steps 3-5 to attach the remaining studs, arranging them so that they carry out the plan indicated by the chalked design.

APPLYING PRONGED RHINESTONES

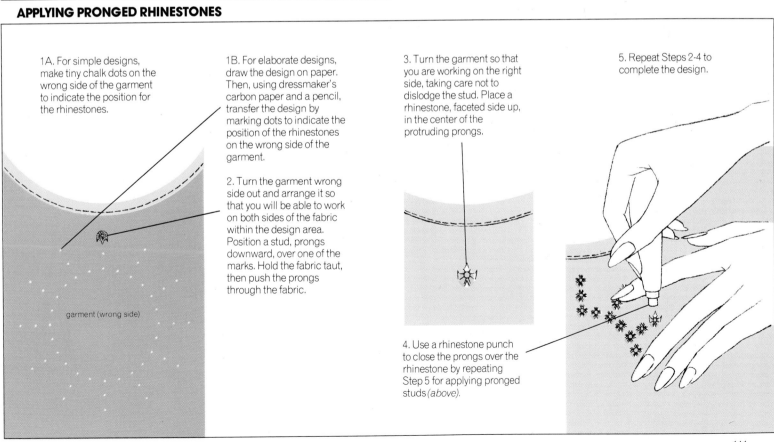

1A. For simple designs, make tiny chalk dots on the wrong side of the garment to indicate the position for the rhinestones.

1B. For elaborate designs, draw the design on paper. Then, using dressmaker's carbon paper and a pencil, transfer the design by marking dots to indicate the position of the rhinestones on the wrong side of the garment.

2. Turn the garment wrong side out and arrange it so that you will be able to work on both sides of the fabric within the design area. Position a stud, prongs downward, over one of the marks. Hold the fabric taut, then push the prongs through the fabric.

3. Turn the garment so that you are working on the right side, taking care not to dislodge the stud. Place a rhinestone, faceted side up, in the center of the protruding prongs.

5. Repeat Steps 2-4 to complete the design.

garment (wrong side)

4. Use a rhinestone punch to close the prongs over the rhinestone by repeating Step 5 for applying pronged studs (above).

TRIMMING WITH BEADS AND SEQUINS

A PREPARING THE DESIGN

1A. To make an elaborate design, pin over the area to be decorated a piece of organza that is the same color as the garment. Trace the outline of the garment section—a neckline in this example—with chalk. Unpin the organza. Draw guide lines for the design on the organza. Stretch the organza on an embroidery hoop.

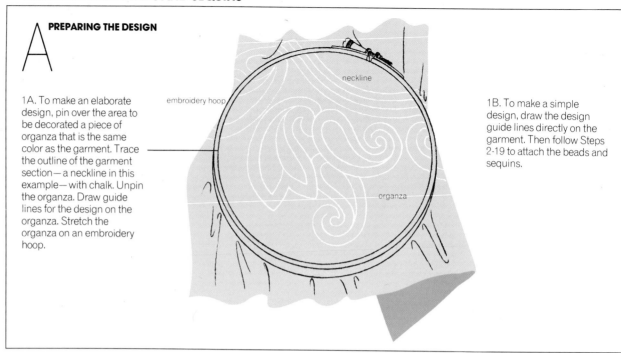

neckline

embroidery hoop

organza

1B. To make a simple design, draw the design guide lines directly on the garment. Then follow Steps 2-19 to attach the beads and sequins.

B ATTACHING THE BEADS

2. Using a knotted double thread coated with beeswax (*Glossary*) and a needle that will slip easily through the hole in the bead, bring the needle up from the wrong side of the fabric. If you are right-handed, begin at the right side of the chalked design; if you are left-handed, start at the left and reverse the direction of all stitches. Pull the thread taut.

3. String four to six beads onto the needle, and draw them down the thread to the fabric.

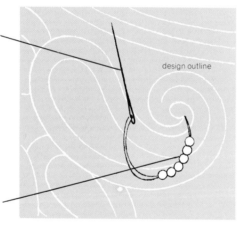

design outline

4. Insert the needle into the fabric at the end of the last bead strung. Make sure to keep the beads on the design as you work around curves.

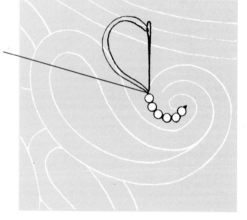

5. To anchor the beads, bring the needle out at a point between the second and third beads strung, just below the thread on which the beads are strung. Pull the needle through.

6. Insert the needle into the fabric just above the thread. Pull the needle through.

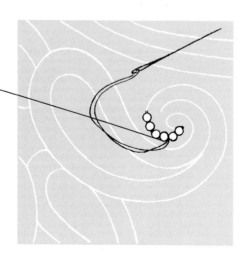

7. If you have strung four beads, skip to Step 8. For six beads, bring the needle out between the fourth and fifth beads strung, and repeat Step 6. Catch the thread underneath the fabric in the anchoring stitch.

8. After the last anchoring stitch, bring the needle out at a point next to the last bead strung.

9. Repeat Steps 3-8 to attach the remaining beads. End off with a fastening stitch (*Appendix*) on the wrong side of the fabric.

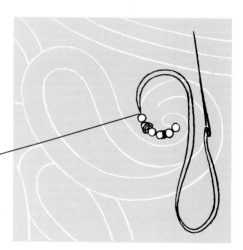

ATTACHING THE SEQUINS

10. Using a single thread coated with beeswax, make several tiny fastening stitches on the wrong side of the fabric. If you are right-handed, start at a point on the right side of the chalked design. If you are left-handed, start at the left, and reverse the direction of all stitches.

11. Bring the needle up from the wrong side, and pull the thread through. Insert the needle through the hole of the sequin from its wrong side. Slide the sequin onto the thread.

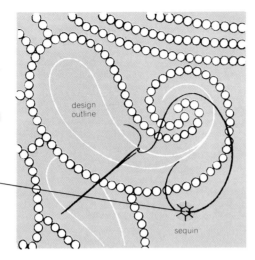

12. Hold the sequin flat against the fabric, and insert the needle at the right-hand edge. Pull the needle through.

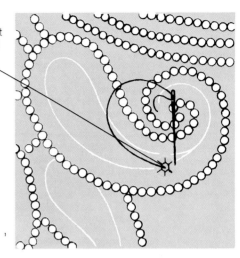

13. Bring the needle up through the hole in the sequin and pull it through. Then insert the needle into the fabric at the left-hand edge of the sequin. Pull the needle through.

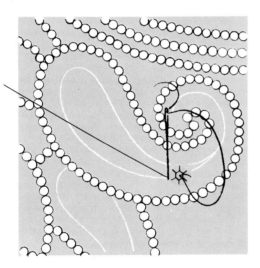

14. Bring the needle up from the wrong side on the guide line, making a stitch that equals one half the diameter of the sequin.

15. Place the second sequin wrong side up, and insert the needle through the hole in the center. String the sequin onto the thread.

16. Insert the needle again at the left-hand edge of the first sequin. Pull the needle through.

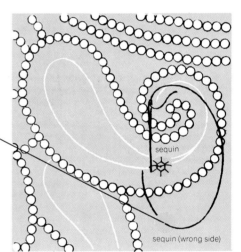

17. Bring the needle up from the wrong side on the guide line, making a stitch equal to one half the diameter of the sequin.

18. Pull the thread through and, at the same time, flip the second sequin over so that it is wrong side down and overlaps the first sequin.

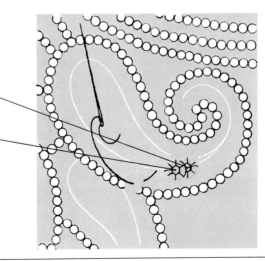

19. Continue to add sequins by repeating Steps 15-18. End with a fastening stitch on the wrong side of the fabric.

continued

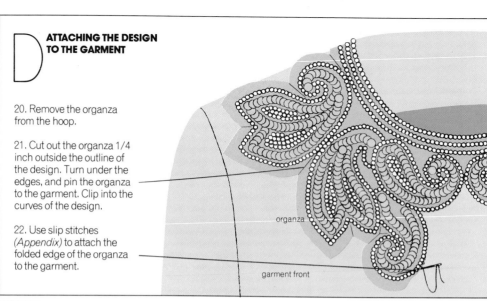

D ATTACHING THE DESIGN TO THE GARMENT

20. Remove the organza from the hoop.

21. Cut out the organza 1/4 inch outside the outline of the design. Turn under the edges, and pin the organza to the garment. Clip into the curves of the design.

22. Use slip stitches (*Appendix*) to attach the folded edge of the organza to the garment.

TRIMMING WITH FEATHERS

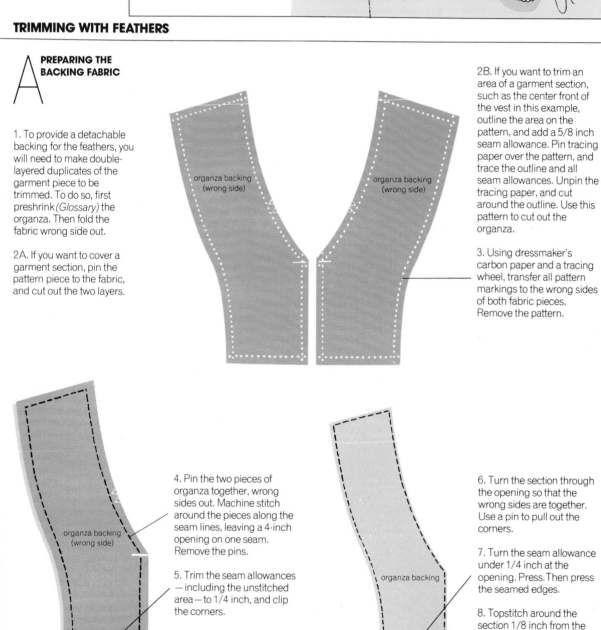

A PREPARING THE BACKING FABRIC

1. To provide a detachable backing for the feathers, you will need to make double-layered duplicates of the garment piece to be trimmed. To do so, first preshrink (*Glossary*) the organza. Then fold the fabric wrong side out.

2A. If you want to cover a garment section, pin the pattern piece to the fabric, and cut out the two layers.

2B. If you want to trim an area of a garment section, such as the center front of the vest in this example, outline the area on the pattern, and add a 5/8 inch seam allowance. Pin tracing paper over the pattern, and trace the outline and all seam allowances. Unpin the tracing paper, and cut around the outline. Use this pattern to cut out the organza.

3. Using dressmaker's carbon paper and a tracing wheel, transfer all pattern markings to the wrong sides of both fabric pieces. Remove the pattern.

4. Pin the two pieces of organza together, wrong sides out. Machine stitch around the pieces along the seam lines, leaving a 4-inch opening on one seam. Remove the pins.

5. Trim the seam allowances —including the unstitched area—to 1/4 inch, and clip the corners.

6. Turn the section through the opening so that the wrong sides are together. Use a pin to pull out the corners.

7. Turn the seam allowance under 1/4 inch at the opening. Press. Then press the seamed edges.

8. Topstitch around the section 1/8 inch from the edge, making sure that you catch the seam allowances inside.

B ATTACHING THE FEATHERS TO THE ORGANZA

9. If you have purchased feathers already joined together into clusters, skip to Step 16.

10. If you are using single feathers, determine the arrangement desired by positioning the feathers on top of the organza.

11. Working on a piece of plastic—for neatness and to prevent the feathers from sticking—turn two feathers wrong side down. Apply rubber cement to the shafts and downy parts, brushing from the bottom of the shafts toward the tips. These feathers will be used as a base for the cluster.

feather

feather

feather (wrong side)

shaft

12. Turn another feather wrong side up. Apply rubber cement to the area that will be glued to the base feathers.

13. Let the glue dry. Place the two base feathers side by side, and glue the single feather on top.

14. Apply rubber cement to the right side of a fourth feather and the wrong side of a fifth feather. Repeat Step 13, placing the fourth feather next to the base feathers and the fifth on top.

15. To make subsequent rows, glue single feathers over the completed rows to form a shingle-like design. Small clusters, about 4 inches by 4 inches, are easiest to work with when attaching the clusters.

16. Turn the organza section to the side that will face out on the finished garment.

17. To keep the organza from shrinking as glue is applied to it, pin the fabric to a piece of 1/4-inch cardboard, pulling the fabric taut as you pin. To prevent the fabric from sticking to the cardboard, cover it with a plastic bag.

18. Arrange the clusters of feathers on the organza to determine the way in which you want the clusters to overlap. Then remove the clusters.

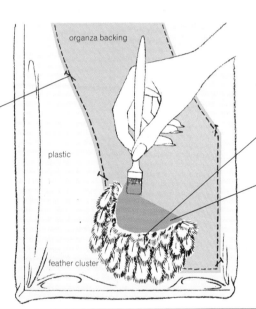

organza backing

plastic

feather cluster

19. Starting at one edge, insert a pin through the center of the first cluster, and pin it to the organza.

20. Lift back the feathers at the top of the cluster, and apply a flexible water-soluble glue to the organza. Finger-press the cluster to the organza.

21. Repeat Step 20 at the bottom of the cluster.

22. Glue the remaining feather clusters to the organza by repeating Steps 19-21.

C ATTACHING THE ORGANZA TO THE GARMENT

23. Attach the organza to the garment with short basting stitches. When the garment requires cleaning, remove the organza and feathers by taking out the basting stitches. Then rebaste after the garment has been cleaned.

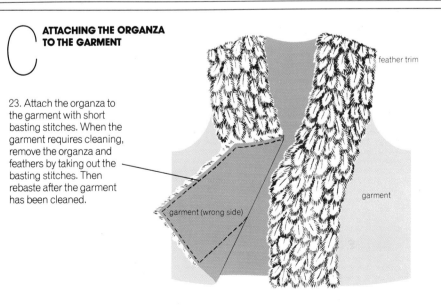

feather trim

garment

garment (wrong side)

Embroidered details on knitwear

Adding embroidery to simple knitted or crocheted garments is an easy way of giving them the individual-ized charm of folk craftwork. The three-dimensional roses blooming on this vest are made from bullion knots *(right),* their stems and leaves with stem and lazy daisy stitches. Other more complicated embroidery ideas may require a pattern and should be traced on a gauzy fabric that is basted to the garment, then snipped away after it has served as guide and reinforcement.

MAKING BULLION KNOT FLOWERS

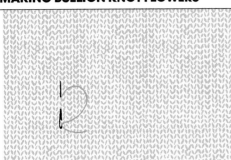

1. Thread a crewel or tapestry needle, make a knot, then pass the needle through one of the wool threads on the wrong side of the garment. Make a fastening stitch.

2. Bring the needle up through the center of one of the wool threads. Draw the yarn through.

3. Point the needle away from you, and insert it to the wrong side the desired length of the stitch below the hole from which the yarn emerged in Step 2. Bring the needle partially up at the original hole.

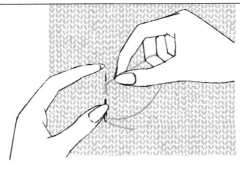

4A. Holding the needle firmly with your left thumb, wind the yarn counterclockwise around the needle until the coil equals the distance between the holes.

4B. If you are left-handed, hold the needle with your right thumb and wind the yarn clockwise.

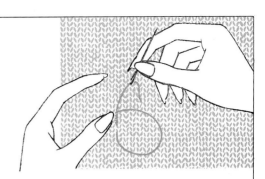

5. Hold the coil with your thumb, and pull the needle and the yarn through the coil.

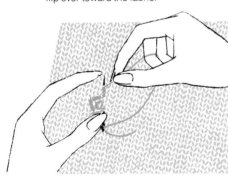

6. When the yarn is completely through the coil, gently pull the yarn toward you. As you pull, the coil will flip over toward the fabric.

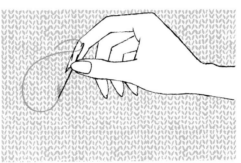

7. To complete the stitch, insert the needle to the wrong side at the bottom of the stitch, and pull the yarn through.

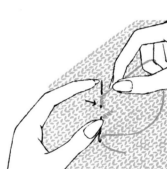

8. Bring the needle up again (arrow) 1/4 inch away from the ends of the first stitch. Repeat Steps 3-7 to make a second stitch. Make a third stitch at the bottom of the V formed by the first 2 stitches so that the 3 stitches form a triangle. This will be the center of the flower.

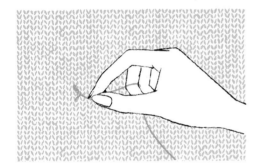

9. Now work a series of bullion stitches around the triangle. Make these stitches slightly larger, and add a few extra twists to the coil so that the stitches will curl slightly. Overlap the ends of the stitches as shown. You will now be working in a circle.

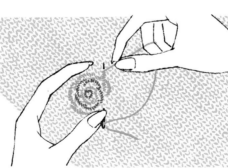

10. Continue to make bullion stitches, working round and round, until the flowers are the desired size. Make the stitches slightly larger each time you start a new ring.

11. If you wish to use another color for some of the petals, fasten off the first color and, using the new color, repeat Steps 1-7.

12. For a raised effect, like the flowers in the photograph at left, form the center of the flower with a series of 3/4-inch-long bullion stitches, rather than the small triangle. Wind the coil loosely, and do not pull the stitch flat against the fabric when drawing the foundation thread toward you (Step 6). If the coil is uneven, smooth it out along the foundation thread with the side of your needle.

13. Work bullion stitches around the vertical stitches made in the previous step to form the flower petals. Change colors as desired.

EMBROIDERING A COMPLICATED DESIGN

A SELECTING THE DESIGN

1. Transfer the design you have chosen for your embroidery onto tracing paper, enlarging or reducing the size as desired, following the instructions in the Appendix.

2. Select the stitches you wish to use. Indicate their placement on your diagram, using letters as a key, as shown in the drawing at right. (Instructions for making bullion knots are on the previous page; the other stitches are in the Appendix.)

tracing paper

STITCH GUIDE
A bullion knots
B French knots
C whipped spider web
D lazy daisy
E satin
F straight
G split
H stem
I chain

B MAKING A PAPER PATTERN

3. Place the garment to be embroidered—in this case, the front of a cardigan sweater—on a flat surface. Position the traced design over it.

4. Move the design until you have determined where you wish to locate the embroidery. Decide how many times you wish to repeat the original design, if any, and whether it should be reversed on corresponding sides.

5. Make paper patterns for the complete design, including all repeats and reverses as determined in Step 4. Outline the edges of the garment on the paper to help you position the pattern accurately. Use your original diagram as a guide, and trace over it as many times as necessary.

6. Make a separate pattern for each area to be embroidered. In this example, there are two patterns—one for each side of the sweater front. The original design (upper left) was reversed and repeated once, directly below; then this design was reversed to make the pattern for the other side.

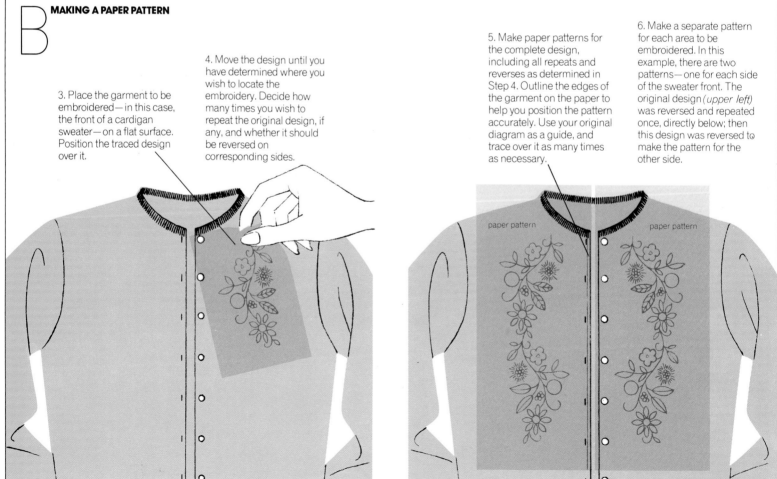

paper pattern   paper pattern

C MAKING A FABRIC PATTERN

7. For each pattern, cut out a piece of sheer fabric —organza, organdy, chiffon or fine batiste— that measures about 2 inches longer and wider than your pattern. Press the fabric.

8. Place the fabric over the pattern, and pin them securely together.

9. Hold the fabric and the pattern down firmly so that they do not slip. Using a hard pencil, carefully trace the design and the garment edges onto the fabric. Remove the pins.

paper pattern

sheer fabric

D ATTACHING THE FABRIC PATTERN

10. Place the garment on a flat surface. Slip a piece of cardboard inside the garment to keep the front and back pieces separated.

11. Place the fabric pattern on top of the garment in the position determined in Step 4.

12. Match the outline of the garment on the pattern with the edges of the garment. Pin, then baste around the edges and from corner to corner as shown. Remove the pins.

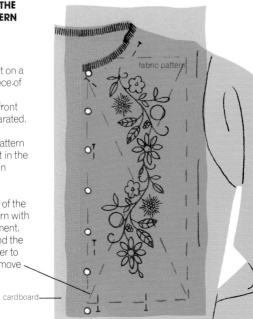

fabric pattern

cardboard

E EMBROIDERING THE DESIGN

13. Thread a crewel or a tapestry needle that has an eye large enough to accommodate the yarn you have selected. Knot the yarn.

14. Select an embroidery hoop designed with a screw. Adjust the hoop so that it is loose enough not to pull the garment out of shape. Place the work in the hoop, then tighten the screw.

15. Embroider the design. Sew through the fabric pattern and the garment. Work the stitches with an even, medium tension— if they are too tight, the garment will pucker and bunch up; if the stitches are too loose, they might get caught and pull out when the garment is worn.

16. Remove the hoop when you are not working to avoid stretching the garment.

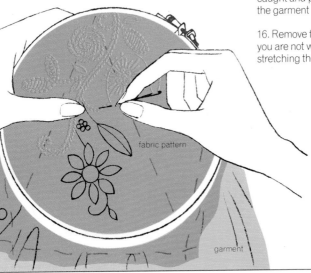

fabric pattern

garment

F REMOVING THE FABRIC PATTERN

17. When the entire design is completed, remove the bastings made in Step 12.

18. Using small, sharp scissors, carefully snip away the fabric pattern around the embroidery stitches. Be careful not to cut the garment.

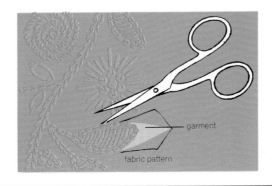

garment

fabric pattern

19. At solid stitches, such as the satin stitch, stretch the garment slightly around the stitch; any remaining fabric will disappear under the stitches.

20. Along line stitches, such as chain or stem stitches, clip and pull the fabric away; also remove any remaining threads under the stitches with tweezers.

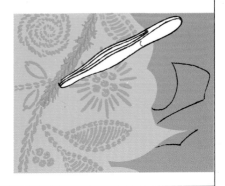

Sculpturing designs into smooth satin

The rich relief of trapunto quilting (*pages 94-95*) makes raised whorls and scrolls for this pocketed stole and its matching crew hat, turning the two simple designs into posh dress-up for a party. Trapunto's embossed effect depends on two fabrics, which must be carefully selected. The fabrics here—sumptuous satin acetate backed with sturdy muslin—lend themselves perfectly to the technique, but you can use anything from jersey to flannel as long as the top fabric has enough give to rise above the stitching and the bottom one is firm enough to provide a strong backing.

Instructions for the trapunto stole and hat

To make the trapunto quilted stole and hat on pages 120-121, you will need 2 1/2 yards of satin, 2 yards of muslin for backing, 14 yards of cotton cording 1/4 inch in diameter, 5 spools of buttonhole twist, 3/4 yard of 3/4-inch-wide grosgrain ribbon and a small amount of polyester batting. Basic instructions for trapunto are on pages 94-95.

Preparing the patterns for the stole and hat: Partial patterns for the areas with designs on the stole and complete patterns for the hat are shown in reduced scale on the diagrams at right. To make a final-size pattern, mark a piece of tracing paper with a grid of 1-inch squares. Then copy the designs freehand onto your enlarged grid, square by square. The hat is for an average size 22, with the brim somewhat larger to allow for the fabric taken up by the quilting. To determine your correct hat size, measure the circumference of your head, then add 1/2 inch to 3/4 inch for a comfortable fit. Enlarge or reduce the pattern accordingly.

Cutting out the stole: For the stole itself, cut two rectangles of satin, each measuring 9 3/4 inches by 67 inches. Then cut one rectangle of muslin the same size for the backing. For the pockets, cut four rectangles of satin, each measuring 10 inches by 11 inches. Then cut two rectangles of muslin the same size for the pocket backings. Make sure to cut all pieces with the length in the direction of the lengthwise grain.

Transferring the designs to the muslin backings: Following the instructions in Box A on page 94, Steps 4-6, transfer the design for the stole to each end of the stole backing and the design for the pocket to each of the pocket backings. Make sure to flop the designs so that the finished design on one end is the reverse of the other.

Preparing to quilt: Draw quilting lines for the cording on the stole and pocket backings in the areas indicated on the design in gray, following Step 9 in Box B on page 94. Then, following Steps 11-15 in the same box, attach the backings to one of the stole pieces and two of the pocket pieces, and stitch on the quilting lines. Put the other satin stole piece and the two satin pocket pieces aside. These will be used to line the stole and pockets.

Quilting the designs: Work the cord through the cording channels, following the instructions in Box D on page 95. Then stuff the enclosed design areas with batting, following Box C on page 94. To pad larger areas, make several openings in the backing so that you can reach all corners. Do not pad the lower ends of the designs on the stole where the pockets will be attached.

Lining the pockets: Pin the quilted pockets and the linings together wrong sides out. Baste just outside the top curved line of quilt stitching of the pocket design. Change the sewing machine bobbin thread to regular sewing thread, reset the gauge to 12 stitches to the inch and attach a zipper foot. Then stitch as close as you can to the top line of stitching, following its curve. Trim the seam allowances to 1/4 inch, and clip around the curves. Turn the pockets so that the wrong sides are together, and press. Then baste the three layers together and trim off the excess linings around the edge.

Assembling the stole: Place the quilted stole wrong side down on a flat surface. Position the lined pockets, lining side down, on each end of the stole, matching the designs and aligning the raw edges. Pin and baste the pockets to the stole. Then place the stole lining wrong side up over the stole and pin and baste all the layers together around the edges. Trim off any excess lining. Next, stitch 5/8 inch in from the edges, leaving a 5-inch opening on one long edge near the center of the stole. Trim the seam allowances to 1/4 inch and clip the corners diagonally. Turn the stole inside out through the opening. Then close the opening, using a slip stitch (Appendix). Press the stole lightly.

Cutting out the hat: With the satin folded wrong sides out, cut out the crown section patterns and the brim pattern, making sure to align the grain-line arrows with the lengthwise grain of the fabric. Next, using the same patterns, cut out backing pieces from the muslin the same way, but cut only one brim piece. Transfer all pattern markings onto the backing pieces.

Preparing and quilting the brim: With each of the three brim pieces wrong side out, close the center-back seam by pinning and then stitching on the seam line. Trim the seam allowances to 1/4 inch, and press open the seam. Put one of the satin pieces aside. It will be used as a lining. Then prepare the brim for quilting, following the instructions in Box B on page 94 and quilt it, following the instructions in Box D on page 95. Make sure to draw the quilting lines on the wrong side of the brim backing and to match the center-back seams when you stitch the satin and backing pieces together.

Lining the brim: Pin the quilted brim and brim lining together wrong sides out. Baste just outside the outer line of quilt stitching. Change the sewing machine bobbin thread to regular sewing thread, reset the gauge to 12 stitches to the inch and attach a zipper foot. Then stitch as close as you can to the outer line of quilt stitching. Trim the seam allowances to 1/4 inch, and clip at close intervals. Turn the brim so that the wrong sides are together, and press. Then baste the three layers together and trim the excess lining around the inner edge.

Assembling the crown: On the wrong side of each satin crown piece, pin the corresponding muslin backing piece also wrong side up. Working two adjacent sections at a time, pin and baste together the sections, muslin sides out, making sure to match the notches. Stitch the sections to-gether; start each seam at the bottom and finish by back-stitching at the top. Trim the seam allowances to 1/4 inch, and finger-press them to one side.

Finishing the hat: With wrong sides out, pin, baste and stitch the crown to the brim, making sure to match the notches. Trim the seam allowances to 3/8 inch. Next, make the inside hatband by cutting a length of grosgrain ribbon 1/2 inch longer than your hat-size measurement. Sew the ends of the ribbon together, making a 1/4 inch seam. Press the seam open. Then pin and baste the band, seamed side down, to the hat seam allowances, matching the band seam with the center-back seam of the crown and aligning the lower edge of the band with the hat seam line. Stitch close to the lower edge of the band. Remove all bastings. Do not press the hat.

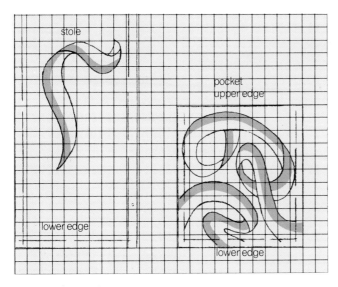

In these patterns for the trapunto designs on the stole and pockets *(left)* and the hat brim and the crown *(below)*, each square equals 1 inch. The gray on the stole and pocket patterns represents the areas to be quilted with 1/4-inch-wide cotton cording; the rest of the design should be quilted with batting. The entire brim of the hat should be quilted with channels of cording; the white areas are seam allowances. The crown should not be quilted.

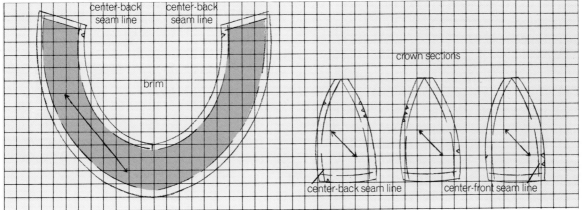

Plumage to adorn a filmy blouse

The bronze sheen of pheasant feathers highlighted by tips of white ostrich turn a plain chiffon blouse into a fanciful topper so light it looks as if it would fly away. The blouse is made from any simple pattern. The feathers are available, prefabricated in clusters, at millinery stores.

Instead of being sewed directly to a garment, feathers are glued to panels of organza that serve as firm, but lightweight, backing. This way the organza can be hand basted into place and easily removed while the blouse is being cleaned.

Instructions for making the feather blouse

The feather blouse on pages 124-125 is made by adapting a commercial pattern for a shirt-style blouse—waistline darts and full shirt sleeves are necessary. The pattern is shortened to waist length and modified to eliminate the button front and to replace the collar with a V neckline.

For the blouse fabric, which is chiffon in the photograph, you will need the yardage specified on the pattern. You will also require 3/4 yard of organza, to which the feathers will be glued. These pieces of organza, cut in the shape of the bodice front and the cuffs, are then basted to the blouse so that the feathers can be removed when the blouse is cleaned. Purchase three dozen clusters or pads of pheasant feathers and 12 of white ostrich feathers (which are produced commercially on farms in South Africa) from a millinery store. The white ostrich tips are glued to the feather clusters with rubber cement, and the clusters are attached with household glue.

To shape the feathers around the bust, use a tailor's ham and a padded bra cup in your size. (A dress form serves as well.) To shape the cuffs, use a jar with a circumference that approximates your wrist size.

Modifying the bodice front pattern: To draw a V neckline, mark the shoulder seam line 1 inch from the neck seam line. Then mark the desired depth of the V neckline at the center front and connect the two marks. Draw a cutting line 1/4 inch outside the new neck seam line.

To eliminate the front overlap, draw a cutting line 1/4 inch outside the center front from the end of the V neckline to the waistline mark on the pattern. To shorten the pattern, draw a line from the waist mark across the pattern to the side seam and a cutting line 1/4 inch below that line. Then trim the pattern along the new cutting lines.

Modifying the back pattern: Make a mark on the shoulder seam line 1 inch from the neck seam line. Then make a mark 3/4 inch from the neck seam line at the center back, and connect the two marks with a smooth curved line. Draw a cutting line 1/4 inch outside that line.

Shorten the pattern by drawing a line from the waist mark across the pattern to the side seam. Then draw a cutting line 1/4 inch below that line. Trim the pattern along the new cutting lines.

Cutting and marking: Set aside any bodice front and collar facing pattern pieces and the collar pattern piece. Then follow your pattern instructions to cut and mark the fabric, using the modified bodice pattern pieces.

Use the bodice front and cuff pattern pieces to prepare the organza backing sections, following the instructions on page 114, Steps 1-3.

Assembling the blouse: Stitch the darts, the side and shoulder seams, and assemble and insert the sleeves following your pattern instructions. Use French seams (Glossary).

Attaching the bias binding: To determine the length of the bias binding to be made, measure the blouse front around the entire length of the front and neck openings, and around the edge of the blouse at the bottom. From the remaining chiffon, cut and join double bias strips, following the instructions for making bias strips (pages 100-101).

Attach the bias strips around the front opening and the waist edge, following the instructions for attaching a bias strip (page 102). Then miter the outside edges at the front corners (page 103) and join the ends (page 104).

Sew a hook and eye to the binding at the point of the V neckline. Then sew snaps down the front and at the waist. Also sew snaps to the cuff.

Attaching feathers to the bodice: Prepare the organza backing for the bodice section, following the instructions on page 115, Steps 16 and 17. The bodice section will not lie flat in the bust area. Arrange feather clusters at the waist edge of the organza so that the tips of the feathers just overlap the bottom edge. Place several ostrich feathers with the pheasant feathers for highlights. If the ostrich feathers are also in clusters, carefully loosen smaller clusters of feathers or individual feathers.

After you have determined the placement of the feathers, remove them from the organza. Cover the work surface with plastic from a dry-cleaner's bag, then brush rubber cement on the front of the shafts and downy parts of the ostrich feathers. Cement the back of the clusters in the area in which you want to place the ostrich tips. When the cement dries, finger-press the tips to the clusters.

Attach the feather clusters to the organza, using the arrangement you have determined and following the instructions on page 115, Steps 19-22. Work up from the bottom edge to the start of the bust shaping. Then arrange one row of clusters at the shoulder edge of the organza so that the tips of the feathers just overlap the shoulder edge. Cement ostrich tips to the clusters as before, then glue the clusters to the organza at the shoulder.

Shaping the feathers over the bust dart: Place a padded bra cup that is your size over the small end of a tailor's ham. Cover them both with plastic to keep the glue from sticking to the cup. Place the bodice section over the bra cup so that it fills out the bust dart. Glue the clusters to the organza (drawing 1), with the tips of the feathers pointing down. Work up the organza to the clusters at the shoulder.

To cover the shafts at the bottom of the shoulder clusters, carefully loosen small clusters of feathers from the

large clusters, and glue them in a spray, adding highlights as desired (drawing 2).

Attaching the feathers to the cuffs: Place an organza cuff section flat, and carefully loosen smaller clusters from the larger ones. Then arrange these feather clusters and os-

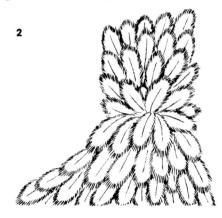

trich tips as desired. Make sure the tips of the first cluster overlap the edge of the organza. They will conceal the closure. Then take the clusters off the organza and cement the tips to the individual clusters.

Position the organza around the jar, and glue the feathers to the fabric (drawing 3). Attach the feathered organza to the bodice and cuffs, following the instructions on page 115, Step 23.

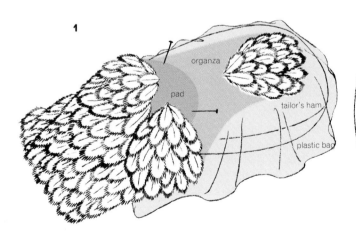

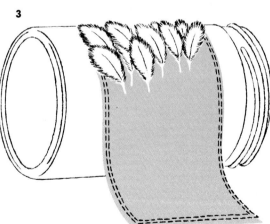

5
GLEAMING SPOOLS AND GLOWING YARN

Crocheting, knitting and macramé are staples among the arts and crafts that give boutique fashions their individualistically handmade look. Any of these crafts afford a ready means for creating unique garments from scratch—starting with nothing more than an idea and the inspiration contained in the color and textures of cords or yarns like those shown on the preceding pages. All of them, moreover, are fundamentally so

FLUID PATTERNS FROM RIVERS OF KNOTTED CORD

simple to do that they invite even beginners to experiment and innovate.

Macramé designer Carolyn Bell, who produced the delicately nubbed but vividly colored confection of a vest shown on pages 142-143, says: "As soon as you start doing macramé, you get designs—you can't help it. It's almost hypnotic. There is something magic about all the cords flowing together with colors and shapes. I hope that anyone who makes my vest will abandon the directions halfway through and start making their own patterns. That's the fun of it."

Knitting and crocheting are just as much fun, but while these are familiar handcrafts that boutique designers employ for everything from jackets and sweaters to hats and socks, macramé is a late bloomer and less understood. Like knitting and crocheting, the art of macramé— or decorative knotting, as it is sometimes called— creates a textile by interlocking strands of cord together. But where a knitter needs needles and a crocheter requires a hook to form the strands into stitches, a macramé artisan uses only fingers to turn the strands into hand-tied knots. Depending on the yarn or cord used and how the knots are made and mixed, the finished result may be soft and silky or rough and nubbly, tightly intertwined or as loose and open as lacework. The texture of the knots and of the strands gives macramé a distinctive, fascinating surface.

For all its appearance of complexity, macramé utilizes only variations of two basic knots—the square knot and the half hitch—each of which can be tied in different directions and combinations to create the design. At the start, the cords are hung in vertical rows from a board with pins or attached to a holding cord (following pages). As the cords are knotted together in groups of two, four, six or more they can be made to change direction—going vertically down the length of the textile or sideways across it to create straight rows, diagonals or even curves. Cords can be added or tied off so that the piece may be shaped into a variety of silhouettes with areas inside it left open or opaque.

Despite all its potential and the pleasure of making it, macramé was something of a lost art up to the late 1960s. First developed by Arabian weavers as a means for tying the loose threads at the ends of fabric into fringe, the art was brought to Europe via Spain in the Eighth Century, during the Moorish occupation. The Spanish taught the French and the Italians; the modern word macramé is an Italian adaptation of the original Arabic *migramah.* During the 19th Century, sailors whiled away idle hours by making ditty bags and rum-bottle covers with a type of macramé known as square knotting, and ladies of the day refined the art by making fringes on such articles as parasols and bellpulls.

But macramé fell out of favor along with bellpulls and other Victorian frills until young people began to revive old crafts a few years ago. At first their macramé projects were of the simplest sorts— belts and headbands, mostly, worked in plain square knots and half hitches from hanks of uncolored wrapping cord. But the possibilities of elaborating on the decorative knotting process proved too appealing to resist.

As the youngsters' macramé took on intricate knot variations and dizzying colorations in bib fronts and boleros, their enthusiasm infected other craftsmen as well. The result is that modern macramé, like modern boutique ideas for knitting and crocheting, is hardly drab and pallid—and certainly not Victorian. Though the craft is easy to master, it stimulates spontaneous design, tantalizing the artisan with its unlimited creative possibilities.

Versatile art from simple macramé

The basic knots of macramé are simple enough to master in an evening. Yet when worked in different combinations and in contrasting cords, they produce varied textures for such items as the sturdy purse and lacy vest on pages 136, 142 and 143.

The only equipment you need is cord, composition board (the kind used for bulletin boards) for a knotting surface, and T pins, pushpins or glass-headed pins to anchor the work. To guide the macramé, pin a piece of paper to the board, marking it in 1-inch squares with indelible ink.

Almost any kind of cord from rope to embroidery thread is suitable for macramé, but whichever you use, it must be firm enough to tie into shapely knots. A good cord for beginners is satin rattail cord.

The cords are attached to the horizontal holding line with a lark's head knot. The work shown here is done with the familiar square knot and double half hitch knot. The cords being knotted (knotting cords), as well as those to which knots are attached (anchoring cords), may run vertically, horizontally or diagonally or they may change direction.

The secret of macramé is practice. To accustom your hands to the process, work a sampler, combining the knots in different ways and experimenting with the methods for adding cording.

MOUNTING WITH THE LARK'S HEAD KNOT

1A. Cut a length of cord for a holding line. The cord should be 6 inches longer than the desired finished width of the piece.

2A. Tie an overhand knot at one end of the cord. Then pin the knot near one edge at the top of the board. If you are right-handed, pin the knot at the left edge. If you are left-handed, pin the knot at the right edge.

1B. If you plan to mount the project on a ring or stick, use the mounting as the holding line.

2B. Bracket it securely to the top of the board with pins.

3. Cut lengths of cord that measure 6 times the desired finished length of the piece.

4. Double one length of cord, forming a small loop at one end.

5A. To make a lark's head knot, first insert your thumb and forefinger into the loop, and grasp the cords, bringing the loop over them *(arrow).*

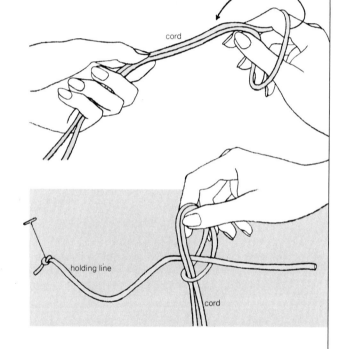

6A. Pull the doubled cord through the initial loop so that the cord forms a second loop. Then slip the second loop onto the free end of the holding line, and push the cord next to the knotted end. Tighten the loop to complete the lark's head knot.

5B. To form a lark's head knot on a ring or stick, hold the cord so that the loop points down, and slip the loop under the holding line.

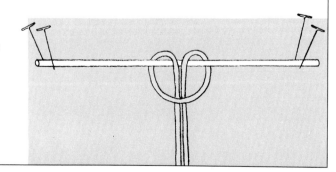

6B. Grasp the two ends of cord, and bring them over the holding line and through the loop. Tighten the loop to complete the lark's head knot.

7. Repeat Steps 5 and 6 to attach the desired number of cords, sliding each cord next to the previous one.

MAKING BUTTERFLY BUNDLES

1. To keep the cords from tangling as you work, make bundles out of long cord ends.

2. Place your forefinger under one cord at the point you want the bundle to fall. If you are right-handed, use your left hand; if you are left-handed, use your right.

3. Spread apart your thumb and forefinger 2 to 3 inches.

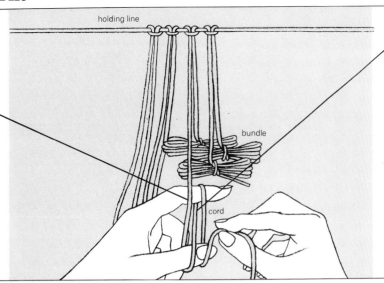

4. With your free hand, bring the cord around your thumb. Then wrap it around your forefinger in a figure eight.

5. Repeat Step 4 until you reach the end of the cord.

6. Carefully slip the wound cord off your fingers, and wrap a rubber band around the center of the bundle. The cord will unwind from the rubber band as you work.

THE SQUARE KNOT

A MAKING THE FIRST HALF KNOT

1. Slip the fingers of your left hand from left to right under the first four cords. The middle cords will be anchoring cords; the first and fourth cords will be knotting cords. (This half of the square knot may be awkward if you are left-handed. After you have practiced the knot, reposition your hands comfortably.)

2. Place the fourth cord over the anchoring cords and under the first cord, leaving a loose loop at the right of the anchoring cords.

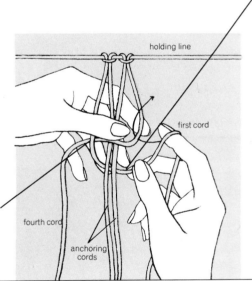

3. Hold the fourth and anchoring cords in your left hand. Then with your free hand, reach behind the anchoring cords and bring the first cord underneath them.

4. Slip the end of the first cord through the loop from the bottom up (arrow).

5. Using whichever hand is more comfortable, hold the anchoring cords taut with your thumb and middle finger, and pull the knotting cords to tighten the knot. Slide the knot to the top of the anchoring cords as you do so.

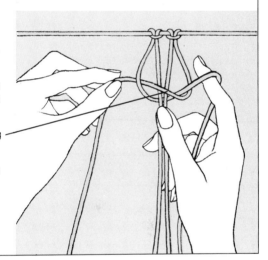

B MAKING THE SECOND HALF KNOT

6. Slide the fingers of your right hand from right to left under the first four cords. (This half of the square knot may be awkward if you are right-handed. After practicing the knot, comfortably reposition your hands.)

7. Place the first cord over the anchoring cords and under the fourth cord, leaving a loose loop at the left of the anchoring cords. Hold the first and anchoring cords with your right hand.

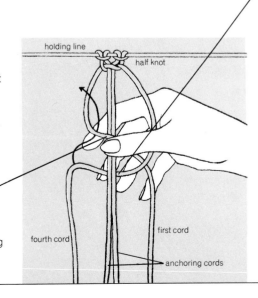

8. Reach behind the anchoring cords with your free hand, and bring the fourth cord underneath them.

9. Slip the end of the fourth cord through the loop from the bottom up (arrow).

10. Using whichever hand is more comfortable, hold the anchoring cords taut with your thumb and middle finger, and pull the knotting cords to tighten the knot. Slide the knot to the top of the anchoring cords as you do so.

11. To make a horizontal row of square knots, repeat Steps 1-10, working each group of four cords across the row.

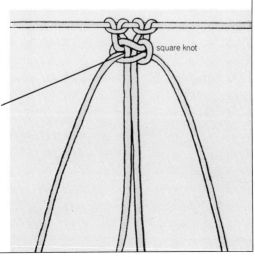

ALTERNATING ROWS OF SQUARE KNOTS

1. Make square knots across the first horizontal row, following the instructions for making a square knot (*page 133*).

2. On the second horizontal row, skip the first two cords and make the first square knot, using the third and sixth cords as the knotting cords and the fourth and fifth cords as the anchoring cords.

3. Continue to make square knots across the row. There will be two unknotted cords at the end of the row.

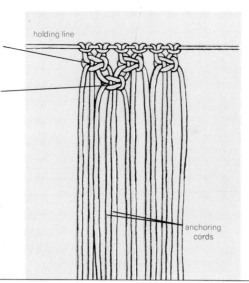

4. On the third row make square knots across the row as in row 1. Tighten the knots on a line parallel to the previous row, leaving a space between the first and third rows of knots.

5. Make alternate rows down the cords by repeating Steps 2-4 to complete the pattern of alternate square knots.

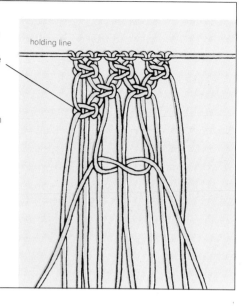

THE DOUBLE HALF HITCH WORKED HORIZONTALLY

1. Insert a pin between the first and second cords just below the holding line.

2. With your right hand, pull the first cord taut across the other cords and parallel to the holding line. This cord will become the anchoring cord, and the other cords will be the knotting cords.

3. With your free hand, bring the second cord up and across the anchoring cord, leaving a loose loop below the anchoring cord.

4. Insert the end of the second cord behind the anchoring cord and through the loop formed in Step 3.

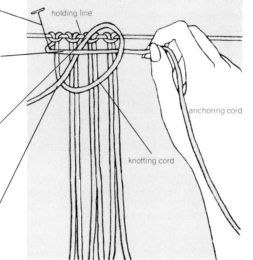

5. Tighten the knot by pulling the knotting cord down perpendicular to the holding line. Then pull the anchoring cord, keeping it parallel to the holding line. Allow the knotting cord to slacken as you do so. Repeat as necessary.

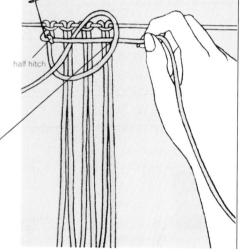

6. To make the second half of the double half hitch, repeat Steps 3-5 with the second cord.

7. Repeat Steps 3-6 on each cord across the row.

8. Insert a pin between the anchoring cord and the last knotting cord at a point just below the last row of knots.

9. Pull the anchoring cord across the knotting cords with your left hand.

10. Repeat Steps 3-6 to make the second row, beginning with the last knotting cord.

11. Work horizontal rows by alternately repeating Steps 1-6 and 8-10.

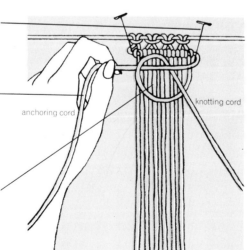

12. If the anchoring cord runs out, add extra cord in the body of the work rather than at the ends. First cut another length of cord. Then overlap the end of the anchoring cord with the end of the new cord and hold it in place.

13. Continue to hold the cords together as you work several double half hitches over them.

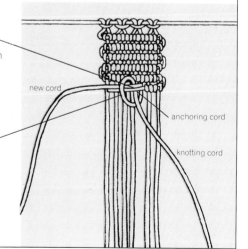

THE DOUBLE HALF HITCH WORKED DIAGONALLY

1. To work the double half hitch knot diagonally, repeat Steps 1-7 for working the double half hitch knot horizontally *(page 134)* but slant the anchoring cord.

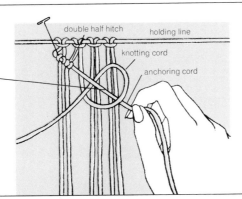

2. At the end of the row, insert a pin between the anchoring cord and the knotting cord at a point just below the previous row.

3. Work back across the row by repeating Steps 8-11 for the double half hitch worked horizontally. Slant the anchoring cord at the desired angle.

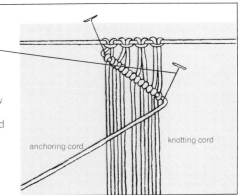

THE DOUBLE HALF HITCH WORKED VERTICALLY

1. Cut and mount the first cord to measure at least three times longer than the other cords — it will be the only knotting cord; all others serve as anchoring cords.

2. Insert a pin between the first and second cords just below the holding line.

3. Bring the knotting cord under the anchoring cord.

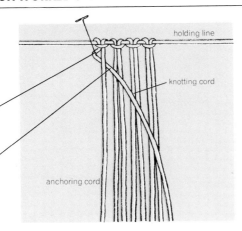

4. With your free hand, bring the knotting cord back across the first anchoring cord, leaving a loose loop to the right of the anchoring cord.

5. Insert the end of the knotting cord under the anchoring cord and through the loop formed in Step 4.

6. Pull the knot tight by pulling the knotting cord out —parallel to the holding line. Pull the anchoring cord down, keeping it perpendicular to the holding line. Let the knotting cord slacken as you do so. Repeat as necessary.

7. To make the second half of the double half hitch, repeat Steps 3-6.

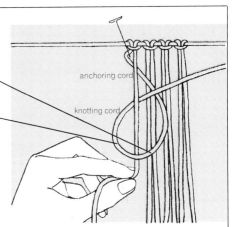

8. Make a double half hitch with the third cord by repeating Steps 3-7.

9. Repeat Steps 3-7 on each cord across the row.

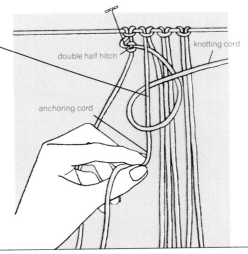

10. At the end of the row, insert a pin between the knotting cord and the last anchoring cord.

11. Slip the knotting cord under the last anchoring cord.

12. Repeat Steps 4-9 back across the row.

13. To make rows of double half hitch knots, repeat Step 10 to begin the rows, then alternate Steps 3-9 and Steps 11 and 12 to work across the cords.

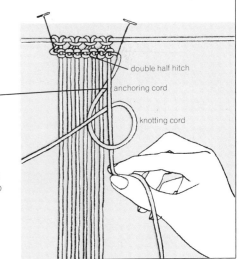

ADDING CORDS TO A WORK IN PROGRESS WITH A SQUARE KNOT

1. Cut a length of cord to six times the desired finished length. Fold the cord in half, and pin the folded cord into the board at the point that you want the knot to fall.

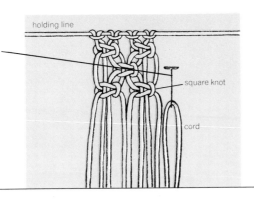

2. Make a square knot *(page 133, Steps 1-10)* with these cords and the last two cords from the body of the work.

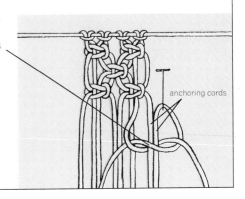

Bag and belt from one knot

One simple knot, the double half hitch, is virtually all you need master to make this striking macramé shoulder bag and a matching belt that doubles as a headband. The intricacy of the chevron design comes from working the knot both diagonally and vertically in a rich variety of yarn colors and textures.

The bag uses 14 colors, a series of browns and yellows contrasting with wine, fuchsia and maroon, while the belt/band uses nine. Lustrous silk cord and heavyweight satin rattail cord blend with the woolly texture of 5-ply knitting worsted to produce an unusual sculptured effect.

The finished bag is folded in thirds, then the strap is laced into the sides with a tapestry needle and wool. Long braided fringes are added to the belt/band to finish the ends.

Instructions for the bag and belt

The shoulder bag and belt pictured on the preceding pages are made from 5-ply bulky knitting worsted wool or rug yarn, heavy-weight satin rattail cord and silk cord. Yarn is sold by the skein. Satin and silk cords can be purchased in spools or by the yard.

To achieve the symmetrical designs on the shoulder bag and the vest, each row is made in three steps: In the first two steps, the left half of the row is knotted toward the left-hand edge and back again toward the center. In the third step, the right half of the row is knotted toward the right-hand edge and then back toward the center.

THE SHOULDER BAG

The bag is made of double half hitch knots worked diagonally (*page 135*) and vertically (*page 135*). An overhand knot, explained in the directions, serves as a filler.

PREPARING THE CORDS

You will need 1 skein—at least 23 yards in length—of 5-ply bulky knitting worsted or rug yarn in each of the following colors: harvest gold, yellow, brown, dark brown, rosewood, light brown, burnt orange, fuschia, maroon, beige and natural beige. You will also need 12 yards of red and 7 yards of gold heavyweight satin rattail cord and 18 yards of wine silk cord. Cut two 120-inch lengths of the gold heavyweight satin rattail, two 105-inch lengths of the yellow yarn, four 100-inch lengths of each of the remaining color cords, plus two extra 100-inch lengths each of the dark brown and the brown yarn for a total of 56 cords.

MOUNTING THE CORDS

The body of the bag is one piece. The back of the bag is knotted first, then the front and flap are worked. To keep the cords for the front and flap out of the way as you knot the back, mount the cords so that those for the front of the bag hang over the back of the board. Tie knots at the center of each of the 100-inch-long cords and 5 inches from the center of the remaining cords. Pin the knots to the board side by side, using the mounting order given below, so that half of the 100-inch-long cords and the shorter sections of the other cords hang down the front of the board.

Mount half the cords from the center of the board to the left edge in the following order: 1 odd length of gold satin;

1 length of harvest gold yarn; 1 odd length of yellow yarn; 1 length each of harvest gold, brown, dark brown, rosewood, and light brown yarns; 2 lengths of burnt orange yarn; 1 length each of light brown, rosewood and fuschia yarn, wine silk cord and maroon yarn; 2 lengths of red satin; 1 length each of maroon yarn, wine silk cord and fuschia, dark brown, brown and beige yarn; 2 lengths of natural beige yarn; and 1 length each of beige, brown and dark brown yarn. Mount the other half of the cords from the center of the board to the right edge in the same order.

Tie the end of each cord in a butterfly bundle (*page 133*) on the front and back of the board.

MAKING THE BAG BACK

Row 1: To knot the 2 center cords, insert a pin between them. Using the cord on the right of the pin as the anchoring cord, make 1 double half hitch knot diagonally from right to left. Step 1: Knot double half hitch knots diagonally from the center of the board to the left edge in the following manner: Using the left center cord as the anchoring cord, knot each of the next 5 cords. Skip 2 cords, then use the next cord (the 9th cord from the center) as the anchoring cord; knot each of the next 3 cords. Skip 3 cords. Using the 16th cord from the center as the anchoring cord, knot each of the next 4 cords. Skip 3 cords. With the 24th cord from the center as the anchoring cord, knot each of the last 4 cords. Step 2: Work back to the center, making double half hitch knots diagonally with the unknotted cords; using the 5th cord from the left as the anchoring cord, knot the first 3 unknotted cords. To hold those knots in place on the board, insert a pin in the 3rd one. Using the anchoring cord as a knotting cord, make 1 double half hitch knot over the next cord (the 9th cord from the left). This knot—and subsequent knots at this point on the design—will pull the segments of knots together. Repin the cords if necessary so that they meet (*drawing 1*). Now using the 13th cord from the left as the anchoring cord, knot the next 3 unknotted cords. Insert a pin in the 3rd one, using the anchoring cord as a knotting cord, and make 1 double half hitch knot over

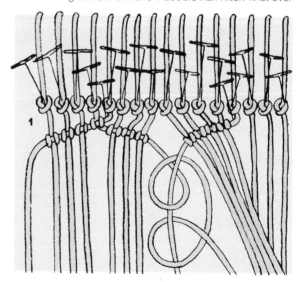

the next cord. Then using the 20th cord from the left as the anchoring cord, knot each of the next 2 unknotted cords. Insert a pin in the last knot. Finally using the anchoring cord as a knotting cord, make 1 double half hitch knot over the next cord. Step 3: To knot the other half of the cords from the center to the right edge, first repeat Step 1 from the center to the right edge, knotting from left to right, then repeat Step 2 to work from the right edge back to the center, knotting from right to left.

Rows 2 and 3: Repeat Row 1.

Row 4: Insert a pin between the 2 center cords. Using the cord at the right of the pin as the anchoring cord, make 1 double half hitch knot from right to left. Make 4 overhand knots with the right-hand cord—the knotting cord from the last knot—incorporating the left-hand cord in the knot (*drawing 2*). Repeat these knots across the macramé at the

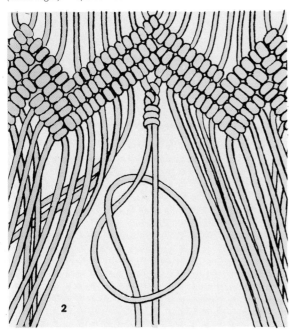

point of each inverted V, making sure you use corresponding colors on both halves of the design.

Row 5: Step 1: Knot double half hitch knots diagonally from right to left in the following manner. Using the left center cord as the anchoring cord, knot each of the next 5 cords. Skip 3 cords, then use the next cord (the 10th cord from the center) as the anchoring cord; knot each of the next 2 cords. Skip 4 cords, then use the 17th cord from the center as the anchoring cord; knot each of the next 3 cords. Skip 4 cords. With the 25th cord from the center as the anchoring cord, knot the last 3 cords. Step 2: To knot the unknotted cords on the left half of the macramé, repeat Row 1, Step 2. Step 3: To knot the right-hand cords of the macramé, repeat Row 1, Step 3.

Rows 6 and 7: Repeat Row 1.

Row 8: Repeat Row 4.

Row 9: Repeat Row 5.

Row 10: Beginning with this row, the double half hitch knot is also worked vertically (*page 135*) as indicated. Join the 2 center cords with 1 double half hitch knot worked diagonally. Step 1: Knot the double half hitch knots vertically toward the left. Using the left center cord as the knotting cord, knot over each of the next 5 cords. Skip 2 cords, then use the next cord (the 9th cord from the center) as the knotting cord; knot over each of the next 3 cords. Skip 3 cords, then use the 16th cord from the center as the knotting cord; knot over each of the next 4 cords. Skip 3 cords. With the 24th cord from the center as the knotting cord, knot over the last 4 cords. Step 2: To knot the unknotted cords on the left half of the macramé, repeat Row 1, Step 2, making double half hitch knots diagonally from left to right as before. Step 3: To knot the right-hand cords of the macramé, repeat Row 1, Step 3.

Row 11: Repeat Row 1.

Row 12: Repeat Row 4.

Row 13: Repeat Row 5.

Row 14: Join the 2 center cords with a double half hitch knot worked diagonally. Step 1: To knot the cords from the center to the left edge, repeat Row 1, Step 1. Step 2: To knot the unknotted cords on the left half of the bag, make double half hitch knots vertically toward the center; with the 5th cord from the left as the knotting cord, knot each of the next 4 cords. With the 13th cord from the left as the knotting cord, knot over each of the next 4 cords. With the 20th cord from the left as the knotting cord, knot over each of the last 3 cords. Step 3: To knot the right-hand cords, repeat Row 1, Step 3.

Row 15: Join the 2 center cords with a double half hitch knot worked diagonally. Then repeat Row 5.

Row 16: Repeat Row 4.

Rows 17-19: Repeat Rows 9-11.

Row 20: Repeat Row 4.

Rows 21-23: Repeat Rows 13-15.

Row 24: Repeat Row 4.

Rows 25-27: Repeat Rows 5-7.

Row 28: Repeat Row 4.

Rows 29-31: Repeat Rows 5-7.

Rows 32-33: Join the 2 center cords with a double half hitch knot worked diagonally. Then repeat Rows 5 and 6.

MAKING THE BAG FRONT

Unpin the macramé and untie the knots used to mount the bag back. Repin the bag to the top of the board so that the unknotted cords hang down the front of the board. Knot the remaining cords by repeating Steps 1-33, pulling the first row of knots tight against the top row on the back of the bag. Then make the flap by knotting double half hitch knots diagonally in the following manner:

Row 1: Using the left center cord as the holding cord, knot each of the next 5 cords from right to left. Now using the right center cord as the holding cord, knot each of the next 5 cords diagonally from left to right.

Rows 2-5: Repeat Row 1, decreasing one knot at the end of each row by leaving one cord unknotted at both edges.

MAKING THE STRAP

Cut eight 120-inch lengths each of beige, natural beige,

brown, dark brown, maroon and fuschia yarns and wine silk and red satin cords.

To mount the cords, first tie a knot at the center of each one. Then pin the knots to the board so that half of each cord hangs down the front and the other half down the back. Mount the cords on the board in the following order: beige, natural beige, brown and dark brown yarns, wine silk cord, maroon yarn, red satin cord and fuschia yarn. Tie both ends of each cord in butterfly bundles. To make the strap, knot double half hitch knots diagonally.

Row 1: Using the 4th cord from the right as the anchoring cord, knot each of the 4 cords next to the left edge. Then using the 5th cord from the left as the anchoring cord, knot each of the 3 cords next to the right edge.

Rows 2-5: Repeat Row 1.

Row 6: Repeat Row 4 of the shoulder bag directions at the center of the strap.

Row 7: Using the 5th cord from the right as the anchoring cord, knot each of the 3 cords next to the left edge. Then using the 5th cord from the left as the anchoring cord, knot each of the 3 cords next to the right edge.

Rows 8 and 9: Repeat Row 1.

Row 10: Repeat Row 4 of the bag instructions.

Row 11: Repeat Row 7.

Row 12: Using the 4th cord from the right as the anchoring cord, knot each of the 4 cords next to the left edge. Then using the 5th cord from the left as the anchoring cord, knot each of the 3 cords next to the right edge.

Row 13: Repeat Row 1.

Rows 14-74: Repeat Rows 10-13, 15 times.

Unpin the macramé and untie the knots used to mount the first half of the strap. Repin the strap to the top of the board so that the unknotted cords hang down the front of the board. Knot the remaining cords by repeating Steps 1-74, pulling the first row of knots tight against the top row on the knotted side of the strap. Work down the length of the cords, then trim the excess cord at both ends of the strap to 6 inches.

CONSTRUCTING THE BAG

Thread the end of one of the cords at the top of the bag through a tapestry needle. Darn the cord end through several loops on the inside of the bag and trim. Repeat on the remaining cords on both ends of the bag. Fold the bag lengthwise into thirds so that the flap edge just hangs over the bottom folded edge of the bag. Mark the center of the bottom fold on each side of the bag with a pin. Align the center of each strap end with the pin at the bottom of the bag. Then darn one of the cords at the center of the strap through the nearest loop on the inside of the bag. Remove the pin, and darn each of the remaining cord ends through successive loops on each side of the center. Tie cord ends together in pairs, then continue to darn the ends through 6 or 7 more loops before trimming off the excess cord (drawing 3, right).

Using a tapestry needle and a strand of dark wool, lace the loops on the edges of the strap with those on the bag. Make a lining if desired and slip stitch it to the inside of the bag.

3

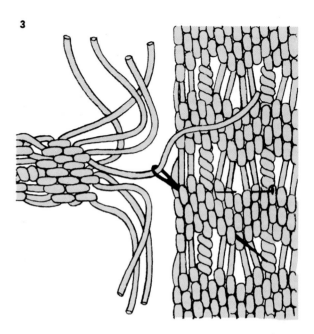

THE BELT

You will need 1 skein—at least 8 yards in length—of 5-ply bulky knitting worsted or rug yarn in each of the following colors: beige, brown, dark brown, maroon, fuschia, light brown and harvest gold. You will also need 8 yards of red heavyweight rattail cord and 8 yards of wine silk cord. The belt is made of double half hitch knots worked diagonally (page 135) and vertically (page 135). An overhand knot, explained in the directions, serves as a filler.

MOUNTING THE CORDS

To make a 23-inch belt, cut two 115-inch lengths of beige, brown and fuschia yarn and two 140-inch lengths of each of the remaining colors (for a total of 18 cords). To make a longer or shorter belt, add or subtract 5 inches of cord for each 1-inch difference in the belt size.

To mount the cords, first tie a knot in the center of each one. Then pin the knots to the board side by side with half of each cord hanging down the front and the remainder hanging over the top and down the back. Mount half the cords from the center of the board to the left edge as follows: 1 cord each of beige, brown and dark brown yarn, wine silk, maroon yarn, red satin and fuschia, light brown and harvest gold yarn. Mount the remaining cords in the same order from the center to the right edge. Tie both ends of each cord in butterfly bundles (page 133).

KNOTTING THE CORDS

Row 1: To knot the 2 center cords, insert a pin between them. Using the cord on the right of the pin as the anchoring cord, make 1 double half hitch knot diagonally from right to left. Step 1: Make double half hitch knots diagonally in the following manner: Using the left center cord as the anchoring cord, knot each of the next 2 cords toward the left-hand edge. Step 2: Using the outside left cord as the anchoring cord, knot the next 5 cords toward the center. Insert a pin into the fifth knot. Then, using the anchoring cord as a knotting cord, make 1 double half hitch knot toward the center—knot the 6th cord from the left-hand edge over the next cord (drawing 1, page 135). This knot—and the corresponding knot on the other half of the belt—will pull the segments of knots together. Step 3: To knot the other half of the cords from the center to the right edge, first repeat Step 1—working from the right center cord toward the right-hand edge. Then repeat Step 2, working from the right edge toward the center.

Rows 2-5: Repeat Row 1.

Row 6: Insert a pin between the 2 center cords. Using the cord at the right of the pin as the anchoring cord, make 1 double half hitch knot. Make 4 overhand knots with the right-hand cord—the one used as knotting cord for the double half hitch—incorporating the other cord in the knots (drawing 2, page 139).

Row 7: Repeat Row 1, Steps 1-3. Do not connect center cords.

Rows 8-10: Repeat Row 1.

Row 11: Make double half hitch knots diagonally in the following manner: Step 1: Using the 4th cord to the left of the center as the anchoring cord, knot the 3 cords to the right of it toward the center. Join the 2 center cords with a double half hitch worked diagonally. Step 2: Using the 4th cord from the center as the anchoring cord, knot the last 5 cords toward the left-hand edge. Step 3: Knot the right-hand cords similarly by repeating Steps 1 and 2—without joining the center cords.

Rows 12-14: Repeat Row 11, 3 times.

Row 15: Using the 3rd cord to the left of the center as the anchoring cord, make 1 double half hitch knot diagonally with the 4th cord from the center. Make 4 overhand knots with the 4th cord from the center incorporating the 3rd cord from the center in the knots (drawing 2, page 139). Repeat on the right side of the center, using the 3rd and 4th cords from the center.

Row 16: Step 1: Using the 3rd cord to the left of the center as the anchoring cord, knot the 2 cords to the right of it toward the center. Join the 2 center cords with a double half hitch knot worked diagonally. Step 2: Using the 6th cord from the left as the anchoring cord, knot the next 5 cords toward the left-hand edge. Step 3: Knot the right-hand cords similarly by repeating Steps 1 and 2—without joining the center cords.

Row 17: Step 1: Using the 4th cord to the left of the center as the anchoring cord, knot the 3 cords to the right of it toward the center. Join the 2 center cords with a double half hitch knot worked diagonally. Step 2: Beginning with this step, work the double half hitch knot vertically in the following manner: Using the 6th cord from the left edge as the knotting cord, knot over each of the next 5 cords toward the left-hand edge. Step 3: Knot the right-hand cords similarly by repeating Steps 1 and 2—without joining the center cords. Repeat Row 1, Step 3.

Row 18: Step 1: Repeat Row 17, Step 1. Steps 2 and 3: Repeat Row 16, Steps 2 and 3.

Row 19: Repeat Row 15.

Rows 20-31: Repeat Rows 16-19, 3 times for a 23-inch belt. Subtract or add this sequence once for every inch you want to subtract from or add to the finished belt.

Row 32: Repeat Row 16.

Row 33: Make double half hitch knots diagonally as follows: Step 1: Using the 4th cord to the left of the center as the anchoring cord, knot the 3 cords to the right of it toward the center. Join the 2 center cords with a double half hitch knot worked diagonally. Step 2: Using the 4th cord to the left of the center as the anchoring cord, knot over the last 5 cords to the left-hand edge. Step 3: Knot the right-hand cords similarly by repeating Steps 1 and 2—without joining the center cords.

Row 34: Step 1: Using the 3rd cord to the left of the center as the anchoring cord, knot 6 cords toward the left-hand edge. Step 2: Using the 3rd cord to the left of the center as the anchoring cord, knot the 2 cords to the right of it toward the center. Join the 2 center cords with a double half hitch knot worked diagonally. Step 3: Knot the right-hand cords similarly by repeating Steps 1 and 2—without joining the center cords. Repeat Row 1, Step 3.

Row 35: Using the 4th cord to the left of the center as the anchoring cord, knot the 3 cords to the right of it toward the center.

FINISHING THE BELT

Unpin the macramé and untie the knots used to mount the first half of the belt. Repin the belt to the top of the board so that the unknotted cords hang down the front. Knot the remaining cords by repeating Rows 1-35, pulling the first row of knots tight against the top row on the first half of the belt. Work down the cords. Then unpin the belt.

Braid the 4 center cords on each end of the belt for 15 inches, and secure the ends with 3 overhand knots of alternating colors (drawing 4). Braid the 3 outside cords on both sides and at both ends of the belt for 15 inches (draw-

4

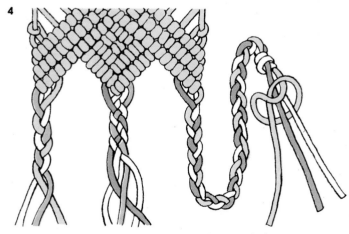

ing 4) and secure the ends with overhand knots as before. Trim the cord ends to 5 inches from the overhand knots. Thread the unbraided cord ends one at a time through a tapestry needle. Then darn them through the 5 or 6 knot loops closest to the end of the belt. Trim off the ends.

A multi-use macramé vest

Swinging with fringe, this hand-knotted vest leads a double life. Worn as shown here it functions as a demure bib that ties in a deep V in back. Turned around, with the V in front, it becomes a garment worthy of Mata Hari. It is made with rayon-covered cord in colors shading from peach to blue; its surface shimmers with a blend of two kinds of cord, one flat and called soutache, the other rounded and called rattail. Two basic knots, the square knot and the double half hitch, account for most of the vest's elaborate pattern.

Instructions for the macramé vest

The vest pictured on the preceding pages is made from satin soutache and rattail cords, knotted within the outline of the back pattern piece of a commercial vest pattern. The pattern determines only the size and general outline of the vest; in the process of tying the knots shown in these instructions, the armholes will become deeper, the shoulders narrower.

To achieve the symmetrical design of the vest, make the knots on the left side, then repeat them on the right side, but in the opposite direction. In order to make the square knots themselves symmetrical, follow the instructions for the square knot on page 133, Steps 1-10, for the left side of the vest. For the right side of the vest, follow the instructions for Steps 6-10 to make the first half of the square knot and the instructions for Steps 1-5 to make the second half.

These instructions are for macraméing a small (sizes 6-8) vest. Any changes necessary for a medium (sizes 10-12) or large (sizes 14-16) vest appear within parentheses—medium first, large next. For all sizes you will need one spool of satin soutache cord at least 144 yards long in each of the following colors: light blue, orange, peach and salmon. You will also need two 144-yard spools of blue soutache cord and one 144-yard spool of light blue thin rattail cord.

PREPARING THE PATTERN

Purchase a commercial vest pattern—with a front opening and no shoulder darts—in your size. Fold the back pattern piece along the outside seam lines. Then, on the knotting board, trace along the folded edges across the shoulders and down both sides.

THE VEST FRONT

The vest front is knotted starting from the shoulders, using alternating rows of square knots of 4 and 8 cords each. The center design is composed mostly of double half hitch knots worked diagonally (page 135) and vertically (page 135). Vertical rows, or sennets, of square knots and chain knots join rows of hitches on the center-front design, as explained in the vest directions. The design is worked in numbered rows.

MOUNTING THE CORDS

Cut eight 20-foot lengths of blue and orange soutache and four 20-foot lengths each of peach, salmon and light blue soutache and light blue rattail cord for a total of 32 cords. As additional cords are called for, cut them to 20-foot lengths unless the instructions specify otherwise.

Tie knots at the center of each cord and pin the knots side by side to the knotting board in the order given below. To keep the cords for the vest back out of the way as you knot the front, mount the cords so that half of each one hangs down the front of the board and the other half hangs over the back.

Mount half the cords across the left shoulder from the neck edge outward in the following order: 2 lengths each of blue soutache, light blue rattail, orange soutache, peach soutache, orange soutache, salmon soutache, light blue soutache and blue soutache. The cords will cover only part of the shoulder line. Mount the other cords across the right shoulder from the neck edge outward in the same order. Leave the cord ends free.

STARTING THE VEST FRONT

Begin by working 3 (6, 9) alternating rows of square knots (page 134).

Row 1: To start the neckline shaping, fold a light blue rattail cord in half and pin it at the fold to the inside edge of the left half of the vest. Then, starting with the inside 4 cords, make square knots across the row (page 135). Now add a folded light blue rattail cord to the inside edge of the right half of the vest and, starting with the inside 4 cords, make square knots across the row.

Rows 2 and 3: Work in alternating rows of square knots across both halves of the vest.

Row 4: Repeat Row 1, adding 1 folded blue soutache cord.

Rows 5 and 6: Repeat Rows 2 and 3.

Row 7: Repeat Row 1.

Rows 8 and 9: Repeat Rows 2 and 3.

Row 10: Repeat Row 1, adding 1 folded light blue soutache cord.

Row 11: Step 1: Repeat Row 10. Step 2: To form the front neckline, pin enough folded cords across the board to connect the vest halves. Starting in the center and working toward the left, mount 8 folded cords side by side in this order: 2 folded lengths of salmon soutache, 2 of peach soutache, 1 of orange soutache, 1 of light blue soutache, 1 of blue soutache and 1 of light blue rattail. If you need more cords to fill in the gap, mount blue cords only in groups of two in this order: 1 folded length of light blue soutache, 1 of blue soutache, 1 of light blue rattail and 1 of light blue soutache. Step 3: Starting in the center and working toward the right, pin an equal number of cords in the same order. Step 4: Make square knots with the additional cords across the row.

Rows 12-14: Work in alternating rows of square knots across the vest for 3 rows.

Rows 15-18 outside cords: Make alternating rows of square knots on the left half of the vest, knotting 8 cords in each knot (*drawing 1*). Make the first knot with the 11th-18th cords to the left of the center and work toward the left-hand

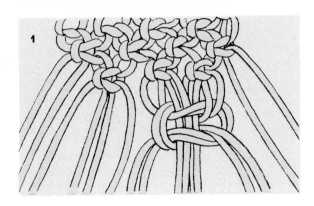

edge. Then knot the right half of the vest similarly. Leave the center cords free.

Row 19 outside cords: Step 1: Make 1 row of 4-cord square knots on the left half of the vest, starting with the 11th-14th cords to the left of center and knotting 4 of the 8 cords from the previous row in each knot. Knot the last 4 cords at the left-hand edge. Step 2: Knot the right half of the vest similarly.

Row 15 center design: Using the left center cord as the anchoring cord, make double half hitch knots diagonally with the next 13 cords toward the left-hand edge of the design. Then knot the right half of the design similarly.

Row 16 center design: Step 1: Repeat Row 15. Step 2: At the left-hand edge of the design, make a square knot, using the anchoring cords from the 2 previous rows and picking up the next 2 free cords. Then make square knots across the row to the outside edge of the vest. Step 3: Knot the right half of the vest similarly by repeating Step 2.

Row 17 center design: Using the left center cord as the knotting cord, make double half hitch knots vertically over the next 11 cords toward the left-hand edge. Then knot the right half of the vest similarly.

Row 18 center design: Step 1: Using the left center cord as the knotting cord, make double half hitch knots vertically over the next 10 cords toward the left-hand edge. Step 2: At the left-hand edge of the design, make 1 square knot, using the 2 knotting cords from the previous 2 rows of vertical half hitch knots and picking up the next 2 free cords. Then make square knots across the row to the left edge. Step 3: Knot the right half of the design similarly then work across the right side of the vest.

Row 19 center design: Step 1: Pin 2 folded light blue rattail cords between the halves of the design, on a line with the

bottom of the previous row of knots. Then make 1 square knot with these 4 cords. Step 2: Using the second cord to the left of the center (the left-hand knotting cord from the square knot) as the anchoring cord, make double half hitch knots diagonally with the next 14 cords toward the left-hand edge. Step 3: Knot the right half of the design similarly.

Row 20 center design: Using the left center cord as the knotting cord, make double half hitch knots vertically over the next 14 cords toward the left-hand edge. Then knot the right half of the design similarly.

Row 21 center design: Repeat Row 15.

Row 22 center design: Repeat Row 15.

Row 23 center design: Step 1: Tie a vertical row—called a sennet in macramé—of 3 chain knots down the first and second cords to the left of the center of the design. Work the chain knots by first making a single half hitch. Then switch the knotting and anchoring cords and make another single half hitch. Alternate the cords on each knot down the sennet (*drawing 2*). Step 2: Tie 3 chain knots down the first and second cords to the right of the center. Step 3:

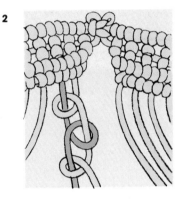

Using the center 4 cords—the 4 cords from the chain knots—make a sennet of 4 square knots. Step 4: Tie one sennet of 4 square knots with the 4 cords to the left of the center sennet, and another sennet of 4 square knots with the 4 cords to the right of the center sennet.

Row 24 center design: Step 1: Using the 6th cord to the left of the center as the anchoring cord, make double half hitch knots diagonally with the next 5 cords toward the center. Step 2: Knot the right half of the design similarly. Step 3: Join the 2 anchoring cords at the center with a double half hitch knot.

Row 25 center design: Repeat Row 24.

Rows 22-24 outside cords: To make the outside cords correspond to the knotted rows of the center design, make 3 alternating rows of 8-cord square knots with the unknotted cords on each half of the vest, starting at the design edge.

Row 26 center design: Step 1: Use lark's head knots to attach two 10-foot lengths of light blue rattail cord to the loop at the outside edge of the design formed by the previous 3 rows of square knots *(drawing 3)*. Step 2: Make 1 square knot with the 4 new cords. Step 3: Make 1 square knot us-

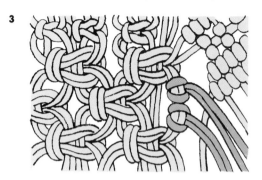

ing 2 of the new cords on the left-hand side and picking up the next 2 cords toward the center of the design. Step 4: Make square knots across the row, using 2 cords from the preceding square knot and picking up the next 2 cords toward the center. Tighten each knot on a line with the bottom of the preceding knot. There will be 2 unknotted cords at the center. Step 5: Knot the right half of the design by repeating Steps 1-4. Step 6: Make 1 square knot with the center 4 cords.

Row 27 center design: Repeat Row 26.

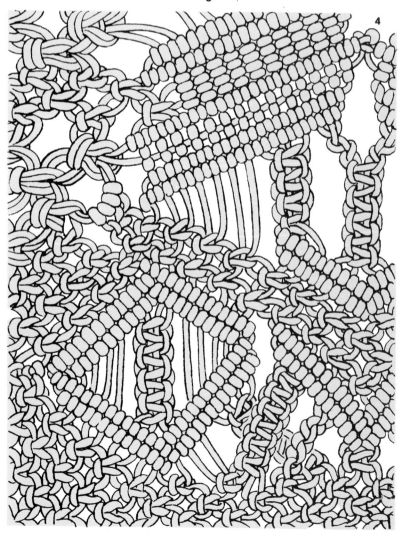

Rows 25-30 outside cords: Make 6 alternating rows of square knots starting the first row at the design edge with the 17th-20th cords to the left of center and working to the outside edge. Begin each successive row by leaving 2 more cords unknotted next to the edge of the design. Step 2: Knot the right half of the design similarly.

Now work the 2 motifs (designated as Rows A and B) at this point on the design *(drawing 4)* in this manner:

Row 28A center design: Step 1: Using the 8th cord to the left of the center as the anchoring cord, make double half hitch knots diagonally with the next 7 cords toward the center. Step 2: Knot the right half of the design similarly. Step 3: Join the 2 anchoring cords at the center with a double half hitch knot.

Row 29A center design: Repeat Row 28A.

Row 28B center design: Step 1: Using the 16th cord to the left of the center as the anchoring cord, make double half hitch knots diagonally with 7 cords toward the center. Step 2: Using the 16th cord to the left of center as the anchoring cord, make double half hitch knots diagonally with 7 cords toward the left-hand edge. Step 3: Knot the right half of the design similarly.

Row 29B: Repeat Row 28B.

Row 30A center design: Step 1: Using the 15th-18th cords to the left of the center, make a sennet of 4 square knots. Step 2: Using the 9th cord to the left of the center as the anchoring cord, make double half hitch knots diagonally with 7 cords toward the left-hand edge. Step 3: Using the 23rd cord to the left of the center as the anchoring cord, make double half hitch knots diagonally with 7 cords toward the center. Step 4: Knot the right half of the design similarly.

Row 31A center design: Repeat Row 30A, Steps 2-4.

Row 30B center design: Step 1: Using the 9th-12th cords to the left of the center, make a sennet of 6 square knots. Step 2: Make a square knot sennet of 6 knots with the 5th-8th cords to the left of the center. Step 3: Make a chain knot sennet of 8 knots with the 3rd and 4th cords to the left of the center. Step 4: Knot the right half of the design similarly. Step 5: Make 1 square knot with the 4 center cords.

Row 31B center design: Step 1: Join the last sennet to the center cords by making 1 square knot with the 1st, 2nd, 9th and 10th cords to the left of center, bringing the square knot sennet behind the work. Step 2: Make 1 square knot with the 5th-8th cords to the left of center. Step 3: Make 1 square knot with the 11th-14th cords to the left of center. Step 4: Make 1 square knot with the 7th-10th cords to the left of center.

FINISHING THE OUTSIDE CORDS

Work down to a point on a line with the top of the side seam line, making alternating rows of square knots on both halves of the vest. Begin each row at the center with 4-cord square knots and knot the last 16 cords with 8-cord knots.

Shape the armholes in the following manner: Step 1: Working only with the outside 12 cords, make alternating rows of square knots on the left half of the vest until the segment is long enough to touch the side seam line. Step 2: Use a lark's head knot to attach a 10-foot-long folded blue cord to each of the inside loops formed between the rows of square knots. Add at least 7 (12, 17) cords to shape the vest over the bust. Step 3: Add knots and cords to the right half of the vest similarly. Step 4: Make alternating rows of square knots across the vest. Start every other row by making a square knot with 2 of the new cords and the next 2 free cords. Work to within the last 7 added cords.

FINISHING THE CENTER DESIGN

Row 32: Step 1: Make an 8-cord square knot with the 8 center cords. Step 2: Make an 8-cord square knot with the next 8 cords on each side of that knot.

Row 33: Step 1: Make four 8-cord square knots with the 32 center cords.

Row 34: Step 1: Repeat Row 32, Step 1. Step 2: Make two 8-cord square knots with the next 16 cords on each side of that knot.

Row 35: Repeat Row 33.

Row 36: Repeat Row 32.

Row 37: Make two 8-cord square knots with the 16 center cords.

Row 38: Repeat Row 32, Step 1.

Rows 39-42: Step 1: Using the 20th cord to the left of the center as the anchoring cord, make double half hitch knots diagonally over the next 19 cords toward the center. Step 2: Knot the right half of the vest similarly. Step 3: Join the 2 center cords with a double half hitch knot.

Rows 43-45: Make alternating rows of 8-cord square knots with the 40 center cords. Work from the center toward the outside edges.

FINISHING THE VEST FRONT

To complete the vest front, knot 4-cord square knots across the vest, incorporating all of the added cords at the outside edges as before. Leave a decreasing number of cords unknotted at the bottom edge to achieve the desired V-shaping at the bottom of the vest.

THE VEST BACK

Unpin the macramé and untie the knots used to mount the cords. Then repin the macramé to the board so that the unknotted cords hang down the front of the board.

MAKING THE VEST BACK

Begin by working 12 (18, 24) alternating rows of square knots across each shoulder.

Row 1: Step 1: To start the neckline shaping, fold a light blue rattail cord in half and pin it—at the fold—to the inside edge of the left half of the vest on a line with the bottom of the previous row. Then, starting with the 4 inside cords, make square knots across the row. Step 2: Pin a folded light blue rattail cord to the inside edge of the right half of the vest and—starting with the 4 inside cords—make square knots across the row.

Rows 2 and 3: Work in alternating rows of square knots across both halves of the vest.

Row 4: Repeat Row 1, adding 1 blue soutache cord to each half of the vest.

Rows 5 and 6: Repeat Rows 2 and 3.

Row 7: Repeat Row 1.

Rows 8 and 9: Repeat Rows 2 and 3.

Row 10: Repeat Row 1, adding 1 light blue soutache cord to each half of the vest.

Rows 11 and 12: Repeat Rows 2 and 3.

Row 13: Repeat Row 1.

Rows 14 and 15: Repeat Rows 2 and 3.

Row 16: Step 1: Using the first 4 inside cords on the left half of the vest, make a square knot sennet of 14 (21, 28) knots. Step 2: Use a lark's head knot to attach 1 folded cord to each inside loop of the sennet (*drawing 5*). Alternate or-

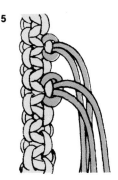

ange and peach cords down the sennet, then finish with 2 blue cords. Step 3: Repeat Steps 1-2 on the right half of the vest, starting with the first 4 inside cords.

FINISHING THE VEST BACK

Make alternating rows of square knots to a point on a line with the top of the side seam line. Incorporate the new cords at the inside edge on every other row. Shape the armhole as on the vest front, incorporating the new cords into the knots on both edges.

FINISHING THE VEST

Unpin the halves of the vest back. Then pin the front of the vest and the left back section to the board side by side so that they meet at the base of the underarm seams. Using 2 cords from each side, make 1 square knot to join them. Unpin the vest, then pin the front and right back sections to the board and join them similarly. Leaving the vest on the board and repinning it as needed, start at the outer edge of the right back section and make square knot sennets with each group of 4 cords all around the vest to shape the bottom edge. Repin as necessary.

Starting again at the right back outer edge, skip 2 cords and then join each pair of sennets around the bottom of the vest with a square knot—using 2 cords from each sennet. Leave the final 2 cords on the left back edge unknotted. Now, starting again at the right back outer edge, make an overhand knot (*page 139*) with the first 2 cords. Then make overhand knots with each group of 4 cords around the vest, finishing with a 2-cord knot. Once again, starting from the right edge, skip 2 cords and make a second row of 4-cord overhand knots.

MAKING THE FRINGE

Determine the length desired for the fringe and tie 4 overhand knots on each cord at that point. Trim any excess cord from below the knots.

Double dash for a sweater

Striped bandoleers across the shoulders and more bands around the hem and the cuffs not only spice this tunic-length sweater with dashes of color, but also simplify the construction of the garment.

Because the modified kimono sleeves simply flow out of the bodice, the sweater itself can be knitted in four separate pieces, all worked in the familiar stockinette stitch. The pieces are then sewed together and the bodice seams are covered by individually knitted striped bands. Similar bands finish the bottom edges of the sweater.

Instructions for knitting the striped band sweater

The banded sweater shown on the preceding pages is knit in an unconventional manner. The body of the sweater is simply two rectangles, with no armhole or neck shaping. Furthermore, it is knit from side seam to side seam, rather than from the bottom up, so that the rows run horizontally rather than vertically. The sleeves are also made differently. The fronts of both sleeves are made at the same time; in the process, the neck shaping is accomplished. Then the sleeve backs are made. After the body sections and sleeves are completed, they are sewed together and bands are attached, concealing the seams, as in the drawing at right.

The instructions that follow are written for a woman's size 10. Changes needed for sizes 12, 14, 16 and 18 follow in parentheses in that order. For the body sections and the sleeves you will need 21 (23, 25, 27, 29) one-ounce balls of plum-colored mohair yarn.

Make the striped bands with either light-weight bulky yarn or knitting worsted. For this trim you will need 1 four-ounce skein of either yarn you select in each of the following colors: medium pink (color A), royal blue (color B), light gray (color C), plum (color D) and dark gray (color E).

When you work with the mohair, use Size 6 straight needles and a double strand of yarn. Work in the stockinette pattern—knit 1 row, purl 1 row—to a gauge of 4 stitches and 6 rows to the inch. For the trim, use Size 10 straight needles and a single strand of the bulky yarn or a double strand of the knitting worsted. With either yarn, work in a gauge of 7 stitches to 2 inches and 4 garter-stitch—all knit—rows to the inch.

To check the gauge, knit a sample 4-by-4-inch swatch, using the yarn, needles and pattern stitch indicated for each part of your garment. Without binding off, remove the swatch from the needles, then, using a ruler, count the number of stitches to the inch across the swatch to obtain the stitch gauge. To determine the row gauge, measure and count the number of vertical rows to the inch. Basic stitches and techniques—such as casting on and increasing and decreasing stitches—are in the Appendix.

THE BODY SECTIONS

The back: Starting at the bottom right corner, cast on 14 stitches for all sizes. Using the stockinette stitch, work 4 rows on the 14 stitches. At the end of the last row—a purl row—cast on 16 stitches for all sizes. Work even on the 30 stitches for 4 rows. At the end of the last row, cast on 16 stitches again. Work even for 4 rows on the 46 stitches of the row. At the end of the last row, cast on 30 stitches; work even on the 76 stitches until the piece measures 8 (8 1/2, 9, 9 1/2, 10) inches from the point where the last 30 stitches were cast on; end with a purl row.

To indicate the underarm of the right-hand side of the back, place a marker—a short length of contrasting color thread tied in place—on the last stitch of the group of 30 stitches you cast on. Place another marker at the end of the last purl row on the 76 stitches to indicate the top cen-

ter of the back. Work even on the 76 stitches for 8 (8 1/2, 9, 9 1/2, 10) inches, ending with a purl row. At the end of this row, place another marker to indicate the underarm of the left-hand side of the back.

At the beginning of the next knit row, bind off 30 stitches, then work 4 rows even on the 46 stitches. At the beginning of the next knit row, bind off 16 stitches, and work even on the 30 stitches for 4 rows. At the beginning of the next knit row, bind off 16 stitches again. Work even on the remaining 14 stitches for 4 rows; bind off.

The front: Follow the instructions for the back.

THE SLEEVES

The sleeve fronts: Starting at the bottom of the left sleeve, cast on 40 (42, 44, 46, 48) stitches. Work even in the stockinette stitch until the piece measures 15 inches in all, or the desired length to the underarm; end with a knit row.

Place a marker at the end of this row to indicate the length of the sleeve to the underarm. Continue to work on the 40 (42, 44, 46, 48) stitches for 6 (6 1/2, 7, 7 1/2, 8) inches, ending with a purl row. The piece should measure 21 (21 1/2, 22, 22 1/2, 23) inches, plus or minus the rows for your sleeve length.

Place a marker at the end of the last purl row just made to indicate the top of the work at the start of the neck shaping. Begin to shape the left-hand side of the neck. Starting on the next knit row, bind off 3 stitches at the beginning of the row. Knit across the remaining 37 (39, 41, 43, 45) stitches. Purl the next row without binding off. On the next row, bind off 3 stitches at the beginning of the row, then knit across the remaining 34 (36, 38, 40, 42) stitches. Purl the next row without binding off. Continue in this manner —binding off 3 stitches at the beginning of every knit row and purling even on the next row—until 16 (18, 20, 22, 24) stitches remain. You will be ending with a knit row.

Measure the length of the work from the marker at the underarm to the row just completed. The length should equal the distance between the left underarm marker and the center-front marker on the front body section.

On the next row purl the 16 (18, 20, 22, 24) stitches. At the end of the row, begin to shape the right-hand side of the neck by casting on 3 stitches. On the next row, knit the 19 (21, 23, 25, 27) stitches. Repeat the last 2 rows until there are 40 (42, 44, 46, 48) stitches on the row.

Now work the front of the right sleeve. Work even for 6 (6 1/2, 7, 7 1/2, 8) inches. Place a marker at the end of the last knit row to indicate the underarm. Work even until the sleeve measures 15 inches—or the length of the left front sleeve—from the underarm marker. Bind off.

The sleeve backs: Follow the instructions for the fronts.

THE STRIPED BAND TRIM

The bottom band: Using color A, cast on 63 (67, 70, 74, 77) stitches. Work even in the garter stitch—all knit rows—for 4 rows. Break off color A. Continuing in the garter stitch, work 4 rows with color B, 4 with color C, 4 with color D and 4 with color E, breaking off the old color at the end of each stripe and attaching the new one at the beginning of the next stripe. Repeat this sequence; make five more colored stripes—there will be 40 rows on this band. Bind off.

The sleeve bands: Using color A, cast on 67 (70, 73, 77, 80) stitches. Then repeat the sequence of 4 rows of garter stitches in each of the five established colors for 40 rows. Bind off. Make another band in the same manner.

The crossed bandoleers: Cast on 126 (140, 154, 168, 182) stitches, using color A. Repeat the sequence of five colored stripes as on the other bands; this time bind off after completing the first color E stripe. There will be 20 rows on this band. Make another band in the same manner.

FINISHING THE SWEATER

Sewing the seams: Sew the side seams of the body sections. Place the sleeve sections together. Match the markers at the neck edges, and sew the top sleeve seams from the neck to the sleeve bottoms. Now match the markers at the underarms, and sew the bottom sleeve seams from the armholes to the sleeve bottoms. Sew the unattached por-

tions at the bottom center of the sleeve sections to the corresponding tops of the body sections (*drawing, below*).

Attaching the bottom trim: Place the band around the bot-

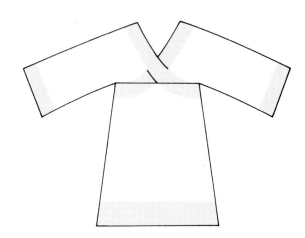

tom of the sweater. Place the two short ends at one side seam. Fold the band to the underside of the sweater at the bottom of the first color C stripe; sew the band along the cast-on row at the bottom of the band. Smooth out the band around the bottom of the sweater—on the outside of the sweater. Sew the bound-off row at the top of the band to the sweater. Join the two short ends of the band by weaving them together along the side seam.

Attaching the sleeve trim: Place a band around each sleeve bottom, with the two short ends of each band meeting at the underarm sleeve seam. Turn the bands to the undersides of the sleeves along the top of the first color E stripe. Sew the bands into place along the cast-on and bound-off rows as you did for the bottom trim. Weave the two short ends together along the underarm sleeve seam.

Attaching the bandoleers: With the sweater front facing up, place the short end of one of the long bands along the left side seam, with the top of the strip at the underarm of that seam and the remaining portion of the short end running down the side seam. Make sure the color E stripe is at the top. Lay the top of the band along the seam connecting the sleeves to the body. At the center front, turn the band up at the V neck, then around the right-hand neck edge, over the shoulder, and down the corresponding neck edge on the back. Align the top of the color E stripe with the neck edges. Continue to carry the strip around the seam connecting the sleeves to the body on the front until you reach the opposite side of the same side seam where you began aligning this band. Sew the band into place along the cast-on and bound-off rows at the bottom and top of the band, then weave the two short ends together at the side seam.

Position the second strip in the same manner, but this time begin and end at the other side seam. Overlap the first band just below the point of the V neck at both the front and the back so that the bands crisscross.

Lively stitched hand warmers

The picot edges on the crocheted mitten and the bright colored out-lines on the knit gloves are more than amusing design elements. The devices join the separately worked palms and backs with crochet stitch-es. Single crochet and two varia-tions, hazelnut and picot, are used for the mittens; the glove is worked in basic rib and stockinette patterns.

The two halves of each mitten are shaped identically with free-form crochet. Each glove half, however, requires different shaping, for the thumb must be made entirely on the palm section.

Instructions for the gloves and mittens

Both knitting and crochet are used for the gloves on page 152, crochet alone for the mittens shown with them. The gloves are made in the stockinette pattern—alternate knit and purl rows—and are joined with single crochet stitches. The mittens are made with single crochet and hazelnut stitches, and are trimmed with picot stitches. Directions for the hazelnut and picot stitches are given in these instructions; other basic knit and crochet stitches and techniques—such as casting on and increasing and decreasing stitches—are in the Appendix.

THE KNITTED GLOVES

These instructions are for the knitted gloves in a small size; if changes are necessary for medium and large sizes they follow in parentheses in that order. To make the gloves in any of these sizes, you will need two 1-ounce balls of a medium-weight mohair yarn in the main color (brown in the photograph) and one ball in the contrasting color (orange). You will also need a pair of Size 6 straight knitting needles, a Size E aluminum crochet hook, a stitch holder designed for knitting (or a large safety pin), and about 1/2 yard of elastic thread.

Work in a gauge of 5 stitches to the inch when knitting. To check the gauge, knit a sample swatch measuring 4 by 4 inches. Without binding off, remove the swatch from the needles. Then, using a ruler, count the number of stitches to the inch across the swatch.

THE RIGHT PALM SECTION

Cast on 19 stitches. Work in a knit 1 stitch, purl 1 stitch ribbing pattern for 4 rows. Change to the stockinette stitch —knit 1 row, purl 1 row—and work in this stitch to the completion of the glove section. Work even until the piece measures 4 inches in all—including the ribbing. On the next row, decrease 1 stitch at the beginning and end of the row. Work even on 17 stitches for another 4 inches.

On the next row, decrease 1 stitch at the beginning and end of the row. Work even now on 15 stitches until the piece measures 10 inches in all, ending with a purl row.

Shaping the top of the thumb: Decrease 1 stitch at the beginning of the next row. Knit across the next 3 stitches. Slip the remaining 10 stitches—which will be worked later —onto a stitch holder or pin. There are now 4 stitches on your needle. Working on these stitches only, decrease 1 stitch at the beginning of the next row, then purl across the remaining 2 stitches. Work even now on the 3 remaining stitches for 2 1/2 (2 3/4, 3) inches. Bind off.

Completing the palm: Cast on 5 stitches. Return to the 10 stitches on the holder, and knit across these stitches. There are now 15 stitches on your needle.

Work even on these stitches for 2 inches, ending with a knit row. Then break off the yarn, and slip these stitches onto your holder.

Completing the thumb: Place the work with the outside facing you. Return to the point at which you cast on the 5 stitches when you were completing the palm. Going across the work horizontally, pick up and knit these 5 stitches. Working on these stitches only, decrease 1 stitch at the beginning and end of the next row, which is a purl row. Work even now on the 3 stitches remaining on the needle for 2 1/2 (2 3/4, 3) inches. Bind off.

Shaping the fingers: To form the index finger, return to the 15 stitches on the holder. With the wrong side of the work facing you, slip the first 4 stitches from the holder onto a needle. Working on these stitches only, purl the first 2 stitches together. Then purl each of the next 2 stitches. You now have 3 stitches on your needle. Work even on these stitches for 2 3/4 (3, 3 1/4) inches to complete the index finger. Bind off.

To form the middle finger, slip the next 4 stitches from the holder, and work them as you did the stitches for the index finger, but this time continue working until this finger measures 3 (3 1/4, 3 1/2) inches.

Work the ring finger next. Begin by slipping the next 4 stitches from the holder; then work them exactly as you did for the index finger.

To make the little finger, slip the 3 stitches that are still on the holder onto your needle. For this finger, do not purl the first 2 stitches together. Instead work even on the 3 stitches until the finger measures 2 1/2 (2 3/4, 3) inches. Then bind off.

THE RIGHT BACK SECTION

To make the back of the glove, work as you did for the palm section up to the point where you began to shape the top of the thumb. Omit this thumb shaping, and instead, continue working on the 15 stitches on your needle until the piece measures 12 inches in all. Then shape the four fingers as you did on the palm section.

THE LEFT GLOVE
Make the palm and back sections as you did on the right glove, but reverse all the shaping.

FINISHING THE GLOVES
Edging the glove sections: Using your crochet hook and the main color yarn, work a row of single crochet stitches around each of the four sections. To do this on the right palm section, start at the upper left corner, and work the crochet stitches down the side edge until you reach the thumb. Work around the top part of the thumb—rounding out the tip—until you reach the other end of the top part. Work around the bottom part of the thumb in the same manner, but going in the opposite direction. Fasten off the yarn.

Join the yarn again at the side edge just below the thumb, and continue making single crochet stitches around each of the fingers, rounding out the tips. Finally, work up the opposite side edge. Fasten off the yarn at the top side edge, without crocheting across the ribbing.

On the left palm section, work single crochet stitches around the edges, as you did for the right palm section.

On each of the back sections, make single crochet stitches around the edges in the same manner, but work down the side edge, around the fingers and up the opposite side edge. Fasten off.

Joining the glove sections: Place the right palm and back sections wrong sides together so that the back of the glove is facing you. Using the contrast color yarn, start at the upper left corner, and crochet the pieces together with single crochet stitches. Work down the side edge, around the fingers, and up the opposite side edge. Fasten off. Turn the glove so the palm is facing you, and attach the yarn again at the outside edge of the thumb. Then join the two thumb pieces with single crochet stitches. Fasten off. Join the left glove sections in the same manner.

The finishing touches: Cut two strands of elastic thread each about 6 inches long. Working on the wrong side of each glove, draw a strand of elastic thread through the bottom row of the ribbing. Block (*Glossary*) the finished gloves.

THE CROCHETED MITTENS
To make the crocheted mittens in a small, medium or large size, you will need 2 ounces of Donegal yarn in each of the following colors: burgundy (color A), apricot (color B), beige (color C), and white (color D). If you prefer, you can substitute equal amounts of lightweight sport or fingering yarn.

Use a Size C aluminum crochet hook. Work in a gauge of 5 stitches to the inch and 6 rows to the inch when making single crochet stitches. To check the gauge, crochet a sample swatch measuring 4 by 4 inches. Using a ruler, count the number of stitches to the inch across the swatch. Then measure and count the number of vertical rows to the inch for the row gauge.

On both mittens, the back and palm sections are the same, which means you will be making four identical pieces.

MAKING THE TRIANGLES
For each mitten, you will need to make six triangles worked in the hazelnut stitch. To make each triangle, use color A yarn, and begin with a foundation chain of 12 stitches.

Row 1: Work in the single crochet stitch on 11 stitches, then chain 1 to turn at the end of the row.

Row 2: Begin to make the hazelnut stitches. To make the first hazelnut stitch—and each subsequent one—start by bringing the yarn over the hook and inserting the hook into the second stitch from the hook. Yarn over the hook again, and draw the yarn through the stitch so that you have three loops on the hook. Bring the yarn over again, and pull it through the first two loops on the hook, leaving two loops. Yarn over, and insert the hook in the same stitch. Yarn over, and draw the yarn through so that you have four loops on the hook. Yarn over, then pull the yarn through the first two loops only, leaving three loops on the hook. Yarn over, insert the hook in the stitch again, yarn over and draw it through so that you have five loops on the hook. Yarn over, and again draw the yarn through the first two loops only, leaving four loops on the hook. Yarn over, insert the hook in the stitch, yarn over, and draw it through so that you have six loops on the hook. Yarn over, and draw the yarn through the first two loops, leaving five loops on the hook. Yarn over, insert the hook in the stitch, yarn over and draw the yarn through so that you have seven loops on the hook. Yarn over, and draw the yarn through the first two loops once more, leaving six loops on the hook. Yarn over, then draw the yarn through all six loops. This forms the first hazelnut.

Make 1 single crochet stitch in the next stitch. Then repeat this sequence—1 hazelnut, 1 single crochet stitch—four more times across the row until five hazelnuts have been completed.

End the row with 1 single crochet stitch in the last stitch. Then chain 1, and turn.

Row 3: Make single crochet stitches only across the first 4 stitches. Decrease 1 stitch, then single crochet across the remaining 4 stitches. You will now be working on 9 stitches. At the end of the row, chain 1 and turn.

Row 4: Work a hazelnut stitch in the second stitch from the hook, and then 1 single crochet stitch in the next stitch. Continue to alternate 1 hazelnut stitch and 1 single crochet stitch across the row, ending with 1 single crochet stitch.

Chain 1 to turn at the end of the row. There will be four hazelnuts on this row.

Row 5: Work across the first 3 stitches in the single crochet stitch. Decrease 1 stitch, then work across the remaining 3 stitches. Chain 1, and turn.

Rows 6-10: Continue to work in the sequence you have established, alternating a hazelnut pattern row with a row of single crochet. On each single crochet row, decrease 1 stitch in the center. On the 10th row, make only 1 hazelnut stitch—to form the point of the triangle—then fasten off. Make 11 more triangles in the same manner.

FORMING THE CENTRAL DIAMOND

Place two of the triangles together at their bases to form a diamond, between points 1 and 2 on the diagram (right). Sew the triangles together, using color A yarn.

Color B section: Attach color B at either the top or bottom point of the diamond. Work 1 single crochet stitch in the first stitch. Then work 52 more single crochet stitches around the diamond, making 11 stitches along each side and 2 stitches at each point. End the round by working 1 more single crochet stitch in the starting point.

Continue to work single crochet stitches around the piece in the same manner, making two more rounds with color B. Remember to work 2 stitches in each point of the diamond as you turn, and 1 stitch in each stitch along the sides.

Color C section: Attach color C, and make two more rounds of single crochet stitches as you did in the color B section.

MAKING THE FINGER SECTIONS

Color D section: Following the diagram, attach color D yarn at point 3. Work 1 single crochet stitch in each stitch until you reach the top center point. Work 3 single crochet stitches at this point. Then work 1 single crochet stitch in each stitch until you are within 3 stitches of point 4. Work these 3 stitches as 1 stitch; then chain 1, and turn.

Continue to work in this manner for 2 more rows if you are making small size mittens. Work for 5 more rows if you are making medium or large size mittens. On each of these rows, remember to work 3 single crochet stitches at the center point and to work the last 3 stitches at the end of each row as 1 stitch before chaining 1 to turn. Fasten off at the end of the last row.

Color C section: Working only on the color D stitches of the previous row, attach color C and make 3 more rows of stitches for a small or medium size; make 5 more rows for a large size.

Continue to work 3 stitches at the top center point, but now work only the last 2 stitches at the end of each row as 1 stitch, before chaining 1 and turning. At the end of the last row with color C, fasten off.

Color B section: Attach color B, and make 3 rows in this color as you did with color C. Fasten off. You have now completed the finger sections.

With the work wrong side up, press the color bands lightly, using a pressing cloth and a steam iron. Be careful not to press directly over the hazelnut stitches of the central diamond.

MAKING THE WRIST SECTIONS

Take a third triangle and match the point with the bottom point of the central diamond. Sew the points together on the wrong side.

Color D section: With the work wrong side down, attach color D yarn in the first single crochet stitch below the stitch level with point 1. Work 1 single crochet stitch in each stitch along the side of the diamond to within 2 stitches of point 5. Work these 2 stitches as 1 stitch. Then work single crochet stitches along the side of the triangle to the cuff edge. Chain 1, and turn.

On the next row, work single crochet stitches back along the side of the triangle to point 5 again. Work the next 2 stitches as 1 stitch. Make single crochet stitches until you are within 3 stitches of the end of the row, then work these 3 stitches off as 1 stitch. Chain 1, and turn.

On the last row, again make single crochet stitches to within 2 stitches of point 5 and work the next 2 stitches as 1 stitch. Then continue making single crochet stitches to the cuff edge, and fasten off.

Color C section: Attach color C in the last stitch of the previous row, and work 3 more rows exactly as you did for the color D section. Remember to decrease in mid-row at the same point.

To fill in the other half of the wrist section, start by attaching color D to the triangle at the cuff edge. On the first row, make single crochet stitches along the side of the triangle to point 6, work the next 2 stitches as 1 stitch. Then make single crochet stitches along the side of the diamond until you are within 3 stitches of the stitch level with point 2. Work these 3 stitches as 1 stitch. Then chain 1 and turn.

Make 2 more rows with color D, then attach color C and make 3 more rows, as you did when you worked on the other side of the wrist section, but remember to work in the reverse order.

Steam press the wrist sections as you did the finger sections. Be careful not to press over the hazelnut stitches.

At this point, you have completed one half of one mitten. Make three more pieces in exactly the same manner. Block (Glossary) all four pieces.

COMPLETING THE MITTENS

Assembling the mitten: Place two halves together with the wrong sides out. Starting at a cuff edge, sew the mittens together along the side for 3 inches. Leave a 1-inch opening for the thumb; then continue to sew around the edges until you reach the opposite cuff edge.

Making the thumb: Turn the mitten right side out. Attach color D yarn at the thumb opening. Work 14 single crochet stitches around the opening then, without joining the rounds, single crochet around the opening on these stitches for 12 more rows. Fasten off. Then sew the seam at the tip of the thumb. Turn the mitten wrong side out, and lightly steam press the thumb.

Making the picot edging: With the mitten turned right side out, attach color A yarn to the top corner of the cuff at point 7. Then make the picot stitch as follows: Work 1 single crochet stitch in each of the first 3 stitches, chain 3 stitches, then work another single crochet stitch into the last single crochet stitch you worked.

Repeat this sequence—make 3 single crochet stitches, chain 3 stitches, and then make 1 single crochet stitch into the last single crochet made before you made the chain —around the entire outside edge of the mitten, including the thumb. Work the picot edging in the same manner around each edge of the cuff opening separately.

Finish the other mitten in exactly the same way.

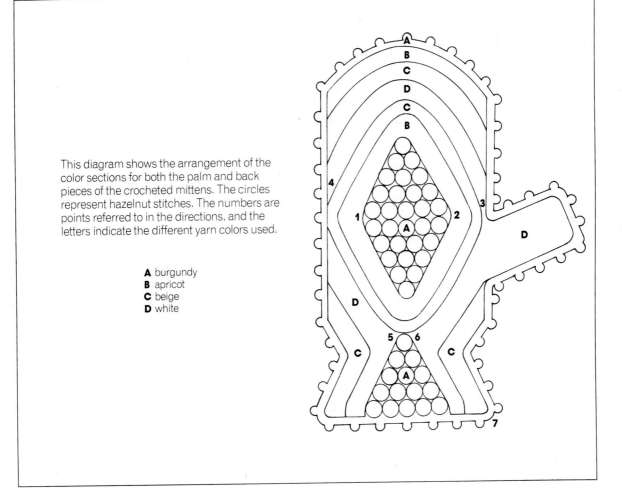

This diagram shows the arrangement of the color sections for both the palm and back pieces of the crocheted mittens. The circles represent hazelnut stitches. The numbers are points referred to in the directions, and the letters indicate the different yarn colors used.

A burgundy
B apricot
C beige
D white

Flamboyant soft shoes

What ends up as extraordinary foot-gear starts out as ordinary knee-high socks. The leather-soled after-ski boots on the left, for example, are enlivened with vibrantly colored free-form crochet. The Japanese-style *tabi* socks, which have shaped big toes so that they can be worn with thong sandals, are knit in a pattern of encircling stripes. To simplify construction and to allow for replacements, both the leather soles on the boots and the solid-colored knit ones on the *tabis* are made separately.

Instructions for the boots and socks

The crocheted boots and the knitted *tabi* socks *(pages 158-159)* use simple stitches. The boots are made with single crochet and edged in picot stitches. The socks are made in the stockinette stitch—knit 1 row, purl 1 row—and a 2-row pattern stitch. Basic stitches and techniques not explained in these directions—such as casting on and increasing and decreasing stitches—are in the Appendix.

THE CROCHETED BOOTS

To make the boots in a small, medium or large women's size, you will need one 4-ounce skein of Donegal tweed yarn each for color A (dark blue in the photograph on page 158), color B (lime green), color C (purple) and color D (emerald green). Equal amounts of medium-weight 4-ply worsted yarn can be substituted. For the soles, you will need about 1/2 yard of cowhide and—for making holes in the leather—a rotary punch, sold in most craft stores.

Use a Size H aluminum crochet hook. Work in a gauge of 4 stitches to the inch and 4 rows to the inch when making single crochet stitches. To check the gauge, crochet a sample swatch measuring 4 by 4 inches. Using a ruler, count the number of stitches to the inch across the swatch. Then measure and count the number of vertical rows to the inch for the row gauge.

In all sizes, these boots measure 15 inches from the top to the heel, 8 1/2 inches around the ankle and 4 1/2 inches across the arch. The length of the foot is 9 inches for a small size, 10 inches for medium and 11 inches for large. The circumference around the calf is 12, 13 and 13 1/2 inches for small, medium and large respectively.

The accompanying diagram *(opposite)* indicates where the color bands bordering the central diamond motifs—as well as the bands forming the foot—are located. The boot is shown spread out flat, as it will be when you are working on it before the front seam is closed.

MAKING THE TRIANGLES

For each boot, make six triangles to form the central diamond motifs. Using color A yarn, begin each triangle with a foundation chain of 13 stitches. Turn. On the first row, work 12 single crochet stitches across the chain; then chain 1, and turn. On the next row, decrease 1 stitch at the beginning of the row. Then continue to make single crochet stitches across the row. At the end of the row, chain 1 and turn. Continue in this manner, decreasing 1 stitch at the beginning of each row until only 1 stitch remains. This stitch forms the point of the triangle. Fasten off. Make 11 more triangles in exactly the same way.

FORMING THE CENTRAL DIAMONDS

Joining the triangles: Place two of the triangles together at their bases to form a diamond. Sew the triangles together, using color A yarn.

Bordering the diamonds with color B: Attach color B at either the top or bottom point of the diamond. Work 1 single crochet stitch in the first stitch. Then work 46 more single crochet stitches around the diamond, making 10 stitches along each side and 2 stitches at each point. End the round by working 1 more single crochet stitch in the starting point. Continue to work single crochet stitches around the piece, making two more rounds of color B. Fasten off.

Working in the same manner, join two more sets of triangles to form diamonds, and border these two diamonds with three rounds of color B.

Joining the diamonds: Following the diagram, line up the three diamond motifs vertically, matching them carefully at points 1 and 2. Sew the diamonds together on the wrong side at the two points. Then, using a pressing cloth and a steam iron, lightly press the diamonds on the wrong side.

MAKING THE SIDE COLOR BANDS

Color C band: With the diamonds wrong side down, attach color C yarn in the third stitch to the left of point 3. Working down the left-hand side of the top diamond, make 1 single crochet stitch in each stitch along the side of the diamond until you reach point 4. Work 3 single crochet stitches at point 4. Then make 1 single crochet stitch in each stitch along the diamond until you are within 1 stitch of point 1. At this point, make a double decrease in the following manner: Insert the hook into the last stitch before point 1; then insert the hook in the stitch in which the diamonds are joined at the point; and finally insert the hook in the first stitch of the second diamond. Bring the yarn over the hook, and pull it through all the loops on the hook, thus decreasing 3 stitches into 1 stitch. Continue to single crochet in each stitch along the second diamond to point 5; then work 3 single crochet stitches at point 5 as you did at point 4. Continue to single crochet in each stitch along the side of the diamond to within 1 stitch before point 2; then make a double decrease at this point as you did at point 1. On the third diamond, work 1 single crochet stitch in each stitch to point 6; then make 3 stitches at this point as you did at points 4 and 5. Continue to make single crochet stitches along the last side until you are within 4 stitches of point 7 at the heel; then work the next 2 stitches as 1 stitch to decrease. Leaving the last 2 stitches before point 7 unworked, chain 1, and turn. Going in the opposite direction now — still using color C — work back along the sides of the diamonds in the same manner. Remember to make 3 stitches at points 6, 5, and 4 and to double decrease at points 2 and 1. Work the last 2 stitches of the row as 1 stitch leaving 2 stitches unworked at the end of the row, as before, to keep the bottom and top edges of the work straight. Break off color C.

Color D band: Attach color D at the top of the work, in the last single crochet stitch of the previous row. Work 2 rows of color D along the sides of the diamonds as you did with color C. Break off color D.

Color A band: Attach color A at the top of the work in the last stitch of the previous row. Then work as you did on the previous color bands, but this time make 3 rows, ending the last row at the heel. Break off the yarn.

Color B band: Attach color B at the bottom of the work in the last stitch of the previous row. Work 2 rows in this color as you did on the other color bands. At the end of the second row, break off the yarn.

Shaping the calf area: Continuing with color B, and starting at the top of the work, make single crochet stitches along the diamonds — increasing and decreasing as before — until you are within 1 stitch before the stitch level with point 5 (arrow). Work the next 2 stitches as 1 stitch; chain 1, and turn. Work back to the top of the work. These rows are sufficient for a small calf. For a medium-sized calf, make 4 more rows; for a large calf, 6 more.

Filling in the small color A triangles: Attach color A to point 8. Work the first 2 stitches as 1 stitch; then make 1 single crochet stitch in each stitch until you are within 1 stitch of point 9. Work the next 2 stitches as 1 stitch. Then make 1

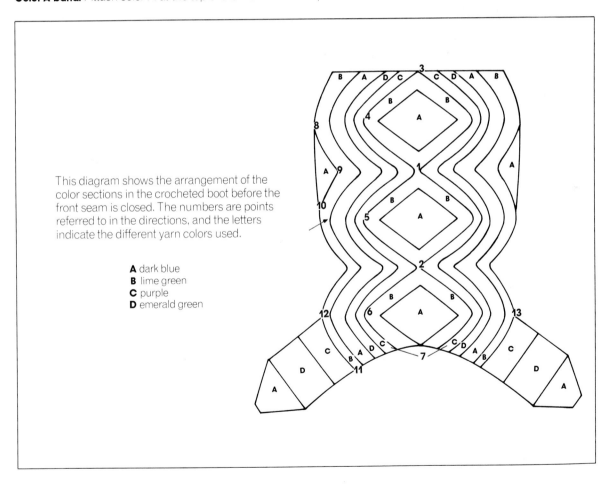

This diagram shows the arrangement of the color sections in the crocheted boot before the front seam is closed. The numbers are points referred to in the directions, and the letters indicate the different yarn colors used.

A dark blue
B lime green
C purple
D emerald green

single crochet stitch in each stitch to within 3 stitches before point 10. Work the next 2 stitches as 1 stitch; then make a single crochet stitch in the last stitch. Chain 1 and turn. Continue to work in this manner until the area is filled in and a triangle is formed, decreasing as on the first color A row. Fasten off.

Making the opposite side: Beginning at the heel (point 7) with color C, work the other side of the boot to correspond to the completed side. End with the last row forming the base of the small triangle, as before.

MAKING THE FOOT

Color C section: With the work wrong side up, start by attaching color C yarn at the bottom of the piece (point 11). Make 1 single crochet stitch in each stitch until you reach point 12, which is the stitch even with point 6. Chain 1 and turn. Work back and forth on these stitches now for 4 more rows. Fasten off.

Color D section: Attach color D, and work even for 5 rows if you are making a small size. For a medium size, work even for 9 rows; for large, 13 rows. In adjusting the size, keep in mind that the row gauge is 4 rows to the inch. Fasten off.

Shaping the toe: Attach color A in the last stitch of the previous row. Then make 1 single crochet stitch in each of the 9 stitches on the row. Chain 1, and turn. Decrease 1 stitch at the beginning of the next row; then work across, making single crochet stitches in each stitch to the end of the row. Chain 1 and turn. Continue in this manner, decreasing 1 stitch at the beginning of every row until only 1 stitch remains. Fasten off.

Shape the foot and toe on the other side in the same manner, beginning at point 13 with color C.

FINISHING THE BOOT

Using a pressing cloth, lightly steam-press the boot on the wrong side. Then block it *(Glossary).*

Closing the seam: Sew the front seam, matching the two color A triangles at the calf to form a diamond. Make sure the striping pattern on the foot and the points of the color A triangles for the toe meet.

Shaping the boot: Insert a tightly rolled turkish towel into the boot. Using a pressing cloth and a steam iron, shape the front seam so that it curves outward at the calf and inward at the ankle.

Making the leather sole: Trace the outline of your foot onto the cowhide with chalk. Cut out the shape. Using the smallest setting on a rotary punch, punch holes all around the sole, spaced about 1/4 inch apart. Sewing through the holes, attach the sole to the bottom edge of the crochet with a sturdy color C thread.

Trimming the boot: Using color C yarn, work a raised row of single crochet stitches around the center-front diamond. Then make raised rows of single crochet stitches along the sides at the point where the vertical color B and color A bands meet and along the back at the point where the color B and color C bands meet. Next make raised stitches across the top of the toe between the color A and color D sections, and then across the top of the foot between the color D and color C sections.

Using color C yarn, work a picot-stitch edging around the top of the boot and around the sole. To make the picot stitches, work 1 single crochet in each of the first 3 stitches; then chain 3 stitches, and make a single crochet stitch into the last single crochet stitch you made before the chain. Repeat this sequence of stitches around both areas to be trimmed.

Make the other boot in exactly the same manner.

THE TABI SOCKS

To make the socks, which are stretchable and will fit most women's feet, you will need two 2-ounce balls of sport-weight yarn in the main color (forest green in the photograph on page 159) and one 2-ounce ball for the contrasting color (beige). You will also need straight knitting needles in Sizes 4 and 6, a stitch holder designed for knitting (or a large safety pin), and about a yard of elastic thread.

Work in a gauge of 6 stitches to the inch and 8 rows to the inch on the Size 6 needles. To check the gauge, knit a sample swatch, measuring 4 by 4 inches. Without binding off, remove the swatch from the needles; then using a ruler, count the number of stitches to the inch across the swatch. To determine your row gauge, measure and count the number of vertical rows to the inch.

THE LEFT SOLE

Starting at the back of the heel and using the Size 6 needles and the main color yarn, cast on 10 stitches. Now working in the stockinette pattern stitch—knit 1 row, purl 1 row—until the completion of the sole, work even for 2 rows. On the next row, increase 1 stitch at the beginning and end of the row. Work the next row even, and then repeat the last 2 rows once more so that you have 14 stitches on the needle. Work even now on these stitches until the piece measures 4 3/4 inches. Increase 1 stitch at the beginning and end of the next row. Work the next row without increasing. Repeat the previous 2 rows—increasing on every other row—until there are 24 stitches. Work even on these stitches until the piece measures 7 inches in all, ending with a purl row. On the next row, decrease 1 stitch at the end of the row. Repeat this decrease 3 times more. Work the next row even, without decreasing.

Shaping the front of the sole: At the beginning of the next row, increase 1 stitch. Knit each of the next 10 stitches. Work the next 2 stitches together to make a decrease. Place the remaining stitches—including the 2 stitches just worked together—on a holder to be worked later. Working on the 12 stitches now, purl the next row. On the next row, decrease 1 stitch at the beginning of the row. Purl the next row. Repeat the previous 2 rows—continuing to decrease 1 stitch at the beginning only of every other row—until 7 stitches remain. Bind off.

Shaping the big toe: Return to the 8 stitches on the holder. Knit across the stitches, and increase 1 stitch in the last stitch of the row. Purl the next row, working on 9 stitches. Work even on these stitches for 4 rows. On the next row, decrease 1 stitch at the end of the row. Work 1 row even, without decreasing. Repeat the last 2 rows once more. Bind off.

THE UPPER PORTION OF THE LEFT SOCK

Shaping the big toe: Using the Size 6 needles and the contrasting color yarn, cast on 9 stitches. Now begin the pattern stitch. On the first pattern row, knit 2 stitches, then slip 1 stitch. Repeat this sequence across the row, ending the row with 1 slip stitch. *(Note:* When making these socks, the multiple of stitches on the needle—resulting from the increases and decreases—will sometimes cause 2 extra stitches at the end of a pattern row. In such cases, end the pattern row by knitting these 2 stitches, rather than by slipping the last stitch as in the row you just completed.) To make the second pattern row, purl each stitch across the row. Continue in this pattern row sequence until the completion of the sock. On the next row, drop the contrasting color yarn, and attach the main color yarn. Repeat row 1 of the pattern, increasing 1 stitch at the beginning of the row. Repeat row 2 of the pattern. Pick up the contrasting color yarn again, and continue to work in this manner—alternating 2 rows of the contrasting color yarn with 2 rows of the main color—but now increase 1 stitch at the beginning and end of every other row, until there are 17 stitches on the needle. Purl 1 row even, then slip these stitches onto a holder to be worked later.

Shaping the section for the other toes: Using the Size 6 needles and the contrasting color yarn, cast on 11 stitches. Follow the instructions for making the big toe—continuing to work the two established pattern-and-color row sequences—until there are 19 stitches on the needle. Purl 1 row even. On the next row, knit across the first 17 stitches. Knit the next 2 stitches together to make 1 stitch. Return to the 17 stitches on the holder. Using the same needles, work the stitches from the holder. Knit the first 2 stitches together to make 1 stitch; then knit the remaining 15 stitches on the holder. There are now 34 stitches on the needle.

Shaping the upper foot section: Work even on the 34 stitches—continuing in the pattern stitch and alternating 2 rows of the contrasting color yarn and 2 rows of the main color—until 10 stripes of each color have been completed. End with a stripe in the main color. At this point work carefully, since you will be increasing or decreasing and changing color sequences simultaneously. Begin the first color sequence. Work 2 rows using contrasting color yarn; then 4 rows with the main color. Work this sequence once more.

Shaping the ankle and leg portions: On the next 2 rows, work in the pattern using the contrasting color. On the next row—the first row of the third main color stripe—increase 1 stitch at the beginning and end of the row. Continuing in the color-and-pattern stitch sequence, repeat this increase on every other row until there are 64 stitches on the needles. On the next row, decrease 1 stitch at the beginning and end of the row, and continue to make this decrease on every other row until 46 stitches remain. Work even on these stitches for 6 rows. At this point, check to see how many main color stripes you have made. At the end of the 11th main color stripe, begin the next color sequence—2 rows with the contrasting color yarn and 6 rows with the main color—and repeat this sequence twice more. At the same time, when you have completed the 6 rows on 46 stitches, make an increase of 1 stitch at the beginning and end of the row. Repeat this increase on every fourth row until there are 84 stitches on the needle. After you have made the third 6-row main-color stripe, begin the next color sequence—2 rows with the contrasting color, then 8 rows with the main color—and repeat this sequence 2 more times. Now work 2 rows with the contrasting color and 10 rows with the main color. Work 2 more rows with the contrasting color. You will now have completed the increases and be working on the 84 stitches. Using the main color yarn, work even on these stitches for 6 more rows.

Making the ribbing: Change to the Size 4 needles. Work in a knit 1 stitch, purl 1 stitch ribbing pattern for 6 rows. Bind off loosely in the ribbing pattern. The sock should measure about 14 inches from the heel to the top of the ribbing.

THE RIGHT SOCK

To make the sole of the right sock, follow the instructions for the left sock reversing all the shaping. To make the upper portion of the right sock, follow the directions for the left sock—again reversing all the shaping—but with these exceptions: begin by making the section for the four toes and then making the big toe. Work the row where the toe sections are joined as follows: starting at the outside edge of the big toe, decrease 1 stitch at the beginning of the row. Work across the next 13 stitches. Decrease 1 stitch again; then work across the stitches from the holder.

FINISHING THE SOCKS

Sew the back seams of the upper portions. With all sections facing wrong side out, fit the soles into their corresponding upper sections, and sew them into place. Measure your calf just below the knee, and cut six strands of elastic thread to fit. On the wrong side of each sock, draw three strands through the ribbed cuff—placing one strand at the bottom of the ribbing, one strand at the center, and one strand at the top.

Hats in knit and crochet

Knitted in brick-red wool, the hat at left adapts a type worn by nomadic Central Asian tribesmen. It has a pebbly texture, and the rolled brim is stuffed with a strip of foam rubber, cut to the proper length, then stitched and curved into a ring.

The close-fitting helmet-shaped black cloche at right is crocheted from a fine rayon-and-wool yarn. Decorating its flipped-up brim are three rows of square metallic studs, attached according to directions in the trim section *(page 111)*.

Instructions for the knit and crochet hats

The instructions that follow are for knitting the Turkish hat and for crocheting the studded cloche pictured on the preceding pages. The hat is worked in the seed stitch pattern—that is, alternating knit and purl stitches across the row, then, on the next row, knitting the stitches that were knitted on the previous row and purling those that were purled. The cloche is worked in the single crochet stitch. Basic stitches and techniques—such as casting on and increasing and decreasing—are in the Appendix.

THE TURKISH HAT

To make the hat you will need 2 two-ounce balls of sport-weight yarn, a pair of Size 6 straight knitting needles and for the brim a strip of 3/4-inch-thick foam rubber cut to measure 10 by 33 inches. Work in a gauge of 6 stitches to the inch. To check the gauge, knit a sample swatch measuring 4 by 4 inches. Without binding off, remove the swatch from the needles, then, using a ruler, count the number of stitches to the inch across the swatch.

THE CROWN

Cast on 110 stitches: Begin the seed stitch pattern as follows: On the first row, knit 1 stitch, purl 1 stitch, then repeat this sequence of stitches across the row. End with a purl stitch. On the next row, purl 1 stitch, knit 1 stitch, and repeat this sequence of stitches across the row. End with a knit stitch. Continue to repeat these 2 rows to work the seed stitch pattern—remembering that on each successive row you must knit the stitches that were knitted on the previous row and purl those that were purled—until the work measures 2 3/4 inches, ending with a row 2 of the pattern.

Begin the first decrease section now. On the first decrease row, work each of the first 8 stitches in the seed stitch pattern. Knit the next 3 stitches together. Work the next 8 stitches in the seed stitch. Repeat this sequence of stitches across the row—knitting 3 stitches together, working the next 8 stitches in the seed stitch—and end by knitting the last 3 stitches together. There will be 90 stitches on the row. On the next row, knit the first stitch—where the 3 stitches were knit together at the end of the previous row. Work the next 8 stitches in the seed stitch. Repeat this sequence of stitches across the row, ending with 8 stitches in the seed stitch pattern. On the next row, work each of the first 8 stitches in the seed stitch, then knit the next stitch. Repeat this sequence of stitches across the row, ending with a knit stitch. On the next row, knit the first stitch, then work the next 8 stitches in the seed stitch and repeat the sequence across the row, ending with 8 stitches in the seed stitch pattern.

Now begin the second decrease section. Work each of the first 6 stitches in the seed stitch. Knit the next 3 stitches together, then work the next 6 stitches in the seed stitch. Repeat this sequence of stitches across the row, ending by knitting the last 3 stitches together. There will be 70 stitches on the row. Following the instructions for the first decrease section, work the next 3 rows, but make 6 seed stitches between each knit stitch, rather than 8 seed stitches as on those rows in the first decrease section.

Now make the 2 rows of the third decrease section. On the first row, work each of the first 4 stitches in the seed stitch. Knit the next 3 stitches together, then work the next 4 stitches in the seed stitch. Repeat this sequence across the row, ending by knitting the last 3 stitches together. There are 50 stitches on the row. Work the next 3 rows as you did on the first and second decrease sections. This time work only 4 seed stitches between each knit stitch.

Begin the fourth decrease section, working the 4 rows as you did on the previous decrease sections but now making only 2 seed stitches between each knit stitch. At the end of the first row of this section, and on the following 3 rows, you will be working on 30 stitches.

Begin the fifth decrease section. Work the first row of this section as you did the first row of the fourth decrease section—2 seed stitches, then knit 3 stitches together. At the end of the row, you will have 18 stitches on the row. Work the remaining 3 rows of this section in the established sequence.

On the next row, knit 3 stitches together across the entire row. There will be 6 stitches remaining on the row.

Completing the crown: Work across the remaining 6 stitches using only purl stitches. Bind off, and leave about a yard of yarn attached to the work. Thread the long strand of yarn onto a large tapestry needle. Place the edges of the crown section together, and sew the back seam.

THE BRIM

Cast on 168 stitches: Work even in the seed stitch pattern until the piece measures 6 1/2 inches. Bind off.

COMPLETING THE HAT

Roll the strip of foam rubber lengthwise, forming a strip approximately 2 inches thick. Stitch the edges firmly in place (*drawing 1*). Turn the strip to form a ring, and sew the short ends together. Cover the ring with the 6 1/2-inch brim piece, turning the lengthwise edges of the piece toward the inside of the ring (*drawing 2*). Join these edges at about the mid-center point of the inside of the ring, and weave the edges together. When you reach the short ends—that

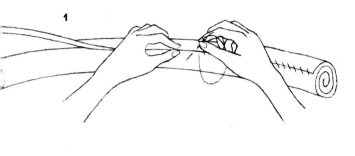

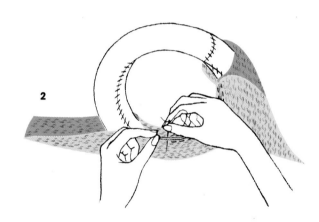

is, the side edges—of the knitted brim, sew them together. Attach the crown to the brim, sewing the bottom edge to the woven seam of the brim inside the ring.

THE STUDDED CLOCHE

To make the cloche you will need 3 ounces of thin, nubby rayon-and-wool yarn and a Size 4 steel crochet hook. You will also need approximately 200 1/4-inch-square silver studs—or their equivalent in other shapes—to make the 3 rows of studs as seen in the photograph. Work in a gauge of 7 stitches to the inch. To check the gauge, crochet a swatch measuring 4 by 4 inches. Using a ruler, count the number of stitches to the inch across the swatch.

THE CROWN

To form the top of the crown, chain 4 stitches; join the last stitch to the first one with a slip stitch to make a ring. To slip stitch, insert the hook through the first stitch, bring the yarn over the hook, then draw the yarn through the stitch and the loop on the hook (the last stitch, in this case).

On the next round, work 6 single crochet stitches through the center of the ring. On the next round, work 2 single crochet stitches in each stitch around the ring. There will be 12 stitches on the round.

Make the next round as follows: Work 1 single crochet stitch in the first stitch, then work 2 single crochet stitches in the next stitch. Repeat this sequence around the ring, ending with 2 single crochet stitches in the last stitch. There will now be 18 stitches on the round.

On the next round, work 1 single crochet stitch in each of the first 2 stitches. Then make 2 single crochet stitches in the third stitch. Repeat this sequence around the ring, ending with 2 single crochet stitches in the last stitch. There are now 24 stitches on the round.

On the next round, work 1 single crochet stitch in each of the first 3 stitches. Then make 2 single crochet stitches in the fourth stitch. Repeat this sequence around, ending with 2 single crochet stitches in the last stitch. You will be working now on 30 stitches.

On each succeeding round, increase 6 stitches, evenly spaced. As you increase, there should be 1 stitch more between each point of increase. When there are 138 stitches on the round, work even on these stitches until the piece measures 5 inches below the last increase row.

THE BRIM

On the next row, work across the first 128 stitches. Chain 1 and turn. Work back and forth on these stitches, only now decreasing 1 stitch at the beginning and end of the next row. Repeat this decrease on every row 4 times more. When these decreases are completed, you will be working on 118 stitches. At the end of the last row, do not chain to turn. On the next row, skip the first stitch. Work a slip stitch in the next stitch. Continue across the row in the single crochet stitch to within the last 2 stitches. Turn without chaining. Repeat this row until you have completed 25 rows. Fasten off. The center portion of the brim should measure about 3 inches. (The single crochet stitches on the brim and those on the crown appear to be different as the brim was crocheted in rows rather than rounds.)

FINISHING THE CLOCHE

Attach yarn to the wrong side of the bottom row at the center back. Work 2 rows of single crochet stitches around the bottom edge. At each curved side edge of the brim—where you are not working into actual stitches but into the ends of the rows—make about 8 stitches. Check to see that you have not made too many stitches so that the work puckers, or too few stitches, which will draw the work too tight. If either situation occurs, rip out the 8 stitches, then add or subtract a few stitches until the work lies flat and the stitches look even. Fasten off. Block the finished work (*Glossary*). Apply the studs around the brim (*page 111*).

GLOSSARY

ACID DYES: Dyes that require the addition of acetic acid or vinegar. Acid dyes can be used on silk, nylon and wool.

APPLIQUÉ: The decoration of fabric by sewing on pieces of other fabrics.

BASTE: To make long, loose stitches by hand or machine to hold together pieces of fabric temporarily or to indicate pattern markings on both sides of a piece of fabric. A line of basting is usually ended with a fastening or backstitch.

BATIK: The technique of creating a dyed pattern on fabric by coating it with wax to block dye from certain areas.

BIAS: A direction diagonal to that of the threads in woven fabric, i.e., the warp and woof, or grains. A true bias is at a 45° angle to the grains.

BIAS BINDING: A folded strip of fabric cut on the bias, so that the strip will stretch smoothly to cover curved and straight edges.

BISCUIT QUILTING: A patchwork of pleated, muslin-backed squares of fabric that are individually stuffed with batting and then sewed together.

BLOCK: To set the final shape of finished knitting or crocheting by pressing it with a warm iron through a damp cloth.

CLIP: A short cut made with scissors into a seam allowance to help the seam lie flat around curves and corners.

CURVED RULER: A special ruler used as a guide in drawing curves.

DART: A stitched fold, tapering to a point at one or both ends, used to shape fabric around curves, such as at the hips.

DIRECT DYES: Dyes that require the addition of salt in order to penetrate fabric. Direct dyes can be used for cotton, linen and viscose rayon.

DRESSMAKER'S CARBON: Heavyweight white or colored carbon paper that is used with a tracing wheel to transfer pattern markings to fabric.

EASE: An even distribution of fullness in fabric, without perceptible gathers or tucks, that enables one section of a garment to be smoothly joined to another slightly smaller section—as in the seam joining a sleeve to its armhole.

FACING: A piece of fabric that is sewed along the raw edge of an opening, such as a neckline, and then turned to the inside to give the edge a smooth finish.

FIBER-REACTIVE DYES: Dyes that require the addition of salt to aid penetration and washing soda to complete the bond of pigment to fabric. Fiber-reactive dyes can be used for silk, cotton, linen and viscose rayon.

FOOT: See PRESSER FOOT

FRENCH SEAM: A seam with enclosed seam allowances. It is made by placing fabric pieces wrong sides together, stitching outside the seam line and trimming the seam allowances. Then the fabric is folded wrong sides out and stitched along the seam line to enclose the seam allowances.

GAUGE: The number of stitches and rows to the inch in a piece of knitted or crocheted material.

GRAIN: In woven fabric, grain is the direction of the threads: the warp (the threads running from one cut end to the other) forms the lengthwise grain; the woof, or weft (the threads running across the lengthwise grain from one finished edge to the other), forms the crosswise grain.

GRAIN-LINE ARROW: The double-ended arrow marked on a pattern piece to indicate how the piece should be aligned with the fabric grains.

HOUSEHOLD DYES: Premixed dyes that generally do not require the addition of other substances to assist penetration or bonding. Household dyes are used for acetates, rayon, nylon and natural fibers.

MACRAMÉ: The art of knotting yarn or cord to create a fabric or fringe.

MITER: A diagonal fold at a corner.

NOTCH: A V- or diamond-shaped marking made on the edge of a garment piece as an alignment guide.

PIECING: The creating of new fabric by sewing together bits of cloth.

PIVOT: A technique for machine stitching around angular corners that involves stopping the machine with the needle down at the apex of a corner, raising the presser foot, pivoting the fabric, and then lowering the presser foot before continuing to stitch.

PRESHRINK: The process of treating fabric to shrink it to an irreducible size before cutting. Washable fabric can be preshrunk simply by washing it as directed by the manufacturer. Nonwashable fabric should be preshrunk by a dry cleaner.

PRESSER FOOT: The part of a sewing machine that holds down fabric while it is being stitched. A general-purpose foot has two prongs of equal length and is used for most stitching. A roller presser has two rollers with grids to prevent bulky or sheer fabric from sticking or slipping while being stitched. A straight-stitch foot has one long and one short prong and can be used for straight stitching and for stitching fabrics of varying thicknesses. A two-pronged even-feed foot, for use on machines that do zigzag stitching, has teeth on the bottom to move two or more layers of fuzzy, slippery or heavy fabric at the same speed. A zipper foot has only one prong and is used to stitch zippers and cording.

RATTAIL CORD: A narrow, tubular satin cord used for trimming and macramé.

SEAM: The joint between two or more pieces of fabric, or the line of stitching that makes a fold in a single fabric piece, e.g., a dart.

SEAM ALLOWANCE: The extra fabric—usually 5/8 inch—that extends outside a seam line.

SELVAGE: The lengthwise finished edge in woven fabric.

SENNET: A vertical row of knots in a macramé design.

SOUTACHE: A narrow braid with a herringbone pattern used for trim and macramé.

STAY STITCH: Machine stitches sewed along the seam line of a garment piece before the seam is stitched to keep the edges from stretching.

STENCILING: The technique of applying thickened dye to fabric through a cutout design.

TIE DYEING: Any of several techniques of creating a dyed pattern on fabric by compressing certain areas so that dye cannot enter them when the fabric is dipped in a dye bath.

TJANTING: A penlike device of Indonesian origin used for applying melted wax to fabric in batiking.

TOPSTITCHING: A line of machine stitching on the visible side of the garment, usually parallel to a seam.

TRACING WHEEL: A small revolving disk attached to a handle and used with dressmaker's carbon paper to transfer pattern markings to fabric.

TRAPUNTO: Quilting in which raised patterns are created by stitching designs into fabric and a backing at the same time, then stuffing filler material into the desired areas through slits in the backing material.

TWILL TAPE: Twilled cotton or polyester tape used to reinforce seams.

ZIGZAG STITCH: A serrated line of machine stitching.

BASIC STITCHES

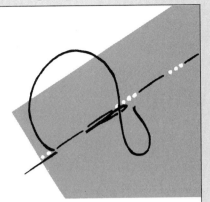

THE FASTENING STITCH

To end a row with a fastening stitch, insert the needle back 1/4 inch and bring it out at the point at which the thread last emerged. Make another stitch through these same points for extra firmness. To begin a row with a fastening stitch, leave a 4-inch loose end and make the initial stitch the same way as an ending stitch.

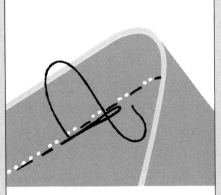

THE RUNNING STITCH

Insert the needle, with knotted thread, from the wrong side of the fabric and weave the needle in and out of the fabric several times, making 1/8-inch, evenly spaced stitches. Pull the thread through. Continue across, making several stitches at a time, and end with with a fastening stitch. When basting, make longer stitches, evenly spaced.

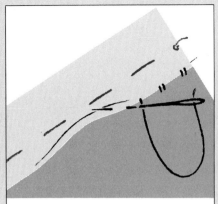

THE SLIP STITCH

Fold under the hem edge and anchor the first stitch with a knot inside the fold. Point the needle to the left. Pick up one or two threads of the garment fabric close to the hem edge, directly below the first stitch, and slide the needle horizontally through the folded edge of the hem 1/8 inch to the left of the previous stitch. Continue across in the same manner and end with a fastening stitch.

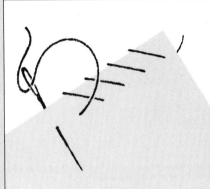

THE OVERCAST STITCH

Draw the needle, with knotted thread, through from the wrong side of the fabric 1/8 to 1/4 inch down from the top edge. With the thread to the right, insert the needle under the fabric from the wrong side 1/8 to 1/4 inch to the left of the first stitch. Continue to make evenly spaced stitches over the fabric edge and end with a fastening stitch.

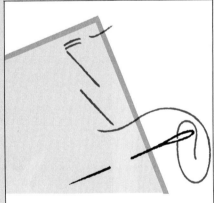

THE DIAGONAL BASTING STITCH

Anchor the basting with a fastening stitch *(above)* through all fabric layers. Keeping the thread to the right of the needle, make a 3/8-inch stitch from right to left, 1 inch directly below the fastening stitch. Continue making diagonal stitches, ending with a backstitch if the basting is to be left in, or a 4-inch-long loose end if the basting is to be removed.

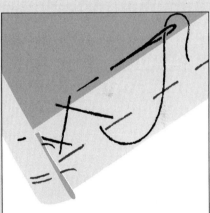

THE CATCH STITCH

Working from left to right, anchor the first stitch with a knot inside the hem 1/4 inch down from the edge. Pick up one or two threads of the garment directly above the hem; pull the thread through. Take a small stitch in the hem only (not in the garment), 1/4 inch down from the edge and 1/4 inch to the right of the previous stitch. End with a fastening stitch.

KNITTING

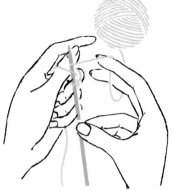

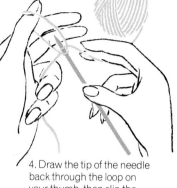

CASTING ON STITCHES
1. Form a slipknot in the yarn, leaving a free end long enough for the number of stitches to be cast on (allow about 1 inch per stitch).

2. Slide a needle through the slipknot and hold the needle in your right hand. Loop the yarn attached to the ball over your right index finger and loop the free end of the yarn around your left thumb.

3. Insert the tip of the needle through the loop on your left thumb and bring the yarn attached to the ball under and over the needle from left to right.

4. Draw the tip of the needle back through the loop on your thumb, then slip the loop off your thumb. Pull the short end of the yarn down to tighten the loop, which is now a stitch. Repeat Steps 2-4 for the required number of stitches.

THE KNIT STITCH
1. Insert the right needle in the front of the stitch closest to the tip of the left needle, as shown. Bring the yarn under and over the right needle.

2. Pull the right needle back through the stitch, bringing with it the loop of yarn. Slide this loop—which is now a stitch—off the left needle and onto the right. Repeat Steps 1 and 2 for each knit stitch.

THE PURL STITCH
1. Insert the right needle into the stitch closest to the tip of the left needle, as shown. Bring the yarn around and under the right needle.

2. Push the needle back through the stitch, bringing with it the loop of yarn —which is now a stitch. Transfer this new stitch to the right needle, letting it slip off the left needle as you do so. Repeat Steps 1 and 2 for each purl stitch.

DECREASING STITCHES
1. Insert the right needle into two stitches instead of one, either from front to back as shown, for a knit stitch, or from back to front as for a purl stitch. Proceed as though you were knitting or purling one stitch at a time.

INCREASING STITCHES
1. On a knit row, insert the right needle through the back of a stitch. Knit the stitch, but do not drop it off the left needle.

2. Knit the same stitch in the ordinary way, and transfer the two stitches to the right needle.

1. On a purl row, insert the right needle from right to left through the horizontal loop at the bottom of a stitch. Make a purl stitch but do not let it slide off the left needle.

2. Now insert the right needle into the vertical loop above the horizontal one. Purl the stitch in the ordinary way, and slide both loops onto the right needle.

BINDING OFF STITCHES
1. Knit (or purl) two stitches. Then insert the left needle through the front of the second stitch from the tip of the right needle.

2. With the left needle, lift the second stitch on the right needle over the first stitch and let it drop.

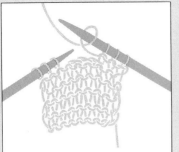

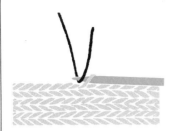

CASTING ON IN MID-ROW

To cast on stitches in the middle of a bound-off row (for example, when making a buttonhole), start by looping the yarn around your left thumb, as you do to cast on a first row. Then insert the right needle into the loop, slide the loop onto the needle, and pull snug.

PICKING UP STITCHES AT AN EDGE

1. To pick up stitches along a finished edge, as when you intend to add ribbing, start by inserting the needle into the first stitch to be picked up. Then wrap another strand of yarn around the needle; draw the yarn through the stitch.

2. Continue in this manner along the edge, drawing the yarn through each successive stitch to be picked up.

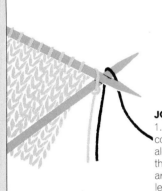

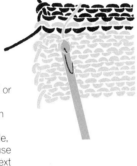

JOINING YARN

1. To introduce a new ball or color of yarn at any point along a row, wrap the yarn that you have been using around the working needle, leaving long ends. Then use the new yarn to knit the next stitch.

2. When you have knitted two or three rows with the new yarn, use a crochet hook to weave the loose ends through nearby stitches on the wrong side of the work.

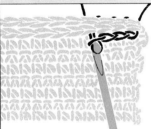

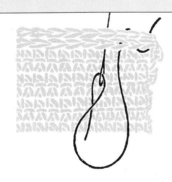

JOINING KNITTED PIECES

1. Knitted garments can be seamed by crocheting, weaving or sewing. For all three, place the edges together, wrong sides out, and align the stitches and rows. To crochet pieces together, insert a crochet hook through the first stitch on each edge, and draw a loop of new yarn through both stitches. Repeat on each pair of stitches, drawing the new loop through the loop on the hook.

2. To weave two pieces together, insert a blunt-tipped tapestry needle through the outermost stitch on each edge. Then turn the needle, and repeat. Continue weaving back and forth until the pieces are joined.

3. To sew two pieces together, insert a blunt-tipped tapestry needle through both pieces 1/4 inch below the aligned edges. Leaving a long end of yarn, insert the needle 1/4 inch to the right of the first stitch, and bring it out, from back to front, 1/4 inch to the left of the first stitch. Continue making stitches in this manner along the edges.

CROCHETING

THE CHAIN STITCH

1. Form a loose slipknot around the crochet hook, about 1 inch from the end of the yarn. Grasp the yarn attached to the ball with the tip of the hook and pull the yarn through the slipknot with the tip of the hook, as shown.

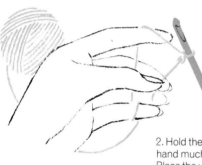

2. Hold the hook in your right hand much like a pencil. Place the yarn from the ball around the left little finger, then up and over the left index finger. Grasp the free end of the yarn between the thumb and middle finger of the left hand.

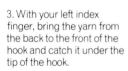

3. With your left index finger, bring the yarn from the back to the front of the hook and catch it under the tip of the hook.

4. Pull the tip of the hook through the loop in the hook, bringing the yarn with it to create the first chain stitch in the foundation chain. Repeat Steps 3 and 4 to form a chain of the desired length.

THE SINGLE CROCHET STITCH

1. To single crochet the first row after a foundation chain, insert the hook through the second chain stitch from the hook (arrow)—do not count the loop on the hook.

2. With two loops now on the hook, bring the yarn over the hook from back to front and catch it under the tip as shown. Then draw the yarn caught under the tip through the loop closest to the tip.

3. Bring the yarn over the hook again and draw it through both of the loops that were on the hook; there is now only a single loop on the hook. Insert the crochet hook into the next chain stitch and repeat Steps 1 and 2. At the end of each row, chain one stitch if the next row is to be worked in single crochet, two stitches for a double crochet pattern, and three stitches for a triple crochet pattern.

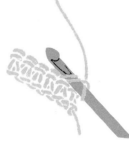

4. Turn the work to crochet back across the previous row. Insert the hook through both loops of the second stitch from the edge, as shown, and all subsequent stitches on this and all rows after the foundation chain.

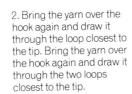

THE DOUBLE CROCHET STITCH

1. To double crochet the first row of stitches after a foundation chain, chain 2 and count back to the third chain stitch from the hook (arrow)—do not count the loop on the hook. Swing the yarn over the hook from back to front, then insert the hook through this third chain stitch.

2. Bring the yarn over the hook again and draw it through the loop closest to the tip. Bring the yarn over the hook again and draw it through the two loops closest to the tip.

3. Bring the yarn over the tip again and draw it through the remaining two loops on the hook. At the end of each row, chain one stitch if the next row is to be worked in single crochet, two stitches for double crochet and three stitches for triple crochet.

4. Turn the work to crochet back across the previous row. Bring the yarn over the hook and insert the hook through both loops of the first stitch from the edge (arrow) on this and all rows after the first.

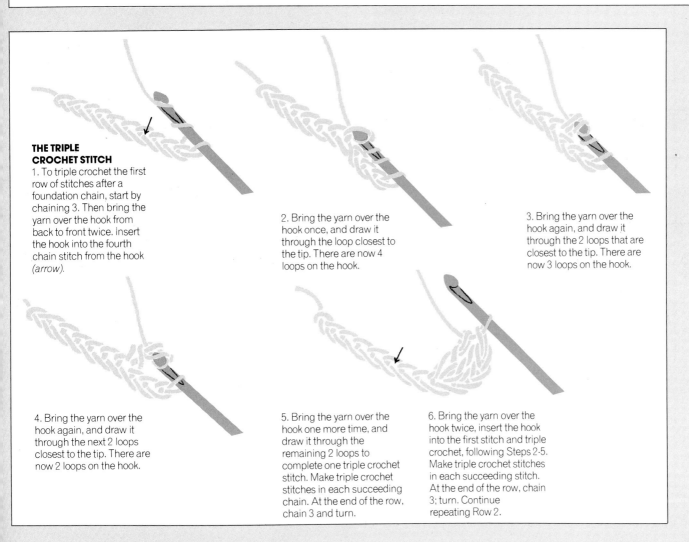

THE TRIPLE CROCHET STITCH

1. To triple crochet the first row of stitches after a foundation chain, start by chaining 3. Then bring the yarn over the hook from back to front twice. Insert the hook into the fourth chain stitch from the hook (arrow).

2. Bring the yarn over the hook once, and draw it through the loop closest to the tip. There are now 4 loops on the hook.

3. Bring the yarn over the hook again, and draw it through the 2 loops that are closest to the tip. There are now 3 loops on the hook.

4. Bring the yarn over the hook again, and draw it through the next 2 loops closest to the tip. There are now 2 loops on the hook.

5. Bring the yarn over the hook one more time, and draw it through the remaining 2 loops to complete one triple crochet stitch. Make triple crochet stitches in each succeeding chain. At the end of the row, chain 3 and turn.

6. Bring the yarn over the hook twice, insert the hook into the first stitch and triple crochet, following Steps 2-5. Make triple crochet stitches in each succeeding stitch. At the end of the row, chain 3; turn. Continue repeating Row 2.

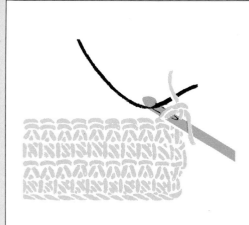

JOINING YARN
1. Join a new ball of yarn at the beginning of a row by drawing it through the first loop; leave a 1-inch-long end. Join a new color at the end of a row, working the last two loops on the hook with the new yarn.

2. When you have crocheted two or three rows, weave the loose ends of the yarn through nearby stitches with the crochet hook.

DECREASING STITCHES, SINGLE CROCHET
1. To decrease in a row of single crochet stitches, insert the hook into both loops of a stitch. Bring the yarn over the hook and draw it through the two loops closest to the tip; this leaves two loops on the hook.

2. Insert the hook through both loops of the next stitch. Bring the yarn over the hook and draw it through the two loops closest to the tip. Bring the yarn over the hook again and draw it through the three remaining loops on the hook.

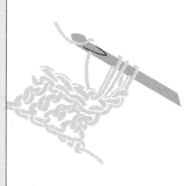

DECREASING STITCHES, DOUBLE CROCHET
1. To decrease in a row of double crochet stitches, bring the yarn over the hook and insert it through both loops of a stitch. Bring the yarn over the hook again, as shown, and draw it through the two loops closest to the tip. Then bring the yarn over the hook again and insert it through both loops of the next stitch.

2. Again bring the yarn over the hook and draw it through the two loops closest to the tip, as shown; there are now five loops on the hook. Bring the yarn over the hook again and draw it through the two loops now closest to the tip. Repeat the process until there are three loops remaining on the hook. Then pull the yarn through the three remaining loops.

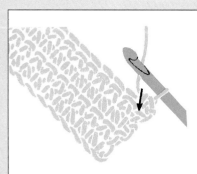
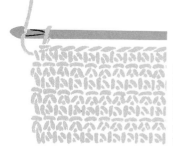

INCREASING STITCHES
To increase stitches, work one stitch—either a single, double or triple crochet, as called for in the instructions—then insert the crochet hook back into the same loop or loops (arrow) and repeat the stitch.

FASTENING OFF
Cut the yarn from the ball, leaving a 2-inch-long end. Pull this end through the loop on the hook to secure it and weave it through one or two nearby stitches.

EMBROIDERY

THE SATIN STITCH

1. Using knotted thread and a hoop to hold the fabric, bring the needle up from the wrong side on the left edge of the design.

2. Insert the needle at a point diagonally across the design. Then bring the needle up just above the first hole, and insert it above the second hole, as shown.

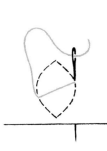

3. Continue in this manner until the top of the design is filled. Then bring the needle up just below the filled part, and make diagonal stitches until the bottom of the design is filled. End off *(page 177)*.

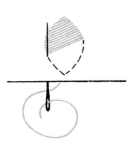

THE FRENCH KNOT

1. Using knotted thread and a hoop to hold the fabric, bring the needle up from the wrong side.

2. Put down the hoop, and loop the thread once around the needle.

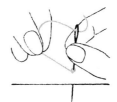

3. Holding the looped thread taut, push the needle tip into the hole from which the thread just emerged. Slide the loop down to the fabric; then push the needle through.

4. For additional French knots, bring the needle up from the wrong side, and repeat Steps 2 and 3. End off *(page 177)*.

THE STRAIGHT STITCH

1. Using a knotted thread, bring the needle up from the wrong side of the material held in the hoop; pull the needle through.

2. Insert the needle down to the wrong side of the material, making a straight stitch of any length or direction desired.

3. Repeat the stitch according to the design you are following, whether in rows, at random or at angles. End off *(page 177)*.

THE CROSS-STITCH

1. Using a knotted thread, bring the needle up from the wrong side of the fabric at the lower right corner of the design. Then insert the needle down at the upper left end of the first diagonal line; bring it out as shown. Continue this diagonal pattern for one row.

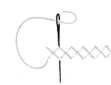

2. At the end of the row, turn and go back over the row, bringing the needle up at the lower left corner of each diagonal line, and inserting it down at the upper right, making a series of "X"s. Secure the last stitch on the wrong side *(Ending Off, page 177)*.

THE LAZY DAISY STITCH

1. Using a knotted thread, bring the needle up from the wrong side of the material at the pointed base of a petal. Pull the needle through and loop the thread from left to right.

2. Insert the needle back in the hole from which it emerged in Step 1 and bring it out again at the outermost curve of the petal, keeping the looped thread under the needle.

3. Pull the needle through, thus tightening the loop to the desired size and flattening it against the material.

4. Insert the needle below the loop to lock the loop in place, then bring the needle up again at the pointed base of the next petal to the left. Complete all of the petals. Secure the thread on the wrong side of the material (*Ending Off, opposite*).

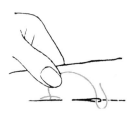

THE SPLIT STITCH

1. Using knotted thread, bring the needle up from the wrong side of the fabric on the guide line. Hold the thread down. Point the needle to the left, and insert it 1/4 inch to the right. Bring up midway to the hole from which the thread emerged. Pull the thread through.

2. Repeat Step 1 with two exceptions: let the thread fall toward you and bring the needle up near the end of the previous stitch so that the needle splits the thread of the stitch. Pull the thread through.

3. Repeat Step 2 until the design is completed. Then secure the last stitch on the wrong side of the fabric (*Ending Off, opposite*).

THE CHAIN STITCH

1. Using knotted thread, bring the needle up from the wrong side.

2. Hold the thread in a loop, and reinsert the needle in the hole from which it just emerged; bring it up directly below, keeping the thread under the needle.

3. Repeat Step 2 until you complete the design. Anchor the last stitch by inserting the needle just below the last loop. End off (*opposite*).

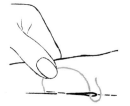

THE STEM STITCH

1. Using a knotted thread, bring the needle up from the wrong side of the material held in the hoop.

2. With your left thumb, hold the thread away from the needle. Point the needle to the left, but take a stitch to the right of the hole made in Step 1. The needle should emerge midway between the beginning of this stitch and the hole made in Step 1.

3. Pull the thread through taut and take another stitch to the right the same size as the one made in Step 2. Continue making similar stitches along the design and secure the last stitch on the wrong side (*Ending Off, opposite*).

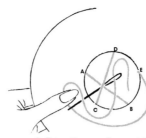

THE WHIPPED SPIDER-WEB STITCH

1. To make the spokes for the stitch, mark five evenly spaced points just inside the circular guide line. Using a blunt-ended tapestry needle and knotted thread, bring the needle up from the wrong side at a mark on the left-hand side of the circle (*point A*). Pull the thread through and insert the needle at a mark on the right-hand side (*point B*).

2. Pull the thread through to the wrong side of the fabric. Bring the needle up again at a mark on the lower part of the circle (*point C*). Pull the thread through; then insert the needle at one of the upper marks (*point D*). Pull the thread through to the wrong side. Be careful not to pull the threads so tight that they pucker the fabric.

3. Bring the needle up at the last mark (*point E*) and pull the thread through. Make a clockwise loop with the thread just below the circle and hold the loop in place. Slip the needle—from right to left—under the crossed threads at the center of the circle. Then bring the needle through the loop so that it passes under the top thread and over the bottom thread.

4. Draw the thread through the loop; then pull it straight up to form a tiny knot at the center of the circle. Make sure the five spokes are of equal length before you pull the knot tight.

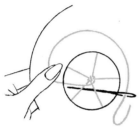
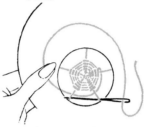

5. Make a clockwise loop. Hold the loop to the left of the circle with your thumb, and slip the needle under the two spokes at the right-hand side of the circle. Pull the thread under the spokes; do not catch the fabric or the thread of the spokes.

6. Repeat Step 5, slipping the needle under two spokes again—this time the second spoke it passed under in the previous step and the spoke to the left of that one. Pull the thread through so that it wraps fairly tightly around the right-hand spoke.

7. Work around the circle in a clockwise direction, repeating Step 6. As you progress, turn the work in a counterclockwise direction, and push the threads covering the spokes toward the center of the circle.

8. When all the spokes are completely covered with thread, carry the thread back over the last spoke. Then insert the needle to the wrong side of the fabric at the tip of the spoke. Pull the thread through and secure the stitch (*Ending Off, below*).

THE UNANCHORED COUCHING STITCH

1. Hold the trim to be couched on the design. Using knotted thread, bring a needle up from the wrong side to the right and 1/4 inch from the end of the trim. Pull through. Insert the needle to the left of the trim and opposite the hole from which the thread emerged. Slant the needle downward and bring it up to the right of the trim. Pull the thread through.

2. Continue making similar stitches. The distance between the stitches is arbitrary but should remain constant throughout the design. Approximately 1/4 inch from the end, secure the last stitch on the wrong side of the fabric (*Ending Off, right*).

ENDING OFF

On the wrong side of the fabric, slide the needle underneath the nearest 3 or 4 consecutive stitches and pull it through. Snip off the excess thread.

TRANSFERRING DESIGNS

TRACING A DESIGN FOR EMBROIDERY

1. Tape the drawing, print or photograph to be traced to a table top or board. Center a sheet of tracing paper over the design and tape it at the top.

2. Trace the design with a fine-tipped black pen.

3. Remove the tracing and fold it into quarters.

4. Unfold it and lightly mark the fold lines with a ruler and pencil.

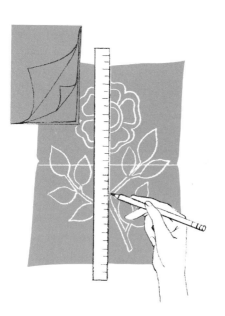

ENLARGING OR REDUCING A DESIGN

1. Trace the design onto a square piece of paper—it must be square to preserve proportions in rectangular designs—and fold the tracing in half across its width, then across its length. Unfold and fold it in quarters and eighths across its width and length to make a grid with eight squares on each side. (For an elaborate design, the paper may be folded into a 16-square grid.) With a ruler and pencil draw lines along the fold marks.

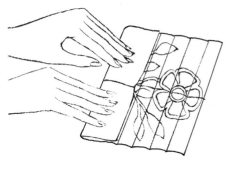

2. Identify horizontal and vertical coordinates as on a map, by penciling letters (A to H) along the top and numbers (1 to 8) down the side.

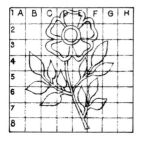

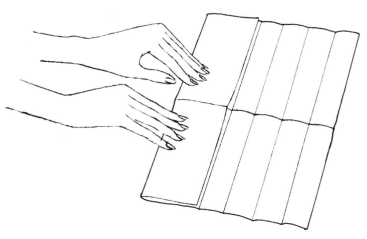

3. Cut a sheet of drawing paper into a square approximately the size you want the embroidery to be.

4. Fold it just as you folded the original and pencil in the same lines and coordinates.

5. Using the coordinates to locate matching squares, copy the design freehand, square by square.

6. Transfer the enlarged or reduced design to the fabric as shown opposite.

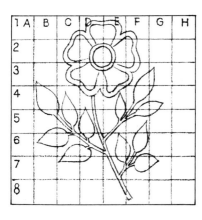

TRANSFERRING A DESIGN TO EMBROIDERY FABRIC

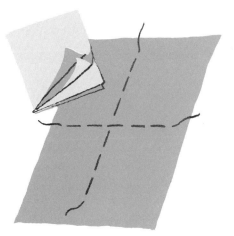

1. Fold the embroidery fabric into quarters and crease the fold lines with your fingers or an iron.

2. Unfold the fabric and baste along the creases, taking long stitches on the visible side for easily followed guide lines.

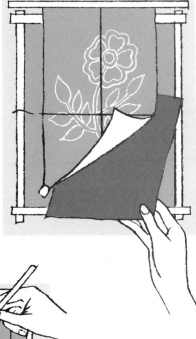

3. Tape the fabric, wrong side down, to the work surface. Then lay the paper tracing over the fabric, aligning its center fold lines with the basting on the fabric, and tape the tracing down along the top. At the bottom corners, put tabs of tape that can easily be lifted as you work.

4. Insert dressmaker's carbon paper, carbon side down, between the tracing or enlarged or reduced drawing and the fabric. (If the carbon paper is smaller then the design, move it as you work.)

5. Trace the design with a dull pencil, pressing hard. From time to time lift the paper and check that the design is coming through distinctly on the fabric. Avoid smudging by working from top to bottom. Remove the fabric and baste around the edges to prevent fraying.

CREDITS

Sources for illustrations and fashions in this book are shown below. Credits from left to right are separated by semicolons, from top to bottom by dashes.

ILLUSTRATIONS: 6,7—Tasso Vendikos. 11—Drawings by Mary Quant. Center photograph by Ronald Traeger. 12 through 17—Arnold Maucher. 18 through 45—Photographs by Ann Spanos Kuhn. Drawings by John Sagan. 46,47—Tasso Vendikos. 50 through 53—Stephen Green-Armytage. 56,57—Jack Escaloni. 58 through 63—Photographs by Al Freni. Drawings by John Sagan. 64,65—Jack Escaloni. 66 through 69—Drawings by Raymond Skibinski. 70,71—Jack Escaloni. 72,73—Drawings by Raymond Skibinski. 74 through 78—Tasso Vendikos. 79 through 87—Drawings by Raymond Skibinski. 88—Tasso Vendikos. 89 through 95—Drawings by Raymond Skibinski. 96—Tasso Vendikos. 97 through 107—Drawings by John Sagan. 108—Tasso Vendikos. 109 through 115—Drawings by John Sagan. 116—Tasso Vendikos. 117, 118,119—Drawings by John Sagan. 120-121—Susan Woods. 123—Drawings by Penny Burnham. 124,125—Susan Woods. 127—Drawings by John Sagan. 128,129—Susan Woods. 132 through 135—Drawings by Jean Held. 136,137—Susan Woods. 138 through 141—Drawings by Raymond Skibinski. 142,143—Susan Woods. 144 through 147—Drawings by Raymond Skibinski. 148,149—Susan Woods. 151—Drawings by Carolyn Mazzello. 152,153—Susan Woods. 157—Drawings by Carolyn Mazzello. 158,159—Susan Woods. 161—Drawings by Carolyn Mazzello. 164,165—Susan Woods. 167—Drawings by Carolyn Mazzello. 169 through 177—Drawings by John Sagan. 178,179—Drawings by Raymond Skibinski except bottom left, drawing by John Sagan.

FASHIONS: 6,7—Jacket by Sarah Penn from Knobkerry Third World Art and Design. 12,13—Blue jean jacket from Nani's Nowhere Else; appliquéd tunic by John Miles from Julie: Artisans' Gallery, Inc.; crocheted vest by Carol Salmon-Orlando; pieced skirt from Tamala Design. 14,15—Quilted jacket by Dana Kent from First of August; appliquéd jacket by Constance Rivemale from Julie: Artisans' Gallery, Inc.; batik dress by Nancy Kotkin of Nani's Nowhere Else. 16,17—Studded top from Giorgio Sant'Angelo's Private Collection; shawl and skirt by Julia Hill from Julie: Artisans' Gallery, Inc.; quilted jacket by Joyce Rothman from Julie: Artisans' Gallery, Inc.; slip dress from Fleury Boutique. 22,23—Cape designed by Jonathan Hitchcock for Jonathan Hitchcock Collection; boots by Herbert Levine; hair styles and make-up by David Frank Ray. 28,29—Tunic from Jackie Rogers. 32,33—Outfit by Judith Shea. 38,39—Jumper design from Nana of Soho Boutique Ltd.; hair styles and make-up by David Frank Ray. 42,43—Top and skirt by Hiroko from Eve Lost, Ltd.; hair styles and make-up by David Frank Ray. 46,47—Dyed fabrics by Anne Hall—Ernst/Reiko Designs—Ellen Backer. 56,57—Tie-dyed fabrics by Ernst/Reiko Designs—Yoshiko Kogo. 64,65—Batiked fabrics by Miso Uno—Carolyn Oberst—Ernest/Reiko Designs. 70,71—Painted fabrics by Ernst/Reiko Designs. 74,75—Hat and body shirt from Giorgio Sant'Angelo's Private Collection. 78—Skirt by Shirley Botsford. 88—Jacket from Henri Bendel. 96—Suede suit from The Farmer's Daughter. 108—Dress from Tamala Design. 116—Sweater by Guiliana Alberti of Milan, Italy. 120,121—Hat and scarf by Lucy Ciancia. 124,125—Blouse by Courtney Boyd Davis. 136,137—Bag, belt and headband by Valya Pavluk. 142,143—Vest by Carolyn Bell. 148,149—Sweater by Guiliana Alberti of Milan, Italy; hat from Eve Lost, Ltd. 152,153—Knit gloves by Annette Feldman; crochet mittens by Carol Salmon-Orlando. 158,159—Crochet boots by Carol Salmon-Orlando; knit socks by Annette Feldman. 164,165—Brim hat from Fiorucci Boutique, Milan, Italy, and adapted by Annette Feldman; cloche hat made by Annette Feldman and studded by Barbara Matera Studio; dress from Jax Manhattan, Inc.

ACKNOWLEDGMENTS

For their help in the preparation of this book the editors thank the following individuals: *in East Hanover, New Jersey:* Raymond Davenport, Sandoz Colors and Chemicals; *in London:* Mary Quant; *in New York City:* Laura Adasko; Carolyn Bell; Susan Bertram; Shirley Botsford; Bonnie Cashin; Lucy Ciancia; Reiko Ehrman; Anne Hall; Fay Halpern; Sally Kirkland; Christine Lightfoot; Carolyn Oberst; Valya Pavluk; Carol Salmon-Orlando; Julie Schafler, Julie: Artisans' Gallery, Inc.; Adam Shapiro, Eve Lost, Ltd.; Alison Stooker, The Softness Group; Geraldine Stutz, Henri Bendel, Inc.; Pat Sukhaprayura; Pauline Trigère; Barbara-Jo Tucker, Gussied-Up, Ltd.; Koos van den Akker; David Wolfson, Hitch, Ltd.; *in San Francisco, California:* Constance Rivemale; *in Watertown, Massachusetts:* Dan Macmillan and Joanna Drew, *Boutique Fashions* magazine; *in Wilmington, Delaware:* G. Robert Stetson, I.C.I. America, Inc.

The editors also thank: *in Amagansett, New York:* Havana 1919; *in London:* The London Museum; *in Nashville, Tennessee:* Betty Boop Nashville; *in New York City:* Aljo Manufacturing Co.; Butterick Fashion Marketing Company; Charivari for Women; Commonwealth Felt Co.; Cordoba; Fashion Institute of Technology Library; Fibre Yarn Co., Inc.; Grand Socco; Henry Lehr; Lune en Papier Antiques; M & J Trimming Co.; Rubicon; Soho Craftsmen Gallery.

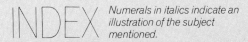

INDEX

Numerals in italics indicate an illustration of the subject mentioned.

☒ Printed in U.S.A.